HARRY MARSH
Kansas State University

HARCOURT BRACE COLLEGE PUBLISHERS

Fort Worth Philadelphia San Diego New York Orlando Austin San Antonio
Toronto Montreal London Sydney Tokyo

Publisher	Ted Buchholz
Senior Acquisitions Editor	Stephen T. Jordan
Senior Project Editor	Cliff Crouch
Production Manager	Melinda Esco
Art Director	Scott Baker
Editorial Assistant	Margaret McAndrew Beasley
Art Assistant	Edie Roberson

Library of Congress Catalog Card Number: 94-79815

International Standard Book Number: 0-15-501948-1

Address for editorial correspondence: Harcourt Brace College Publishers
301 Commerce Street, Suite 3700
Fort Worth, Texas 76102

Address for orders: Harcourt Brace, Inc.
6277 Sea Harbor Drive
Orlando, Florida, 32887
Phone: 800 / 782-4479, or
(*in Florida only*) 800 / 433-0001

Cover illustration by Scott Baker
Interior line art by Bill Alger and Edie Roberson

Printed in the United States of America

4 5 6 7 8 9 0 1 2 3 4 039 9 8 7 6 5 4 3 2 1

CONTENTS

Figures and Boxed Feature Essays v

Preface vii

INTRODUCTION 1

CHAPTER 1
Contemporary Media in the Computer Age
Using a Model to See How Computers Are Changing Mass Media 3

CHAPTER 2
Media Revolutions
Examining How Printing, Indexing, Radio, and Television Have Changed the World 17

CHAPTER 3
The Digital Medium
Considering How Digital Technology Can Bring About a Convergence of the Media 33

CHAPTER 4
The Media Environment
Surveying the Effect of Media on the Environment—and the Environment the Media Have Created for Themselves 47

CHAPTER 5
Freedom in a New Information Environment
The Public's "Right to Know" Confronts the Business of Selling Information 61

CHAPTER 6
The Media in Transition
Incorporating Digital Communication into Existing Media 79

CHAPTER 7
Practical Models
Learning How to Build the Medium of the Future from the Internet, the Associated Press, CDs, and So Forth 99

CHAPTER 8
Users of the Media
Capitalizing on the Advantages of the New Medium to Meet the Needs of Busy Users 115

CHAPTER 9
The Content of Tomorrow's Medium
Telling Stories in a Digital, Multimedia, Hypertext Environment 133

CHAPTER 10
Tomorrow's Media Professionals
Facilitating and Maintaining the New Medium and Its Content 153

CONCLUSION 175

Index 177

Figures and Boxed Feature Essays

Figure 1.1 Claude Shannon's Model of a General Communication System 5

Figure 1.2 The Contemporary Newspaper 7

Box 1.1 The Newspaper Model: Past, Present, and Future 8

Figure 1.3 The Compact Disk Music System 11

Box 1.2 Communication Model of Contemporary Mass Media Systems 13

Figure 2.1 Making Waves 18

Figure 2.2 Literacy and Intuition 21

Figure 2.3 Morse's Digital System 23

Figure 2.4 Digitizing the Wave 25

Box 2.1 A Chronology of Radio and Television Technology 27

Box 2.2 A Chronology of Radio and Television Content 28–29

Figure 3.1 Communication Model of the Future Medium 36

Figure 3.2 The Decoding–Receiving Computer of the Future? 39

Box 3.1 E-Mail from Maria 41

Box 3.2 A Multimedia History of World War II 43–44

Figure 4.1 Why Keep on Truckin'? 52

Figure 4.2 Scheduled vs. Menu-Driven Information 58

Figure 5.1 Identifiers: Henry Ford and Bill Gates 64

Figure 5.2 Al Gore's Vision of the Information Highway 70

Figure 6.1 Encoding Transitions 82

Figure 6.2 Channel Transitions 85

Figure 6.3 Decoding Transitions 89

Box 6.1 One Newspaper's Initiatives in New Technology 96

Figure 7.1 Interstate and Internet 101

Figure 7.2 Adding Content and Feedback to the Shannon Model 103

Figure 8.1 Defining the Media Gap 125

Figure 8.2 The Media User Target 127

Figure 9.1 The Importance of Content 135

Box 9.1 Telling Stories: The Traditional Way. . . 148

Box 9.2 And the New Medium Way 149

Figure 10.1 The Shannon–Weaver Model Emphasizing User and Noise 156

Figure 10.2 Professionals' New Relationships with Users 162

Figure 10.3 An Unmediated Mass Medium 165

Figure 10.4 A Mediated Mass Medium 166

Box 10.1 A Review for the New Medium Professional 171

PREFACE

A textbook should provide students with a frame of reference and a body of knowledge about a subject. The discipline of mass communications abounds with such books. We have a variety of excellent books for courses such as Introduction to Mass Communications or Mass Media and Society. We also have introductory texts in the various fields of mass communications: advertising, journalism, public relations, radio and television, theory and research, and others. The focus of each is on its own frame of reference and its own body of knowledge. To shift the focus is to risk sending a confusing message to students.

Yet the mass media are confronting momentous changes. Can we say where they are going and still claim an authoritative grounding in any of these disciplines? Perhaps. But we will be on better ground some years from now, when the changes now under way have resolved into a clearer picture.

The reason for offering a supplementary text such as *Creating Tomorrow's Mass Media* is to introduce students to what seems to be happening while retaining the sure foundation of existing textbooks. It gives instructors an opportunity to tell their students: "Okay, we've been talking about well-grounded practices and theories in our fields, now let's turn to the broad area of mass communications in the age of digital communications that lies ahead of us."

This is an opportunity to let student readers know that, in choosing a mass communications career, they face the certainty of change—probably more radical change than most of their fellow students in other disciplines. We can let students know that their actions and choices in creating new forms and networks of mass communications will make a true difference. For example, their actions could cause us, as individuals, to lose much of our privacy; or they could cost us, as citizens, much of the access to information we need to participate fully in our government, our economy, and our society.

Most important, we can remind students that participating in change is an opportunity for creativity and perhaps a chance to make a difference for the better. For that reason, *Creating Tomorrow's Mass Media* is upbeat. It does not minimize the problems that lie ahead; but it does say that students can have great expectations and that they have some opportunities for achieving them.

Thus, this book is an exposition of what seems likely to happen to the mass media during the next two or three decades and what issues prospective media professionals need to be aware of regarding these changes. It attempts to look at the topic holistically: how changes in the media affect our environment and ways of life, as well as likely changes in the way mass media will present news, advertising, and entertainment.

Any book about the future is conjectural. This book attempts to be specific enough to allow easy understanding of the material without being overly dogmatic. It is succinct. Existing and developing practices are the basis for conceptualizing what is happening and will happen. The text presumes some familiarity with existing media, and—although it depends on theoretical concepts—it remains an exposition of, rather than the defense or enunciation of, a theory or approach to the study of mass communications. By presenting models and examples it gains some timelessness. It depends upon diagrams and models to analyze mass communication processes.

Most particularly, it depends on the half-century-old model of communication created by Claude Shannon. The Shannon model is used not because it is venerable but because it compartmentalizes the creation, transmission, and reception of a message in ways important to understanding contemporary changes. For example, we can see by using the model how the tangible-paper newspaper has become a part of the channel instead of a part of the encoding process. Unlike the first 300 years of its history, today's newspaper's paper existence is no longer essential to publishing the information; in many cases it now resides pristine in the newspaper's computer.

At the appropriate point in the book the concepts of shared fields of experience and feedback are added to the Shannon model, then elaborated upon to emphasize the importance of paying attention to Users of the media and to their contributions to media content.

The writing style ranges from conversational to non-technical explanatory. Anecdotal examples are sprinkled throughout the text, as are additional one- and two-sentence marginal "short takes." Ancillary textual material of importance is featured in boxes. Charts, diagrams, and cartoons encourage easier comprehension. (A separate table of contents for all these items may be consulted for quick reference.) Jargon, when necessary, is explained as it occurs within the text.

To emphasize major differences likely to exist in mass media, two terms, "New Medium" and "User," are defined here. They are capitalized throughout the book.

The term *New Medium* emphasizes the ongoing convergence of existing media—print, broadcast, cable, and so forth—into a single digitized, multimedia, hypertext medium. For example, intangibles such as "the Net" and the much-touted "information superhighway" represent the channel of the New Medium.

The term *User* emphasizes the participatory nature of receivers or consumers of the New Medium. The term also emphasizes the obsolescence of passive concepts such as viewer and audience.

The text differentiates between hardware, software, and content.

Hardware is the silicon, metal, and plastic that make up the satellites, fiber optics, parabolic antennas, computers, and other tangible aspects of the New Medium.

Software is the complex of mathematical computer language creations that makes the hardware do the many things that the New Medium will do. It is the programming of the computers.

Content is the data that software manipulates. It is the news, art, entertainment, and other information consumed by the User.

Organizationally, *Creating Tomorrow's Mass Media* uses chapters 1 through 4 to review the current state of mass media and describe the characteristics of the emerging digitized mass media. Chapter 5 confronts the implications the emerging media hold for freedom of information and the public's "right to know." Chapters 6 and 7 deal with how the changes are taking place. The last three chapters are a progression focusing directly on, first, the nature of the Users of the New Medium; then on the characteristics of the content the New Medium is capable of providing; and, finally, on the expanded challenges and opportunities that media professionals face.

Keeping up with the ongoing changes in the media is as easy as reading the news media. Business periodicals and sections are especially helpful because they document those changes in which people are willing to invest money. To keep absolutely current with the subject would require searching every index in the library, however, because we are all finding ways to use digitized information and communication resources. Computer- and media-trade magazines and academic communication journals provide technical and theoretical background. The conferences and publications of centers such as the Freedom Forum and the Poynter Institute are also valuable. More and more, the Internet is a fertile source of information, sources, and conversation. Sample some of the available lists: the Computer Assisted Reporting and Research List (CARR-L) is especially useful.

Acknowledgments for the shaping of this book go back to the turbulent 1950s in Mississippi, when Hodding Carter, Jr., was more mentor than publisher to the staff of the *Delta Democrat-Times* in Greenville. By example, he set a high standard; by giving us great leeway, he let us discover how to communicate with an often reluctant readership. Innovation in a sophisticated world marked the example set by editors John Denson and James Bellows at the *New York Herald Tribune* in the 1960s. My bosses at that paper, editorial page editors Dwight Sargent and Raymond K. Price, Jr., let me participate in the innovation. Frederick Williams and Werner Severin at the University of

Texas made sure I understood the importance of communication theory. As an instructor at Baylor who had just done a thesis on computerized print technology, Michael Stricklin introduced me to mass media use of computers. The editors of the *New York Daily News,* the *Waco Tribune-Herald,* the *Arkansas Gazette,* and the *Kansas City Star* provided me with summer faculty internships that kept me abreast of changes through the 1970s. T. C. Sanders of Springdale, Arkansas, provided the funds that let me develop a computerized laboratory at the University of Arkansas. Using resources secured by Carol Oukrop, the director of the A. Q. Miller School of Journalism and Mass Communications, Charles Pearce has acquired the hardware, software, and expertise and provided the patient support required for the past decade at Kansas State University.

My spouse, Ellie Marsh, has made this book possible in three ways: By getting a master's degree in library and information science and allowing me to type her papers, she introduced me to the world of data processing and information handling. By advancing her career to the University of Washington, she gave me a refuge in Seattle, where it rains two-thirds of the time, so that I could write without interruption. By being an efficient reference librarian with a curious mind, she has fed me innumerable pieces of pertinent information.

Finally, a panel of expert reviewers contributed immeasurably to the development of this text. They included James Bernstein, Indiana University; John Bowes, University of Washington; Kathleen Hansen, University of Minnesota–Minneapolis; Susan Lucarelli, University of Tennessee–Knoxville; Dave Sedman, University of Arkansas–Little Rock; and Loy A. Singleton, University of Alabama.

Creating Tomorrow's Mass Media confronts the likelihood of radical change in the media and discusses how media professionals might prepare for it. It is concise and holistic. It provides, without getting mired in technical details, a conceptual framework for where the media are going. By doing this, it gives the New Medium professional and the User of information some idea of what to expect. Providing that insight is a cause we as teachers, students, and readers can join in pursuing. In that spirit, here is my e-mail address:

marfa@ksuvm.ksu.edu

Let's stay in touch.

Introduction

My career in mass communications has spanned the last half of the twentieth century. It's been fascinating. I've felt rewarded by being able to contribute to people's knowledge of the world. Now in the latter years of my career I am amazed to look back and see how much change—how much progress—has taken place in the field.

At the beginning of my career the newspaper was *the* medium of mass communication, always had been (for 300 years anyway), and always would be. I'd read newspapers and magazines as a child and I would listen, with my father, to the 10 P.M. news on the radio. Radio was a valuable but ancillary medium as far as the dissemination of information was concerned. So in college I majored in journalism and, upon graduation, I got a job on a very small daily newspaper. It was during that first year as a reporter that I saw my first television program. What a curiosity it was just to look at the test pattern! I had the same feeling those people must have had who saw the introduction of the printing press, the camera, the telegraph, the phonograph, and the telephone. I again experienced the feeling the first time I used a computer and still am experiencing it.

That feeling—of wonder—is the inspiration for this book. I am convinced that the changes I have seen are as nothing compared to what is ahead. In my youth we talked of The Press, that institution made up of newspapers and magazines that provided the bulk of public information. There were also books. There was the stage, the screen, the pulpit, the soapbox, the platform, broadcasting, and the billboard. Academics began to realize the interrelationships that existed and chose to call the various manifestations of mass communications the

Harry Marsh grew up in West Texas cowtowns; worked on newspapers in Texas, Mississippi, Alabama, and New York City; has taught at Baylor, the University of Arkansas, and Kansas State; and has degrees from Baylor, Columbia, and the University of Texas.

mass media (perhaps thinking that naming them after an ancient deity would lend intellectual prestige to what they were doing).

Now we are seeing all these media spilling over into what we have thought of as public records, as private communications, as libraries. And from all this is emerging a new way of thinking about information—its creation, its storage, its transmission, its reception, and its use. New professions must be created to carry out this transformation. New words must be coined to identify it.

I hope you find what is to follow basic enough for anyone to understand and enlightening enough to hold your interest.

Harry Marsh
Manhattan, Kansas

Contemporary Media in the Computer Age

Using a Model to See How Computers Are Changing Mass Media

As our case is new, so we must think anew and act anew.

—Abraham Lincoln

A politician uttered those words. They are the words of someone who has conviction. As students and professionals in the mass media environment, we must think anew and act anew because in our time there are so many questions.

Why are newspapers getting smaller, losing household penetration, and becoming more expensive? Why are movie companies and publishing houses merging and buying broadcasting companies? How can any viewer intelligently choose among 40—or 500—channels of cable television? How can an advertiser successfully reach a mass audience (or a narrow audience) in this hyperactive, multifaceted media environment?

The key question, which we will proceed to explore, is this: *What effect will the digitization of information and the use of the computer have on this chaotic media environment?* (Digitization means putting all information in digital computer memory.)

What we are going to do and how much we prosper during our professional lives depends upon the answer. As Users of the mass media, the answer will determine in large part how we live our lives, because the media provide us with culture and entertainment, information about products and services, and news about politics and government—as well as news about the people who do all these things and about our friends and neighbors.

Will the effect of computers and digitization of information be another stage in the evolution of the media, which has gone through mechanization, automation, and electrification? Probably not. There are signs all about us that the changes taking place in the way we gather, organize, transmit, and receive information can safely be described as *revolutionary.*

Revolutions create apprehension. As the old order gives way to something new, those of us involved wonder what the future holds. We cannot presume that trends will continue on the present paths. We can't even define the trends at first. However, sometimes a look at previous revolutions can at least provide an estimate of the magnitude of what is happening. In Chapter Two we will examine the effects of two revolutions occurring in the media. A brief reference to the introduction of printing is appropriate here.

A REVOLUTIONARY CHANGE

Certainly the invention of printing changed the way people live their lives.

Almost everyone has heard of Johannes Gutenberg. Historians say he was the first to combine movable type with the printing press. We can lay at the feet of this fifteenth-century German the credit (and the blame) for inventing the mass media. What is a mass medium? It is a way for one source to deliver a message to many receivers. Consider the early newspaper.

Gutenberg's invention resulted in the wide dissemination of Martin Luther's theses, which triggered the Reformation. Electronic mail and the fax machine are widely credited with maintaining the momentum of the pro-democracy movements in Eastern Europe and the former Soviet Union. Again, a technological innovation served as a catalyst in social change.

An editor–publisher like James Franklin would meet the ships sailing into eighteenth-century Boston harbor, talk to the captains, crews, and passengers, and return to his office to take quill pen in hand and jot down their "tydings" from wherever they had embarked. He would listen to coffeehouse gossip, get whatever the government had written down, clip some more "tydings" from newspapers he had received from Philadelphia and elsewhere, and take all these jottings to the typecase. There he and the other printers would select one letter of metal type at a time from the case and place each in a rectangular wood or metal form. The form would go on the press, be inked, and, one sheet at a time, the *New England Courant* would appear. The copies would be distributed around town and sent by post to other towns.

Whereas word of mouth had been the primary way information traveled before printing, now there was a tangible record. The illiterate gathered round the literate to hear the latest "tydings" read. The value of literacy increased dramatically, so most people learned to read.

Once so rare they were curiosities, newspapers today have become so common that they are often nuisances.

A lot of bells and whistles have been added to the printing process, but essentially that's the way newspapers, magazines, and books are produced today. In Franklin's day that was the only way to produce multiple copies. Now there is a quicker, cleaner, easier way of communicating.

USING A MODEL

For a real understanding of how newspapers or any of the mass media communicate, we first need to understand what we do when we communicate. Models help us understand what next year's fashions and cars may look like and whether or not an airplane may fly. An examination of a basic communication model, created in the 1940s by a telephone engineer named Claude Shannon, is enlightening (see Figure 1.1).

Communication: "All the procedures by which one mind may affect another."
—Warren Weaver

You and I along with Mikhail Baryshnikov, Whoopi Goldberg, the late Norman Rockwell, and Barbra Streisand have continually placed ourselves in the Information Source box. Through my mind runs the question, "How can I explain the Claude Shannon model?" Through yours runs, "How can I kid my newspaper reporter friend about how he's going to be out of a job according to this book I'm reading?"

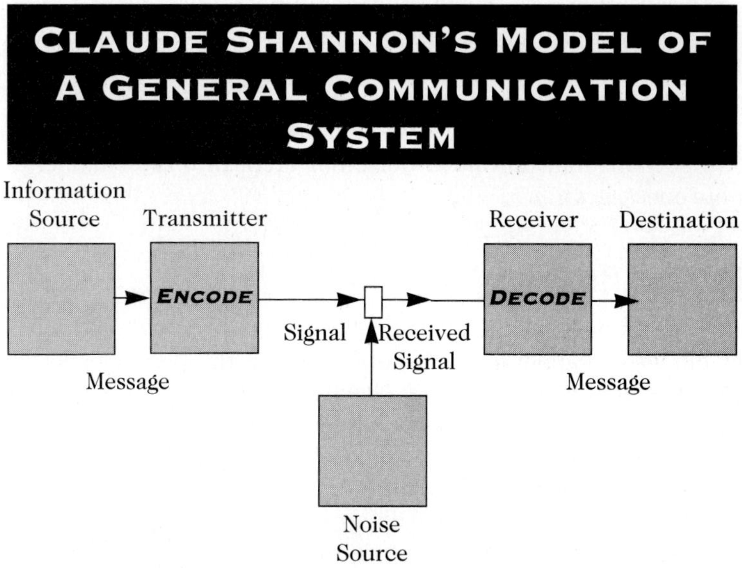

CLAUDE SHANNON'S MODEL OF A GENERAL COMMUNICATION SYSTEM

Information Source
Transmitter
Receiver
Destination
ENCODE
DECODE
Signal
Received Signal
Message
Message
Noise Source

FIGURE 1.1

Through Baryshnikov's runs whatever it takes to make his body do those amazingly graceful things he does. Through Whoopi's runs a wry way of thinking that enthralls us when she acts. Through Norman's ran the essence of grassroots America. Through Barbra's run sounds never yet heard.

Then we all move on to the second box, and that's where the work begins: My typing, floor pacing, and revising to write the book. Your careful crafting of each word and seeking out just the right moment at Friday night's happy hour to zap your reporter friend. Mikhail's powerful and disciplined movements. Whoopi's comic clairvoyance in *Ghost*. Barbra's soaring voice. Norman's painting. We each encode our message.

And we send it on its way down a channel: me to the publisher and bookstore, you across the room to your friend, in a PBS special from the Kennedy Center, on the movie screen, in a Central Park concert, on a calendar or collector plate.

Notice the line that intersects with the channel. It is connected to the word *noise*. A common definition of noise is "an assault on the ears." The definition we need is much broader. Noise in our model is anything that interferes with or modifies the message as transmitted and changes it to something else by the time it is received. It can be actual noise, or off-balance color on a television set, the neighbor's dog barking or biting your ankles, your sister's stereo blaring while you are trying to read this chapter. Some noise interferes with every message. But usually the message gets through.

At the other end of the model the message is heard or seen or both. Through those two senses it enters the mind of the receiver, the audience member, and is interpreted according to knowledge, emotions, and whatever else the mind uses.

As senders, we hope that we've done a good job of encoding and, also important, that not much noise has crept into the channel to distort our messages.

NOISY PRESSES

Houston Chronicle executive Jack Stanley cites some newspaper problems: helping advertisers reach small groups of readers, newsprint recycling, putting the newspaper together, and computer-integrated manufacturing, all of which are related to the printing process.

Upon examining the mass media using this model and analyzing what has been happening very subtly during the past decade or two, we discover that a revolutionary change is indeed under way. What we thought was necessary for the encoding of mass media messages is now a part of the channel through which the message flows and in fact is becoming a noisy part of that channel.

The accompanying chart illustrates this change, using newspapers as the example. The printing press formerly was essential to encoding the newspaper message. Until the paper came off the press the newspaper message was in bits and pieces, paper and metal, all over the composing room. In the 1970s the change began, as Box 1.1 (on the following page) shows. By the end of the 1980s computers were used at some newspapers for every facet of encoding.

Now that the newspaper's computer is its sole encoding device, replacing everything from the copy editor's pencil to the printer's Linotype machine, the newspaper is complete and organized in the computer, easy to read on the screen, and easy to transmit to another computer.

The making of the printing plates and the operation of the presses is now part of the distribution system because that's the way information has been distributed for centuries and because millions of newspaper subscribers have neither computers to capture the newspaper nor the skill and inclination to do so. Inevitably that will change.

In 1990 the *Albuquerque Tribune* began publishing a password in each day's edition. Owners of personal computers with modems dial into the newspaper's computer for information not in the daily edition. In 1987 the *Middlesex News* (Massachusetts) introduced a computer bulletin board for the convenience of its readers. By 1994, forty-one newspapers had or were planning on-line services.

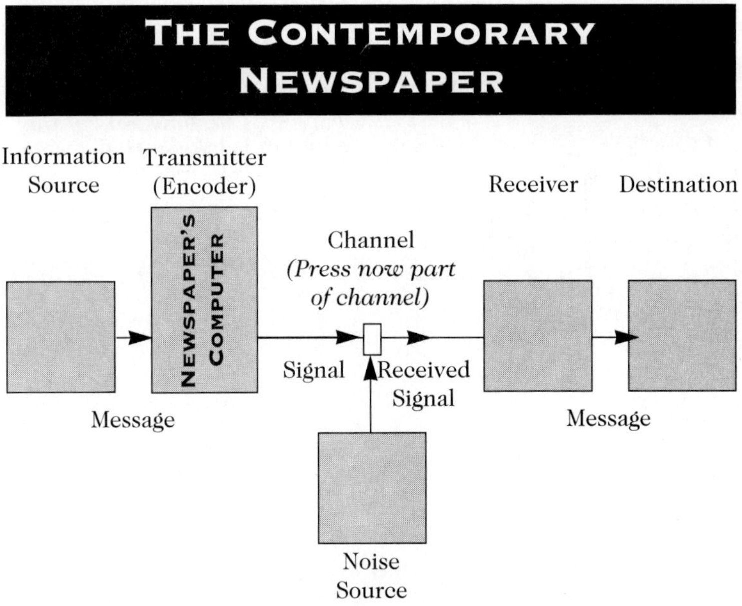

Formidable obstacles stand in the way of making the transition to a newspaper distributed by computer. But there are compelling forces moving in that direction already, and newspapers are already producing digitized editions. Meanwhile, here is a version of our model (Figure 1.2) that is one more reminder of what has already happened: As the description of the contemporary newspaper indicates, the computer is now almost the sole encoding device the newspaper uses; in this revised model of communication the newspaper's computer almost completely fills the encoder box.

THE CONTEMPORARY NEWSPAPER

Information Source
Transmitter (Encoder)
NEWSPAPER'S COMPUTER
Channel *(Press now part of channel)*
Receiver
Destination
Message
Signal
Received Signal
Message
Noise Source

FIGURE 1.2

THE NEWSPAPER MODEL: PAST, PRESENT, AND FUTURE*

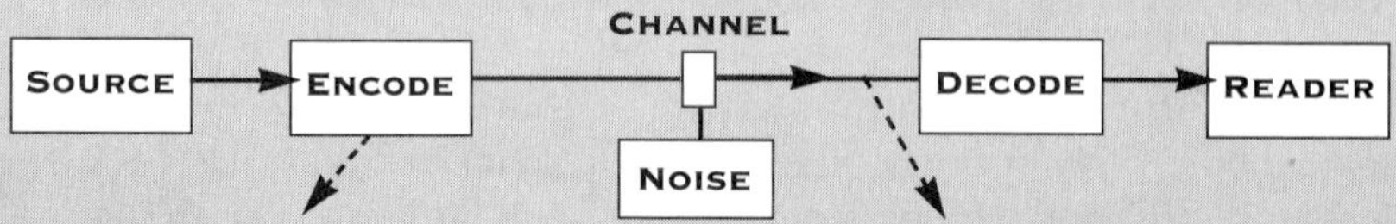

Creating the Newspaper

Traditional

Reporters write stories (1690).
Presses print papers (1690).
Production people turn copy into type (1690).
Editors edit and write headlines (1835).
Artists create graphs, charts (1860).
Designers create page dummies (1860).
Plates are made (1890), put on presses.
Photograghers take pictures (1900).
Editors crop and scale pictures (1900).
Type pasted up (1968).

> ***Not until the paper comes off the press do we have a newspaper we can read.***

Contemporary

Reporters write stories into computers (1972).
Editors edit, write heads into computer (1972).
Ad writers and artists create advertisements on computers (1984).
Artists create charts and graphs on screen (1986).
Editors crop, scale pictures on screen (1988).
Photographers take pictures, scan into computer (1988).
Designers create page dummies and paginate paper on computer (1988).

> ***The newspaper is a complete entity, as readable on computer screen as on paper.***

Future

Same as current newspaper encoding (above), except photographers will use computerized digital cameras, eliminating film and chemical processing. All images will move directly from camera to newspaper computer.

Distributing the Newspaper

Traditional

Papers are bundled (1690).
Papers go to delivery people, post office (1690).
Delivery people throw papers under rose bushes (1860).
Reader in bathrobe with hole in seat searches under bushes to find paper (1860).
Bundles loaded on trucks by route (1910).

Contemporary

Same as traditional newspaper channel (above) except that making the printing plates and printing the newspaper on a press is no longer encoding. It is now essential only to the distribution system. Also, reader in bathrobe with hole in seat gets wet running to pick up damp newspaper in leaky plastic wrap.

> ***Printing the news on paper has now become part of the distribution system.***

Future

(now becoming available)

Newspaper transmitted over phone lines or cable to reader's computer. Reader, with hole in seat of bathrobe and hot cup of coffee in hand, is glad to have a good power-surge protector on computer because of last night's thunderstorm. Turns on computer to see what's happened lately.

> ***News"paper" will reside in reader's computer. Computer searches will aid quick reading.***

*Approximate dates when practice became practical in parentheses.

BOX 1.1

How Computers Communicate

One compelling reason for changing to a computerized newspaper is that all the other mass media are being computerized, as will be shown. To appreciate the major change that has overtaken all the media, it is necessary to understand the language that computers use.

If you can count to one, you can understand how computer language works. That's all that digital computers do, count to one. But they do it at the speed of light (186,000 miles per second), and they do it very accurately. Understand how a light switch works (off = 0; on = 1) and you can understand how a computer works.

When I am hungry, I look in the cookie jar. If a cookie is there, I have something to eat. If no cookie is there, I remain hungry. This cookie story is a demonstration of counting to one. I either have a cookie (one) or no cookies (nothing). If there are fifty cookies in the jar and I am very hungry, I look in the cookie jar fifty times and each time find a cookie (one) and on the fifty-first time, I find no cookies (nothing or zero); however, that's not very important to me because I am no longer hungry. But this little story is very important to understanding binary mathematics, which is what computer science is based on.

Binary mathematics uses one as a base. Most of us ordinary people use the decimal system with ten as a base, I presume because we have ten fingers, which makes it easy to count by tens.

We learn a multiplication table based on tens. We could learn a multiplication table based on two numbers (a binary system), the numbers being zero and one. I know this is true because the first computer I ever worked on, back in 1972, required me to use binary mathematics to get it started. I would turn it on and then flip a series of toggle switches to install the program that would boot it in the rear end and make it work. Each toggle switch was turned on (one) or off (zero). Then that part of the program was entered into the computer. Eventually, if I toggled all those dozens of zeros and ones in correctly (no mistakes), the computer would know how to read perforated paper tape and I could feed in the rest of the program by running a long paper tape through a reader.

A 1972 computerized newspaper photocomposition system had a capacity of about sixteen stories, cost about $40,000 and could out-produce six or seven $15,000 hot-metal Linotype machines. Fifteen years later, a $10,000 Macintosh or PC (personal computer) and laser printer system could easily produce dozens of stories and graphics for a small weekly or daily newspaper, and 99 percent of all Linotype machines had been sold for scrap.

Now all this is handled by binary information stored on the hard disk of my computer. In fact, these days I turn my computer on and very soon it smiles at me and beeps pleasantly, letting me know it is ready to face the new day. Computers are just beginning to be really friendly to ordinary people like me.

Let's look at binary mathematics and the computer another way. If you look through a magnifying glass at a black-and-white photograph just produced by a conventional camera, you will see that black fades evenly into lighter shades and eventually into white (an analog image). But if you look through a magnifying glass at a black-and-white photograph reproduced in a newspaper, you will see lots of black dots on the white paper—small dots where the picture is white or light gray, larger where the picture is dark gray, and almost on top of each other where the picture is black (a binary image).

Now, imagine that all the dots are the same size, but there are none where the picture is white; they are far apart where the picture is light gray and they are closer and closer together in those parts of the picture that are dark gray or black. In the computer each dot represents a one; each point where there is no dot represents a zero. Using this system, a digital computer can represent almost anything—a photograph, a novel, a mathematical formula, or a three-dimensional image of a 1967 Chevrolet Camaro. (The Camaro is garaged in computer storage at the Massachusetts Institute of Technology).

The Media Lab at MIT has been doing research on the future of the media as they relate to computers since the early 1970s, originally as the Architecture Machine Group.

Whole new professions of computer scientists, engineers, and technologists have evolved. They create amazing things, from Pacman to pictures of Saturn, using computers and binary mathematics. For a long time they've worked in the worlds of business and science; now it's their job to make these computers do what us ordinary people need them to do. They should remember that, and especially *you* must remember it. If you think you need access to good roads, good schools, good food, good housing, and good clothes, then right now add good computer access to the list of necessities, or prepare to be an outcast in the information age, living beyond the pale, uncivilized and powerless.

That is because every kind of record and communication can be and now is being encoded, stored, transmitted, and decoded using the new universal language of binary mathematics.

A Universal Language

To demonstrate the widespread use of this new language and to emphasize how far the mass media have gone in achieving computerized encoding, let's look at video (television and the movies) and audio (radio and music).

Manufacturing information processors has become big business: In 1928, it accounted for $180 million in revenues. Half a century later, the figure had reached $7.7 billion for the top five companies.

First, music. In the mid-nineteenth century under the auspices of the impressario P. T. Barnum, the Swedish soprano Jenny Lind toured the United States. We can imagine a bronco-busting cowboy, Jim, riding his recently tamed mustang into Dodge City, spending the evening in a vaudeville house, and then retiring to a saloon for a beer and vowing that Miss Lind was indeed the Swedish Nightingale. Until high-fidelity recordings came into use in the middle of this century, there was no substitute for hearing a performance live.

The elements in the communication model are simple. Jenny sings; Jim listens. Sender and receiver must be at the same place at the same time. Vocal chords complete the encoding; ears begin the decoding and the air in the opera house is the channel.

Now, however, we can imagine Jim's great-great-grandson, a knuckle-busting mechanic also named Jim, leaping into his recently renovated Mustang and tucking a compact disk (CD) into the car's sound system so he can listen to Joan Jett singing "I Hate Myself for Loving You," as he wheels to the supermarket for a six-pack.

The elements in the communication model are much more complicated. Joan sings; the music is recorded; the analog sound is converted into digital information in a computer; CDs are manufactured and distributed; the expensive sound system in the Mustang includes a CD player with a little computer that converts the digital information to analog signals that reproduce the music. A whole new complicated industry has evolved.

Along the way we have had wax cylinders, shellac 78 rpm records, vinyl LPs, 45s, high fidelity, wire recordings, tape recordings, stereo, tape cassettes, and now CDs. The CD has created an entirely different environment for music (and indeed for mass media). The CD usually works perfectly or not at all; no more scratches. But, most

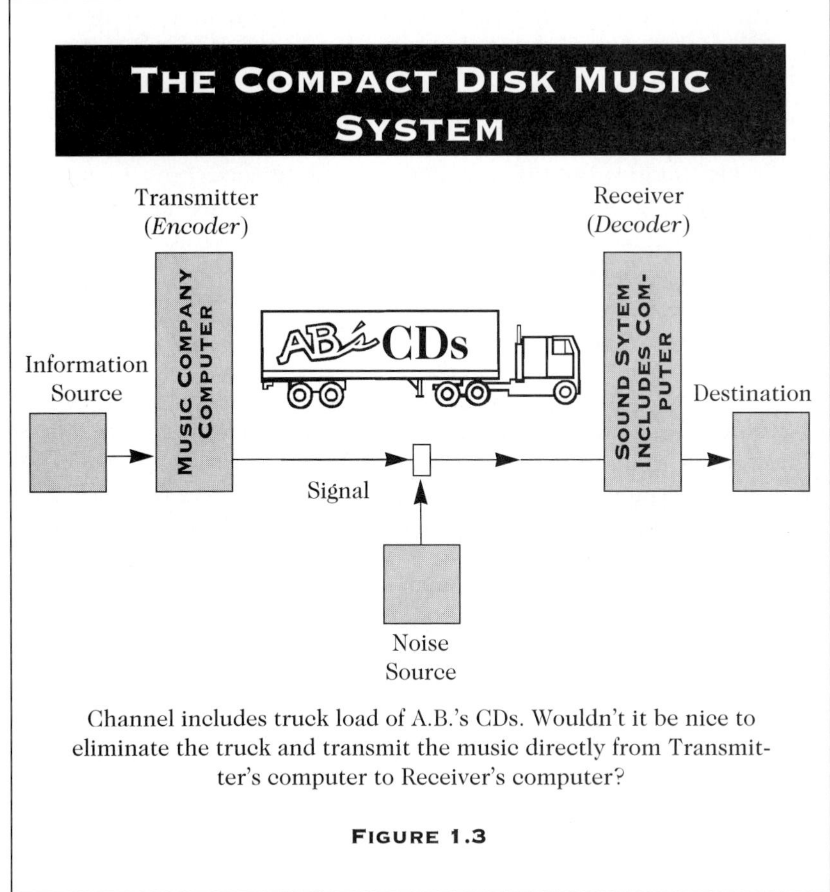

Channel includes truck load of A.B.'s CDs. Wouldn't it be nice to eliminate the truck and transmit the music directly from Transmitter's computer to Receiver's computer?

FIGURE 1.3

important, it requires a computer (tiny though the decoding computer is) at the receiving end. Look at the CD communication model shown in Figure 1.3 (on the preceding page).

Even the imaginative P. T. Barnum would be amazed at the vast array of machines and recording materials that have spewed from the factories, through the stores, and into the cabinets and attics of our homes over the past eight decades. Now, with the digital CD, they are becoming obsolete, as is radio (more on that later).

Video disks are not as common as CDs, but they have been around longer and are frequently used in business and education applications. A teacher of drama or of the motion picture can now use a classroom computer to skip around on a video disk to illustrate points he or she wishes to make, without going through the laborious process of clipping film or editing videotape. Video games illustrate how digitized moving images can be manipulated by the computer so that the player proceeds through increasing levels of difficulty toward that magic maximum score. The "Aspen Movie Map" was created by MIT's Media Lab a dozen years ago. Using this video disk system, you can view the streets of the famed Colorado resort, turning left or right, changing seasons from winter to summer and even stopping and going into buildings.

The video toaster is an off-the-shelf personal computer programmed and adapted to do most of the video editing done by equipment costing ten times as much.

The Aspen Movie Map is more than a fascinating toy. It informs us that (1) video is as amenable to digital technology as any of the other tools used by the mass media, (2) getting access to the specific information the receiver wants is simplified through digital technology, and (3) the receiver (User) can have much greater control over what you get from the mass media.

CROWDED CHANNELS

By the way, if the above indicates paper newspapers are becoming obsolete, it should also become clear that broadcasting and cable as we now know them are becoming obsolete too. Broadcasting and cable never were in the manufacturing business. They have always provided the receiver with an intangible product, to be heard through speakers or seen on a screen. But they have a time problem, a chronology problem. They transmit their messages at their convenience and hope it will be at your convenience too. Prime time for television and drive time for radio are jammed with what the producers consider the best information they have to offer; they can't depend on large audiences at other times. Now, with the proliferation of audio and video channels, no single sender can depend on large audiences at any time. Oh yes, the audio and video people already are using computers at the encoding end of the communication model to a great extent.

A Montreal television station (Tele–Metropole) now offers viewers up to four different views of a baseball game. Viewers can split the screen to see two, three, or four views, or they can select the view of their choice.

If audio and video communicators began dumping their information into your computer's memory on a regular basis, then their

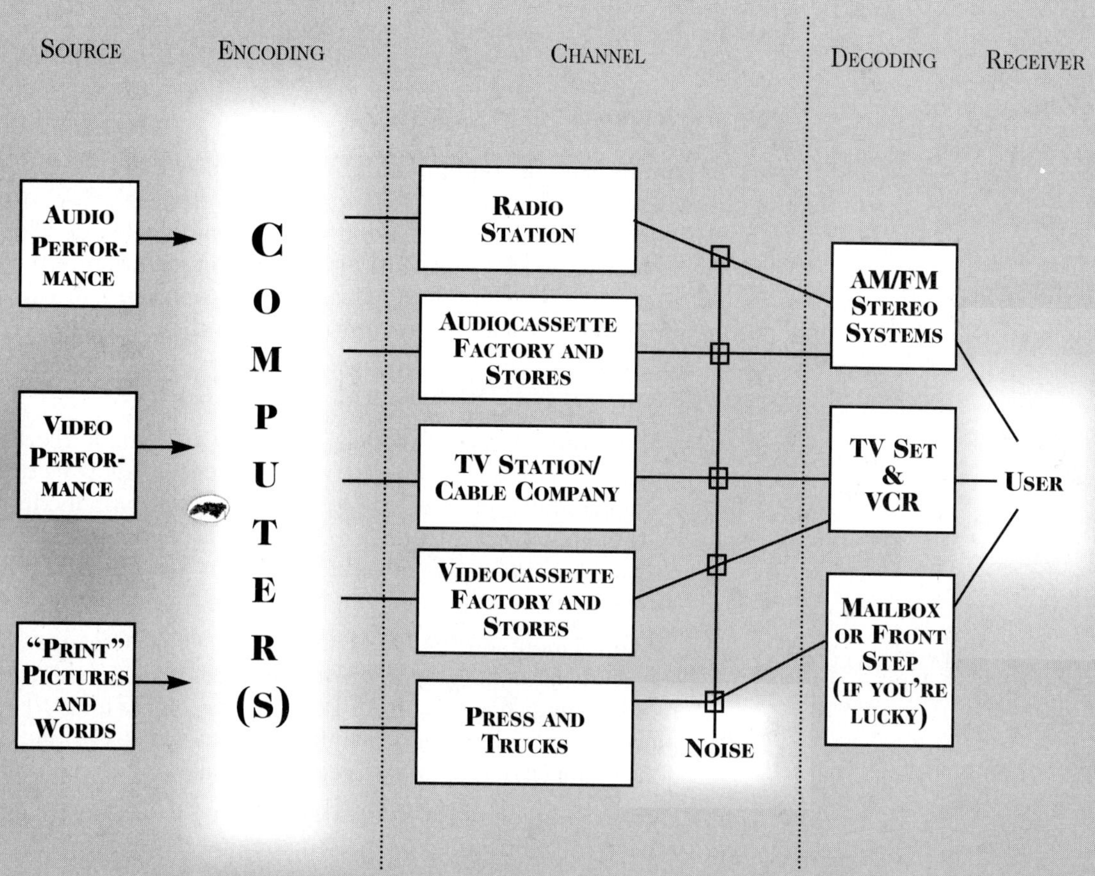

All media can and do use computers as encoding devices. The print media use them almost exclusively and the other media are adapting them rapidly. Theoretically a media giant such as Time-Warner could do all its audio, video, and print encoding on one giant computer. Of course, microphones and cameras are still part of the encoding process.

Keep in mind that cassettes and paper are not information. They *carry* the information, and since the information can be carried more efficiently by digital/electronic means, at some time in the future, these manufactured items may no longer be used as part of the channel. Users may make their own paper or cassette copies for personal storage.

The mailbox and doorstep are really part of the channel for print media. Also, eyes, ears, and hands are part of the decoding process for all the media.

Box 1.2

messages would be there when you had time to watch or listen to them. Instead we have a cacophony of print, audio, and video arriving in our mailboxes, under our rose bushes, by video rentals, and through the purchase of cassettes, CDs, and so forth. Our homes and cars are cluttered with the electronic devices needed to decode many of these gizmos, and with publications often unread because it takes so long to find what we are interested in.

SUMMARY

To summarize the contemporary mass media systems, as Box 1.2 (on the preceding page) indicates, we have late-twentieth-century computerized encoding systems imposed on technologies developed from the sixteenth century through the first half of the twentieth. The channels of distribution and the decoding systems are unwieldy, uneconomical, and obsolete for the most part. We all deserve better.

DISCUSSION TOPICS, PROJECTS, AND EXERCISES

1. Discuss the concept of models. Have you used them in other courses or contexts? Demonstrate how models allow us to understand complicated things by identifying components and relationships. Introduce other models of communication that further illuminate how information is processed and distributed.
2. Do you remember the first time you saw a CD? Create a time-line list of developments in recorded music to show how rapidly things have changed. Do you have access to a CD player or own compact disks? Individually, write critiques comparing CDs and tape cassettes as media.
3. Do a class inventory of computer skills, with class members reporting on how they have used computers. Discuss resources available to improve computer skills.
4. Discuss the disadvantages of using computerized information rather than traditional media.

SUGGESTED READINGS

Brand, Stewart. *The Media Lab: Inventing the Future at MIT*. New York: Viking, 1987. How scientists began to think about using computers for all kinds of communication.

Minow, Newton W. *How Vast the Wasteland Now?* New York: Gannett Foundation Media Center, 1991. A look at contemporary television by one of its keenest critics, a former head of the Federal Communications Commission.

Pavlik, John V., and Everette E. Dennis. *Demystifying Media Technology*. Mountain View, California: Mayfield, 1993. A good handbook for explanations of computerized communication technology.

Shannon, Claude E., and Warren Weaver. *The Mathematical Theory of Communication.* Urbana, Illinois: University of Illinois Press, 1949. This seminal book contains the basic model used in this text.

Media Revolutions

Examining How Printing, Indexing, Radio, and Television Have Changed the World

A word fitly spoken is like apples of gold in pictures of silver.
—**Proverbs 25:11**

We know little of prehistoric humanity. But we do know that the greatest gift our ancient ancestors gave us was not the wheel or fire. It was speech. People learned to articulate their thoughts into sounds, into language. Using speech, what people experienced they could share, discuss, analyze. Past events could be recalled and what one person experienced could be shared with another who had not experienced it. We know so little of these people because their language could not be preserved. Then came writing.

Over the long centuries of human existence pockets of civilization developed from time to time prior to the era in which printing was introduced. We can visit the sites of ancient civilizations on most of the Earth's continents and wonder about them. We are most familiar with the civilizations of the Greeks, Romans, and Israelites because they knew how to write. Because of these writings, these civilizations have had a profound influence on our own. But like those of Egypt, Mexico, and Peru, they were limited in their geographical influence and eventually languished. Only a few people could read and write. Few copies of what was written existed. What we know as the Dark Ages followed.

A person living during the Dark Ages was not likely ever to travel more than 7 miles from his own domicile. Survival was the single most important motivating factor in this person's life—that is, acquiring food, clothing, and shelter. Knowledge was gained by experience and by listening to the experienced. Valuable knowledge was what helped ensure survival. Other knowledge and other activities, such as using one's imagination or questioning the status quo, were often thought to be wasteful, indeed dangerous. Resolution of the anxieties generated by the great unknowns beyond each new day and beyond that 7-mile radius was left to superstition or religious faith.

A new kind of oral tradition is emerging with the onset of radio talk shows and all kinds of 800- and 900-number telephone services, providing recorded voices that offer everything from the current temperature to high-voltage suggestions that will raise one's temperature.

Of course there were traders and there were gypsies and minstrels. These travelers brought tales of strange things, places, and people. They were little trusted but good for an hour or two of entertainment in the flickering light of a campfire, a lamp, or a fireplace.

What laws there were depended largely upon the oral tradition. The older and the wiser related to the magistrate what had happened in the past and that was the precedent that governed, unless the powerful intervened. A "hearing" remains the technical term for presentation of information to officials.

Behind high walls of monasteries what literate knowledge existed was copied and recopied by hand. The clergy read these Latin tomes

MAKING WAVES

To speak, the mind tells the lungs to push air up the throat and through the voice box (larynx), and tells the muscles of the larynx to shape it so the vocal cords vibrate in the rushing air, creating analog wave motions that pass into the open air (or other gas or even water) and to a listener's ears. To hear, the eardrums pick up the vibrations and pass them to the brain, which interprets them.

The pitch (high or low) is determined by the frequency of the wave motions (how many per second): the loudness is determined by the amplitude (or height) of the wave motion. Theoretically all the sounds ever made are still echoing around the atmosphere. Select words carefully. Don't make waves unnecessarily.

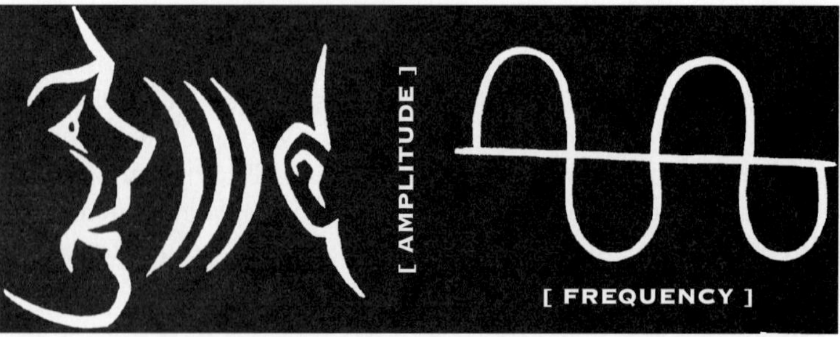

FIGURE 2.1

and interpreted them for the people. The church had power and wealth and so did the strong, who could maintain bands of armed men. Around them gathered artists and craftsmen. The conquests of these strong men uncovered knowledge preserved and created by other cultures. A few affluent people in some Italian cities even hired teachers to spread knowledge of the law, and at these colleges the seeds of renewed civilization began to sprout.

INTRODUCTION OF PRINTING

Into this environment came the printing press. The introduction of movable type and of the printing press by Gutenberg and others had a profound effect on society. It was a primary contributor to what we believe to be an enlightened world, to the expansion of Western civilization across the globe, and even to major changes in our environment. One scholar labeled it "The Day the Universe Changed." There is no evidence that the universe actually changed, but our perception of it changed very rapidly, and our perception of the universe, as much as the reality of the universe and perhaps more, determines how we conduct our lives.

What we are discussing is revolutionary change—not a gradual modification of culture and society, but a major upheaval. There is evidence that a somewhat similar upheaval is now taking place, and an examination of what happened beginning almost five centuries ago can give us a perspective on this new upheaval.

In 1455, 70 copies of the first Gutenberg Bible were published; in 1456, 270 copies of the second were published. By 1500, press runs of 1,000 copies were common. Luther's ninety-five theses were posted on the Wittenberg church door in 1517. By 1564, the Vatican had published an Index of Prohibited Books.

Here are some of the things worth looking into that the introduction of printing did:

- It encouraged literacy.
- It broke the monopoly on information.
- It led to methods of indexing and organizing information.
- It allowed printers to control what information was disseminated.
- It encouraged writers to write and to make their own analyses of what they wrote about.
- It reduced parochialism, encouraging a world view.
- It created a tradition of linear logic, of Gutenberg Man.

Of course at its introduction no one knew it would do all those things. It was seen as one of the mechanical changes that were beginning to take place. Legal and religious books could be produced more quickly. The church's indulgencies, whereby sins were expiated for a price, could be mass-produced. That was the role of printing as perceived by the "great minds" of that time.

It was the printers themselves who became aware of a new power. Now the wisdom of a living wise man could be projected far beyond the reach of his voice. Just as the wisdom of Socrates and Moses had been preserved and multiplied by the scribes toiling with quill and parchment, now words of the living could be scattered far and wide with ease by the type compositor and pressman. The good talker was replaced by those who could read well aloud, and the good listener was soon replaced by the good reader.

Reading had always been the beginning of education and now being a reader was important, so education flourished. The young were no longer tied to the advice and knowledge of the old people they knew. Once they knew how to read they could begin to make independent judgments based on their own knowledge.

Religious treatises, pamphlets, and even cartoons fueled the Reformation and the Counter-Reformation. Just as important, every craft and skill became the subject of a book. Accurate representations of plants and animals, cities, and people, could be made in narrative or with woodcut engravings. People could learn from contemporaries they had never listened to about things that they had never seen. The colleges based on study of the law became universities, teaching and studying the arts and the sciences.

Proponents of multimedia journalism see it as being closely related to story telling, the technique of the oral tradition. Multimedia designer Abbe Don has said, "We make memories."

For a brief period Renaissance Man existed. By reading widely he could truly say that he understood his world. In his family library were a few dozen books. Polite society could discuss all of them. At this point in history we have friends, acquaintances, and perhaps strangers all discussing shared vicarious experiences in the drawing room—a far cry from minstrels telling tales around a campfire.

But more books meant more subjects covered and in more detail. The human mind, not being a computer, could not store every bit of knowledge, nor could it even keep up with where every bit of knowledge, of humor, of beauty was stored.

INDEXING AND NETWORKING

Concepts of organizing and retrieving information emerged. Put books about the same subject together. Create lists of books (bibliographies) about the same subjects. Instead of dealing with whole books, list information about a book on a card that can be filed alphabetically. Create several cards for each book, listing different categories of information first (subject, author, title) so that multiple alphabetical files can be created. Include in the books attributions and references to previous writings that were used in creating the book (footnotes and cross-references).

The introduction and expansion of mercantilism, the buying and selling of products and services, developed at the same time and in conjunction with printing and the spread of knowledge. Knowing who had what and who needed what is power to the merchant. So merchants who had information networks began to produce hand-copied news letters and distributing them to those who would pay for them, and when printing came along, the newspaper was born.

Demand for new information encouraged writers and printers to explore every profitable subject. The vast supply of printed material allowed the reader to pick and choose what was interesting and important. That meant people were taking their own destinies into their own hands.

The minstrels and gypsies had created in the minds of parochial people pictures of things they had never seen. Now books about faraway places and exotic creatures expanded those pictures. Voracious readers became a population with a world view.

A world population of readers and writers evolved into what Marshall McLuhan labeled Gutenberg Man. Advertising genius Tony Schwartz (who revolutionized television political advertising) describes Gutenberg Man as the product of linear, laborious writing and reading. Gutenberg Man takes experience and writes it down. In the process logic is applied. The encoding process includes a careful packaging of

LITERACY AND INTUITION

Like speech, the first writing copied nature: pictographs and hieroglyphics. Chinese and Japanese characters have some images as their bases. But modern English and the European and Middle Eastern written languages are not intuitive. We learn the alphabet, spelling, punctuation, capitalization, and style. Then we work hard to get a job that includes a secretary who can then do all the supposedly nitpicky chores of cleaning up our writing and filing.

For a long time writing was the only way to preserve and transport knowledge, and writing *remains* the most concise, precise, and elegant way. It lends itself to categorization and crossreferencing. Literacy is a hallmark of civilization. A scholar must publish to be recognized. We depend on writing. Then someone types a smiley :-) and we realize the value of the intuitive. (Some more smileys are reproduced below.) I ❤ YOU has a warmth to it. The red octagon says STOP better than the word does. Be on the lookout for ways to use intuitive communication; after all, Apple Computer has made a fortune from it.

FIGURE 2.2

experience into sentences and paragraphs. Then, as if the channel were a train or a moving van, the information is transported to the reader, who in the decoding process unloads and unwraps each paragraph and sentence in order (unless he or she is one of those perverse people who like to read the last chapter first). Gutenberg Man creates a new reality of imagined experience from an orderly presentation of disorderly experiences.

INTRODUCTION OF ELECTRONICS

And so modern people lived in the chaos that is our world, retreating frequently into the Gutenberg world, recording experiences into words and paragraphs and reading these logical representations of a chaotic environment. Then in the mid-nineteenth century Samuel F. B. Morse introduced the telegraph; his first official message sent from the offices of the *Baltimore Sun* to the U. S. Capitol was: "What hath God wrought?" This first electronic message, sent by Gutenberg Man but encoded in near-digital-style Morse code, was a more prophetic question than he dreamed, because the answer has not yet been half-answered.

The telegraph transmitted code, which was almost binary code, over a wire at the speed of light. For the first time communication went beyond our line of sight by moving electrons instead of molecules. This change was revolutionary. Molecules are very heavy and difficult to move, being made up of atoms. Electrons, tiny bits of energy that we visualize as spinning about the nucleus of an atom, are light and easy to move. Molecules in our atmosphere run into the sound barrier at 550 miles per hour. Electrons can travel at the speed of light, 186,000 miles per second.

Benjamin Franklin was a pioneer in both the print and electronic fields. As a writer and printer he proved that journalism and newspapering could be profitable in the late eighteenth century. As a curious genius he was one of the first to investigate the nature of electricity through his experiments with kites during thunderstorms.

For example, let's consider the U. S. Capitol, the *Baltimore Sun,* and the president's annual State of the Union address. Prior to the introduction of the telegraph, the *Sun* and other newspapers north and east of Washington, D. C., would charter a locomotive on the day of the State of the Union address. Reporters would write down the president's words as rapidly as he spoke them, then hasten to the railroad station, and while the locomotive was puffing its way to Baltimore at the breakneck speed of 50 miles per hour, they would make a copy of the speech, which a clerk from the *Sun* would fetch from the train to the newspaper office. With belching smoke, clanging bell, and shrill whistle, the engine would make its way to Philadelphia, Trenton, New York, Hartford, and Boston so that newspaper readers could the very next morning see what the president planned to do to them during the coming year.

A telegrapher's index finger poised over a black button replaced all that, and the newspapers connected to the wires had the speech within minutes of its delivery, no matter how many hundreds of miles

MORSE'S DIGITAL SYSTEM

When Samuel F. B. Morse demonstrated his newly invented telegraph 150 years ago, he also demonstrated a new kind of writing. It was writing for the ear. But it did not depend upon analog sound signals the way speech does. Instead it used a code that was almost a digital system. Digital uses the concept of *something or nothing* (an electrical charge or no electrical charge). Morse used short or long bursts of electricity (dots or dashes). They were separated by short gaps of no electricity. Telegraphers wrote (or transmitted) with a key (or switch), which they tapped. Combinations of dots and dashes represented letters and numerals. At the other end of the telegraph wire, telegraphers read by listening to the dots and dashes and then transcribed into written alphabet what they heard. Soon typewriter keyboards and printers were hooked to the circuits and teletypewriter came into use, eliminating the need to learn the code. But some still do. Tune in a short-wave receiver some night and listen to the dots and dashes of ham radio operators tapping out globe-circling communications.

FIGURE 2.3

they were from the Capitol. And now in our dens we watch the president's every expression and hear his words, probably before the people present at the speech in the upper corners of the House of Representatives gallery hear them.

ELECTRONICS AND EXPERIENTIAL COMMUNICATION

Here, then, are some of the things worth looking at that the introduction of electronic processing of information has already done.

- It has provided information instantaneously.
- It provides information continuously.
- It can provide the same information worldwide.
- It has reduced the need for written description, broadening the sensual spectrum of the media.
- It has reduced the social distance between a mass media sender and a mass media receiver.

- It has blurred the boundary lines between "information" and "entertainment" by presenting both in the same channel using the same methods.
- It has returned us to the environment of Experiential Man.

During the Middle Ages, the arrival of a traveler must have been a matter of intense interest. He might have news of a battle that had happened months before or a plague that had raged somewhere else without the local folk having an inkling of it. Indeed, the Battle of New Orleans (1815) was won against the British by General Andrew Jackson and his rag-tag army of Tennesseans, New Orleans socialites, and Jean Lafitte's pirates *after* the governments involved had agreed to cease hostilities. Well into this century, sports pages carried play-by-play accounts of out-of-town games so the locals could create for themselves the game that was played the day before.

What a change has transpired! On December 7, 1941, all Americans knew before sundown that the U. S. fleet had been bombed at Pearl Harbor. And in 1991, the world watched Scuds and Tomahawk missiles arch through the skies and explode on Saudi Arabia, Kuwait, and Iraq. We watched the Persian Gulf War in real time, all the time.

POINT-TO-POINT COMMUNICATION. Instantaneous and continuous distribution of information began with what is called point-to-point communication. One telegrapher would communicate with another over a wire. The information, in the form of a telegram, would go to a single addressee, who might or might not make it known to friends or publish it in a newspaper. During the World Series a newspaper might set up a large blackboard in its storefront window, and, as a telegrapher tapped out news of balls and strikes, hits, and errors, a staff member with chalk would keep the crowd on the sidewalk apprised of the game's progress while it was happening. How exciting!

Beginning late in the nineteenth century, the telephone allowed one person to speak to another over a wire. Then came wireless. The dots and dashes of Morse code were sent out into the "ether," using the same electromagnetic spectrum that contains light we can see. Guglielmo Marconi demonstrated how ships could communicate with one another and with shore stations, no wires attached. Even when "wireless telephone" or voice radio was introduced, it was seen primarily as a point-to-point communication medium.

BROADCASTING. However, even children who could lay their hands on a battery, a set of headphones, some wire, and a crystal could pick up the dots and dashes out there in the ether, and before World War I, meteorologists in Kansas were tapping out forecasts so ranchers could protect their livestock from storms and farmers would have some idea of when the rain was coming. Like corn kernels in a planter's bag, the dots and dashes and the words were cast abroad. We had broadcasting, a new mass medium.

A new kind of oral tradition was created. Thousands heard a man try to tell them what was happening when the giant hydrogen-filled passenger dirigible Hindenburg burst into flame and was destroyed in a couple of minutes while landing at Lakehurst, New Jersey. The public had to wait a day to see the pictures of the blaze in a newspaper, and a week or two to see the movie newsreel. But with radio, announcers told us what was happening, from before the beginning of the game or the national political convention, continuing throughout and until after the last fan or delegate had departed. The voices continue to let us hear "all about it" all the time, every day.

A century ago, before wireless, different nationalities residing in isolation on an island could live in harmony for months while their mother countries were locked in mortal warfare, until a ship stopped off with news of the strife. But on November 22, 1963, large portions of the Earth's population were shocked and grieved as news of the assassination of the young President of the United States—John Kennedy,

Authorized by the Federal Communications Commission (FCC) in 1948, citizens-band (CB) radios allow anyone to broadcast at low power in the ultra-high-frequency (UHF) band. Twenty-five years later, inexpensive transmitter–receiver sets were marketed, resulting in a CB craze. In 1978 CB was so popular the FCC added seventeen channels to the original twenty-three. Originally used primarily by truckers to share weather, traffic, and law-enforcement information, CB was installed in millions of cars, but when the novelty wore off, the public lost interest because the content of CB communication was so inane.

DIGITIZING THE WAVE

Spoken words in a room use the air to carry the sound waves. A telephone mouthpiece uses sound vibrations to modify an electric current in the phone circuit. A radio transmitter applies the sound vibrations to a carrier wave, modulating the wave. AM radio transmitters modulate the amplitude of the wave; FM stations modulate the frequency. Electric interference causes static, particularly on AM. When the sound is digitized, interference is all but eliminated. Using light as a carrier in fiber optics eliminates the electromagnetic interference of other kinds of carriers.

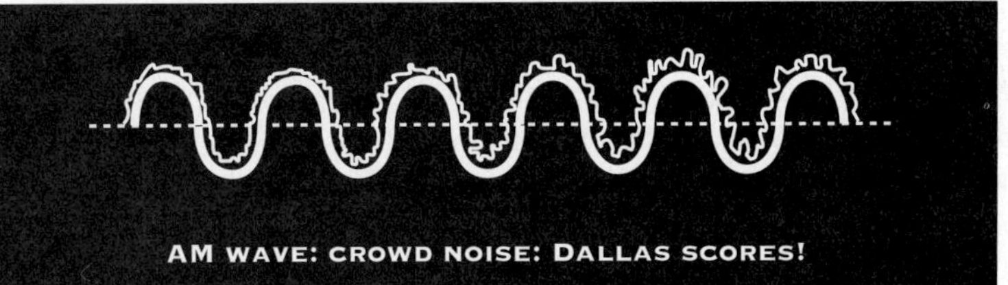

FIGURE 2.4

the man who had created the Peace Corps and comforted the beleaguered citizens of Berlin—flew across the air waves. Now financial wizards watch all the securities and commodity markets worldwide, fingers poised over their computer keyboards ready to trigger dozens of instantaneous and simultaneous buy-and-sell orders.

AN INTIMATE MEDIUM. But the new broadcasting devices were more than instantaneous and universal publications. They were a new medium. Particularly after the introduction of television at the middle of the century, it was readily apparent that they were a different kind of mass medium, different in their sensory stimuli.

When WEAF (New York's pioneer station) broadcast the first commercial, Commerce Secretary Herbert Hoover commented, "It is inconceivable that we should allow so great a possibility for service to be drowned in advertising chatter."

Radio was not an electronic lecture hall. In the 1920s and '30s, the charlatan Dr. John Romulus Brinkley realized that by assuming a bedside manner over the air he could read a listener's letter, "diagnose" the listener's ailment, and "prescribe" a "cure" for thousands of listeners simultaneously and at great financial profit. Radio, it turned out, was person-to-person. The cultivated and confident voice of President Franklin Roosevelt coming quietly from the Oval Office into the living rooms of America during his many "Fireside Chats" reassured a nation during the Great Depression.

In 1949, 2.3 percent of U.S. homes had television sets; by 1954, more than half did; by 1978, 97 percent did; by 1992, 98.2 percent did, and the TV stayed on seven hours a day.

On television in the presidential debates of 1960, the nervous expression and dark jowls of Vice-President Nixon contrasted to his detriment with the assured and youthful demeanor of his opponent, Senator Kennedy. In the early hours of the Gulf War, the news became the frenzied struggle of reporters in Jerusalem to don gas masks, fearing that Iraqi Scud missiles then falling on the city would contain chemical weapons. Viewers around the world perceived the urgency of the moment, although no weapons were in sight and not a word was being uttered.

FACT AND FICTION BLURRED

In the Dark Ages minstrels both informed and entertained. So have the print media. During the century in which magazines were the great national medium of the United States, articles of nonfiction and stories or serial books of fiction appeared on adjacent pages. For example, a nonfiction personality profile about an important manufacturer might appear in an issue of *The Saturday Evening Post,* and elsewhere there might be a short story with a wealthy manufacturer as its central character. The article would identify real places and real events and be accompanied by a real photograph of a real man. The short story would carry a drawing or painting of the imaginary hero and his name and address would clearly be imaginary. (Of course unscrupulous publications sometimes published fiction as fact, such as the *New York Sun*'s description of real people seen on the Moon through a giant telescope that never existed.)

A CHRONOLOGY OF RADIO AND TELEVISION TECHNOLOGY

1820
Hans Christian Oersted showed that current flowing in a wire establishes a magnetic field around it.

1864
James Clerk Maxwell published a theory that said a change in electrical voltage or current creates an electrical disturbance traveling in space at the speed of light.

1888
Heinrich Hertz used oscillating circuits to transmit and receive electromagnetic waves, calculating their velocity at the speed of light.

1895
Guglielmo Marconi built the first practical wireless telegraph system, patented in 1896. He broadcast across the Atlantic in 1901.

1905
Sir Ambrose Fleming developed the diode vacuum tube, permitting detection of high-frequency radio waves.

1906
Reginald Aubrey Fressenden, first voice transmission by radio.

1907
Lee de Forest introduced the triode tube, capable of amplifying radio signals.

1918
Edwin Armstrong introduced the superheterodyne circuit, permitting efficient tuning of receivers.

1933
Armstrong introduced frequency modulation (FM), as opposed to amplitude modulation (AM). FM greatly reduced static interference.

1939
Since 1929 David Sarnoff had been interested in television. NBC spent $50 million on it, using Vladimar Zworykin's all-electronic technology; demonstrated at the 1939 New York World's Fair.

1944
FCC approves twelve very-high-frequency (VHF) and seventy ultra-high-frequency (UHF) channels for television.

1948
Three Bell Laboratories scientists introduced the transitstor, a solid-state device that replaced vacuum tubes and brought about integrated circuit technology, which has made the computer practical.

1950s–1960s
Coaxial cable and microwave systems were built, providing television networks with efficient channels.

1975
RCA launched the first satellite designed for television. By the 1990s there were 65 million satellite television networks.

1992
55 million American homes had cable television.

BOX 2.1

A CHRONOLOGY OF RADIO AND TELEVISION CONTENT

1912 Radio Act of 1912 allowed broadcasts at 360-meter wave length; interference resulted; entry into World War I suspended private use.

1920 Frank Conrad founded KDKA, Pittsburgh, to air news, sports, election returns.

1922 AT&T's WEAF in New York airs first commercial, a ten-minute real estate pitch.

1926 Radio Corporation of America (RCA, owned by Westinghouse, General Electric, and AT&T) bought WEAF and founded the National Broadcasting Company to offer programming to increase sales of radio sets. David Sarnoff was the guiding light.

1927 Columbia Broadcasting System (CBS) was founded; William Paley soon took it over.

1929 Freeman Gosden and Charles Correll created *Amos 'n Andy*, a daily 15-minute comedy drama in which two black men tried to deal with the problems of the Great Depression. Audience: forty million. Their success brought Jack Benny, George Burns, Gracie Allen, and Ed Wynn into radio.

1931 NBC now entirely commercial; profit $2 million.

1934 Broadcasting Act of 1934 created the Federal Communications Commision (FCC); required stations to broadcast for "public convenience and necessity."

1937 NBC lures conductor Arturo Toscanini to New York from Italy, established the NBC Symphony Orchestra, which performed on Sunday evenings.

1938 Drama matures. Orson Welles' Halloween broadcast of H.G. Wells' *War of the Worlds* frightens millions.

1938 CBS sent Edward R. Murrow to Europe to line up lecturers. Instead he aired the Nazis' coup of Austria, beginning what became news coverage of World War II. He hired a team of notable journalists, including Walter Cronkite.

1941 FCC Report on Chain Broadcasting required NBC to sell one of its two radio networks. Upon its sale, the Blue network became ABC.

1947 House Un-American Activities Committee began investigating Communist infiltration of American institutions, including broadcast artists; 151 were blacklisted.

1948 Milton Berle pioneered television comedy.

1950 Murrow and Fred Friendly established *See It Now*, a documentary news program which, among other topics, exposed Senator Joseph McCarthy's lists of alleged Communists or Communist sympathizers. In 1954, McCarthy was censured by the Senate.

1951 Leonard Goldensen of United Paramount Theaters bought ABC and brought in movie industry promotion and programming such as *The Mickey Mouse Club* (1955).

1952 NBC began the *Today* show, with Dave Garroway as host; and in 1953 began *Tonight* with Steve Allen.

BOX 2.2

cont'd...

A CHRONOLOGY OF RADIO AND TELEVISION CONTENT

1955 Among musical extravaganzas, Mary Martin as *Peter Pan* attracted 60 million viewers.

1959 The era of the big quiz show ended with evidence of rigged answers on *The $64,000 Question.* Payoffs of disc jockeys to promote records was a radio scandal.

1960 James Aubrey (CBS) introduced *Beverly Hillbillies* and other filmed comedies; *I Love Lucy* (early 1950s) was the first filmed show, permitting reruns.

1961 FCC Chairman Newton Minow warned that "games, violence, and sadism" were turning television into "a vast wasteland."

1963 A majority of Americans were transfixed by telecasts related to the November 22 Kennedy assassination as the three networks that dominated television suspended all other programming.

1967 The Carnegie Commission urged establishment of a fourth network, publicly operated. PBS (funded by viewers, corporations, and government) was created.

1969 *The Forsyte Saga* of nineteenth–century British life, broadcast on PBS, demonstated the viability of broadcasting to an intellectual niche. Children's Television Workshop's *Sesame Street* was a nonexploitative PBS children's educational and entertainment program.

1971 *All in the Family* (CBS) imported controversial topics into television situation comedies, much as *Amos'n Andy* had in radio.

1972 The Surgeon General and the National Institute for Mental Health warned that television violence encouraged childhood aggression.

1975 Fred Silverman at ABC appealed to youth with *Happy Days* and introduced series spectaculars with *Roots.*

1980 NBC's *Hill Street Blues* brought gritty reality to television dramas.

1985 *The Cosby Show* dissected middle–class family life.

1985–1986 Capital Cities Communication (newspapers and stations) bought ABC; General Electric bought RCA (and NBC); Time Inc. (publishers) merged with Warner Brothers (television and movies).

1980s A period of deregulation, attempting to allow stations and networks to compete with cable television and videocassettes. Satellite technology let superstations like WTBS (Atlanta), owned by Ted Turner, became mini-networks through cable television. Turner surprised the experts when Cable News Network (CNN), 24-hour all-news programming, proved a success.

1990 Rupert Murdoch's Fox network had 133 stations presenting lowbrow programming such as *The Simpsons.*

1990s Radio grew; 4,900 FM stations, 4,200 AM stations. Music networks via satellite and talk–show hosts such as Larry King, Paul Harvey, and Rush Limbaugh were popular.

BOX 2.2

By 1992, 55 million U.S. households had cable television service from the 8,700 cable television systems in service. They were served by sixty-five networks transmitted by satellite. In addition 3-million backyard satellite receiver dishes had been sold.

Through its Astra satellite, Radio Luxembourg is transmitting Direct Broadcast Service (DBS) to 20 million European households. Of these, 2 million households were receiving the service on their own satellite receiver dishes.

The lines have blurred with motion pictures, radio, and television. A crime scene complete with police, victim on a stretcher, ambulance, and curious crowds, looked as legitimate on *NYPD Blue* as it did on the evening news. Indeed the "Old Redhead," Gordon McLendon, used to present fictionalized versions of major-league baseball games on radio while the real games were still in progress. Prevented from being at the games in person, McLendon would receive a play-by-play description telegraphed from inside the stadium and, in the comfort of his broadcast studio, recreate the sound of the bat hitting the ball and the roar of the crowd indicating the ball had soared over the center-field fence, while delivering a colorful but imaginary oral description of the player saluting the applause with lifted cap.

Indeed, after seeing an early demonstration of television in 1938, E. B. White wrote: "A door closing, heard over the air, a face contorted seen in a panel of light, these will emerge as the real and the true. And when we bang the door of our own cell or look into another's face, the impression will be of mere artifice." Three decades later, *The New Yorker* magazine, for which Mr. White wrote so long and so well, published one of its classic cartoons. It depicted a man changing a tire in the rain, shaking his fist and shouting at his children in the car, "But this is the *real world,* I can't change the channel!"

VICARIOUS REALITY

Today's generation gauges its real experiences against those it experiences vicariously on television, radio, and motion pictures. Vicarious reality has changed from the linear written logic of Gutenberg Man to the impressions gained through the electronic media by the new Experiential Man. Douglass Cater has sharpened the contrast between Gutenberg Man and Experiential Man by suggesting that reading and writing are carried out by Gutenberg Man using the left hemisphere of the brain, while the Experiential Man of the Dark Ages and today's electronically stimulated Experiential Man rely on the right hemisphere, or as Cater says, appositional hemisphere of the brain. While this is not the place for a discourse on "left brain, right brain," the concept that a person responds differently to different kinds of stimuli (including those stimuli created by the mass media) is widely accepted.

For example, two great complaints of contemporary educators are that the new generations (1.) can't read, don't read, and won't read, and (2.) television is to blame for subverting the minds of the new generations. How much of this is a legitimate criticism and how much is a failure to understand the nature of experiential learning, even vicarious experiential learning? The contemporary view of what is knowledge is biased toward Gutenberg, linear-logical information. Experiential logic and information are quite different.

The poets understand this. What is a tree? Enough wood pulp to produce a Sunday copy of *The New York Times*? A producer of leaves that fall and must be raked up in the autumn? Things that prevent one from seeing the forest? Something to climb? Something to sit under until an apple falls on one's head and leads one to the theory of gravity? Joyce Kilmer decided that trees were lovelier than poems and that only God truly understood them. What is a rainbow to a 65-year-old man? If we are to believe John Keats, what a rainbow is to a 65-year-old man depends on whether his heart leaped up when he was a boy and saw a rainbow. ("My heart leaps up when I behold a rainbow in the sky . . . the child is but the father of the man.")

Since all kinds of information can now be digitized, put into a computer, and made available through a single medium, the simultaneous understanding of both cold logic and things that make our hearts leap up is important, and may well determine the kind of mass communication messages that evolve now that a new revolution in communication is taking place.

A Technological Dark Age?

There is a dark side to predictions of where the new revolution in communication may go. The onset of the Dark Ages offers an analogy of what could happen in the decades ahead. After the Classical Age, the unmoneyed elite—those who could read and write and communicate what they had reasoned—disappeared from society into the monasteries. Knowledge became an end unto itself. The great mass of society had no access to broad learning. That's why the period that followed has been called the Dark Ages.

Some scholars predict that "a new social class" is emerging made up of those people who can use the new information and communication opportunities. Mirabito and Morgenstern, for example, in their exposition of contemporary communication technology noted that as early as 1986 conferences were being held on the possibility of a deprived social class emerging "for those individuals who do not know how to use a computer or who lack information and management skills."

Summary

The greatest gift of prehistoric man was speech. The classical civilizations gave us writing and words of wisdom. But mass knowledge remained largely experiential until the introduction of the printing press. A revolution in thinking ensued. Gutenberg man, the reader, now views serious knowledge as based on linear logic. The introduction of the electronic media has given people alternatives. Recent generations have both experiential and linear-logical alternatives available in the media. The New Medium—digital computerized mass communication—can combine both. Will the promise of this New Medium be available to all?

Discussion Topics, Projects, and Exercises

1. Play the game Gossip. Whisper a complicated sentence to a class member, who then whispers it to the next student. After the sentence has gone all around the room to each student, ask the last student to say the sentence he or she heard. Compare that sentence to the original. There will be major differences. Discuss these differences in the light of the oral tradition that existed prior to the introduction of printing.
2. Report on or discuss functional illiteracy. How does our world seem to a person who cannot read? How is such a person handicapped? How widespread is functional illiteracy?
3. As a class exercise, write or tell what your perceptions are of (a) a news story you might read of a terrible traffic accident in a distant city; (b) a news story about an accident on your campus; (c) a friend's description of a traffic accident the friend has just seen; (d) the worst traffic accident you have experienced. Discuss the differences in what you "know" about each accident and how you "feel" about each accident. Relate this to linear Gutenberg logic and to experiential logic.
4. View a videotape of *The Day the Universe Changed.*

Suggested Readings

Cater, Douglass, and Richard Adler. *Television as a Social Force*. New York: Praeger, 1975. An early look at the phenomenon of television.

Eisenstein, Elizabeth L. *The Printing Revolution in Early Modern Europe*. Cambridge, Great Britain: Cambridge University Press, 1983. Examination of how printing had unexpected influences on medieval Europe.

McLuhan, Marshall. *Understanding Media*. New York: Signet, 1964. The book about the media that had all America talking and introduced a new way to look at mass communication.

Mirabito, Michael M., and Barbara L. Morgenstern. *The New Communications Technologies*. Boston: Focal Press, 1990. Descriptions of fairly recent technological developments.

The Digital Medium

Considering How Digital Technology Can Bring About a Convergence of the Media

Ted Turner's mastery of cable television and satellite transmission has, in a sense, brought mass media to an end. Success in the future requires constant innovation.

—Donald L. Shaw

Not so long ago a scholar would take a fountain pen and a notebook to the library, look up references in a periodical index or a card catalog, find the citations in the stacks, and sit down at a table to make notes. Some of this note taking could be done back at the scholar's own desk if the books could be checked out. Perhaps an experiment would be conducted in a laboratory or an authority interviewed. Again notes would be taken. From these ink-blotted pages the scholar would synthesize a research report, pecking away at a noisy manual typewriter, diligently applying a rubber eraser to correct errors as they were made. By the use of carbon paper, the scholar could retain a copy of the report while sending the original off for publication or to be evaluated by a teacher.

"Little more than a decade ago, the only people who got to watch movies on demand were motion-picture studio executives . . . and the only people who had car phones were government officials and some phone company executives. . . . [Now] the options are so commonplace that people don't even stop to think about them."

—Alfred C. Sikes

The typewriter and the fountain pen were the great innovations of the previous hundred years. Earlier technological innovation included the steel pen, a great improvement over the goose quill.

What a difference less than a half-century makes. A tape recorder captures every word of an interview or the description of a laboratory experiment as it is conducted. The scholar uses a CD-ROM (CD-Read Only Memory) index and an on-line computerized card catalog today.

Keywords dramatically increase searching ability and efficiency. Articles from journals or chapters from books are inexpensively copied and taken home. Instead of notes, the scholar uses a highlighter to mark the precious passages. Indeed, the scholar may go far beyond the local library through online searching of distant computerized databases and instantaneously secure texts of articles (probably with the assistance of an experienced librarian laboring at a computer keyboard).

The scholar uses a computer word-processing program that can automatically print one or more copies. If the first draft contains errors, the scholar again brings up the report on the screen, corrects them, and prints out a new, clean version.

This is the information world of today; it is still a Gutenberg, linear-logical world, but that is changing.

A visit to the Seattle Museum of Art will demonstrate the change. This new museum, of course, has paintings on the walls, sculpture on pedestals, and ceramics and so forth in cases. A brochure gives the layout of the museum. Brief descriptions on cards accompany each work. A catalog of the holdings can be purchased that gives further printed information. Books about art are available in the store near the entrance—all the Gutenberg accoutrements.

But what sets this museum apart from an information point of view is a computer screen named Viewpoint located in the main hallway. Here any patron may pause and literally at one's fingertips gain an understanding of what is on display from many different perspectives. Icons, or little pictures, invite the patron to see the "Maps" of the museum or a "Glossary" of art terms. By touching the map icon, floorplans of the museum are revealed, and by touching a room on the plan, examples of the art in that room are shown on the screen.

Or perhaps the patron would like a "Guided Tour." Touch that icon on Viewpoint and a choice of "Geography," "Great Themes," or other tours are offered. The "Great Themes" tour has choices of such things as "The Human Form" or "Landscapes" or "Portraits." Touch the "Portraits" icon and a selection of art works—oils from nineteenth-century Europe, a wood mask from Africa, a photograph from Depression America—are offered. Each of these icons offers a full-screen depiction of the art work and another screen that includes text about the artist and a critical description of the work.

Thus Viewpoint cross-references the holdings of the museum in many ways that let the patron's fingers do the walking. The computer can be used for a quick reference to what a patron wants to see, for a lengthy preview of what the museum offers, or for a satisfying review of what one has already seen. The patron views pictures and reads text.

On the fourth floor of the museum is another innovation. A videocassette player, screen, and earphones offer the patron an opportunity to have an American Indian artist give brief oral descriptions of

A CD at the National Gallery in London, similar to Viewpoint, was so popular that people spent hours looking at the screen instead of going through the museum. Access to the CD had to be limited. Now the CD has been marketed to the public by the Microsoft corporation.

her work (shown on the screen) and to hear the music of a contemporary American Indian group that she chose. If the audio and video were digitized and incorporated into Viewpoint on the ground floor, two additional dimensions would be added to the information it contains.

This is an inkling of the medium of tomorrow: easy to use, incorporating audio and video plus oral and written language, and with great flexibility in the way its information can be arranged and accessed. It combines linear-logical information with experiential information.

Viewpoint is a simplified prototype of what the business and home information computer of tomorrow may offer. In the accompanying chart (see Figure 3.1) it would occupy the Decoding computer spot. The chief difference would be that instead of being a stand-alone computer depending entirely on what is in its memory, it would have continuous access to the whole world through a broadband channel of communication. Another difference would be that it would already "know" many of the things its User was interested in and would make them immediately available on command, as well as adapting as future information needs arise.

All the components of this New Medium exist.

SOURCE/ENCODING

As indicated in Chapter One, print media, audio-based media, and video-based media all are using digitized information. The print media, through desktop publishing and digitized still photography, depend on it almost exclusively. The CD has taken the recording industry into the digital world in breathtaking fashion. The Source/Encoding third of the model shown in Figure 3.1 is rapidly falling into place.

In fact, no major technological breakthroughs are required to create a system that offers information to all. The challenge ahead, rather, is to standardize, organize, and schedule. Standardization of the way digital information is manipulated sufficiently to allow a universal network to carry all kinds of information is a goal. Another is to organize information providers sufficiently to allow all of them access to the universal network. Actually getting the information onto the network is a matter of scheduling. These are the kinds of challenges on which good bureaucracies thrive.

On smaller scales, these kinds of challenges are being met all the time. Busy minds have been dealing with how to move digital information into networks throughout the 1980s and into the 1990s. Most of the time the networks provide information for specialized enterprises, such as scientific research organizations, businesses, and the professions. How to deal with the broad spectrum of the public is a new challenge.

COMMUNICATION MODEL OF THE FUTURE MEDIUM

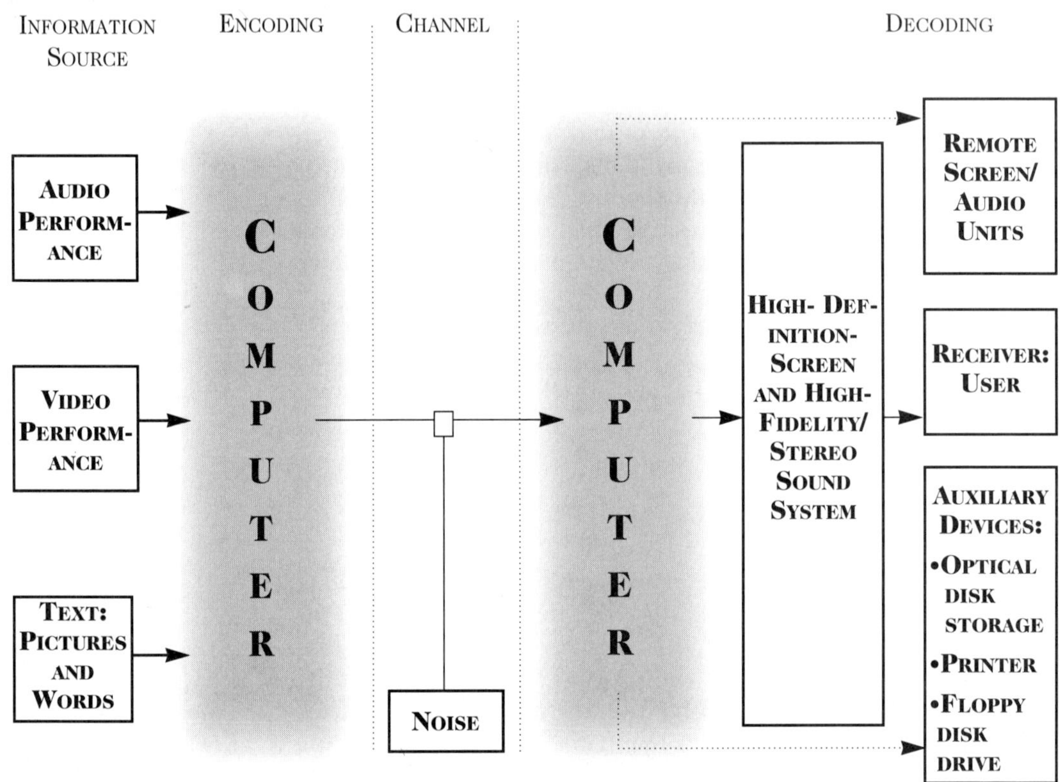

The mass medium of the future will convert all information into digital form and transmit it electronically from the Source's computer to the Receiver's computer. Users of this medium will no longer have to be involved with the tangible aspects of the distribution systems used by contemporary mass media (paper publications, film, cassettes, disks); nor will the users of this medium be constricted by radio, television, and theater time factors (schedules).

Users of the New Medium will encode, transmit, decode, and receive single messages that use both audio and video (sound and sight, including speech and reading) simultaneously. This will allow the Receiver to understand messages easier and quicker.

The amount of information/number of messages that may be transmitted by the Sender and that are available to the Receiver will be vastly increased. At the same time, the Receiver's ability to winnow through information to find what is interesting and necessary is vastly increased by the Decoder's (computer's) ability to search, find, and display almost instantaneously.

FIGURE 3.1

A variety of specialists have expertise to contribute to this challenge; postal-service and parcel-delivery specialists, telephone customer-service specialists, print-media editors, and circulation specialists, broadcast producers, and news directors, to name a few. They need to be a part of the team that determines how and when information is directed into the universal communication channel. They need to adapt their expertise to a new kind of information channel.

Instead of creating a whole new information network for Texas public schools, the Texas Higher Education Network (THENet) became Texas Education Network (TENet), and at a cost of $5 a year, a school or teacher can have access to Internet, university library catalogs, databases, and bulletin boards. Expanding the network was vastly less expensive than creating a new one.

CHANNEL

Video, audio, and text combined is a heavy load of information, and heavy-duty information channels are needed to transport it. Continually expanding artificial-satellite technology and the introduction of fiber-optic networks are providing the broadband channels that can carry the load. Satellites in particular are designed to carry all kinds of communications at once and are accelerating the move to the all-digital information environment. Connectivity is a challenge, but the technology for the Channel portion of Figure 3.1 exists, though what economic and physical form it will take is a matter of intense competition and controversy.

Great corporations are joining forces to grab a piece of this information channel. Public hearings and private convocations have taken it up. In the background is history: the populist and private-enterprise approaches to establishing canals, highways, sea and air lanes, electric power utilities, the postal system, the telegraph, radio, television, and a free press.

The rush toward an integrated medium is on. News items tell how: CNN and Gannett explore interactive media; IBM meets with cable companies on two-way TV services; the FCC lets phone companies enter cable TV; book sellers are abuzz about books in digital form; Apple and CNN hope to test a weekly news magazine; Apple and IBM share in developing multimedia computers.

Even while the corporations cook up deals and the government agencies negotiate, networks are springing up ad hoc. The most noteworthy is the Internet. Originally a U. S. government effort to link computers, it moved into the academic community, and now in less than a decade millions of people who have gained access to Internet have made it into a global network used for the most serious and frivolous purposes—far beyond what its creators could have imagined. The Internet provides an information environment that ranges in quality from professional journals at their best to CB radio at its worst.

Because the Internet was needed and was used, brainpower has been applied to overcome problems such as connectivity, control, and cost, to make the Internet living proof of what a great computerized information system can be.

Two paths to obtaining a universal channel seem to be possible. The first would follow the Internet model: an existing network will prove to be so useful that a high percentage of the population will embrace it. Or, a combination of careful planning and a great leap of faith will result in the channel and its useful content being made available and accepted.

Of course the institution—nation, corporation, whatever—that first creates the channel will assume a leadership role in world affairs.

DECODING/RECEIVER

The Decoding/Receiving portion of the model shown in Figure 3.1, in reality, is a simplified mirror image of the Source/Encoding portion with its own specialized functions. The technology exists in disparate appliances throughout many homes: a computer with a modem connecting it to a telephone line, cable television, radio and television sets, speaker systems, and so forth. Pulling it all together is the challenge, a challenge that has the sale of 100 million or more units as an incentive.

The decoding/receiving computer and software would go beyond what the existing appliances do (see Figure 3.2). It would:

1. accept all kinds of digital signals,
2. provide for easy movement between them,
3. provide a large amount of easily accessible storage,
4. provide appropriate categories of information (movies, music, news, mail, and so forth, with subcategories for each),
5. provide an information-needs inventory for the User so the decoder could continually search for important information and immediately have it on tap the next time the User is available,
6. provide for permanent storage of appropriate information, and
7. provide a regular purge of temporary information.

The ability of a computer to do these things has been and is being tested. But these kinds of applications are not widely used now. A detailed description of what could be useful is appropriate.

First, here is what the decoding/receiving computer would do with the digital signals received:

- Identify them as to information category: text, graphics, audio, video, service to system;
- Store them appropriately;
- Categorize messages by content, source, and priority of importance: entertainment or factual, personal or general information, requested data (and by whom), or message consigned by an information service;
- See which messages match the User profile;
- Prioritize the message for easy decision making by the User as to how much time to spend with each;

The Decoding–Receiving Computer of the Future?

The Medium Decoder
needs a computer–
- a link to the world
- a good screen
- great speakers
- and maybe a printer–

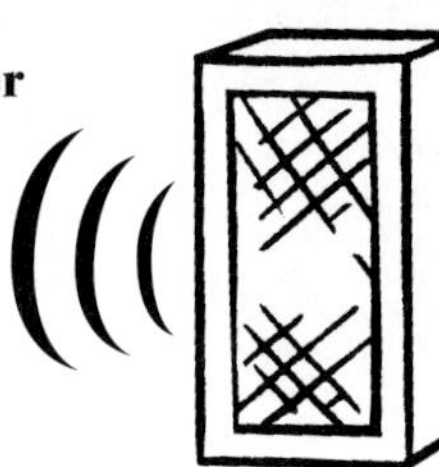

plus lots of
memory for all
kinds of information

–also needs a detective
who can find
anything instantly–

and a granny who knows what
you want before you ask for it.

Figure 3.2

- Save permanent information;
- Purge temporal information.

Second, here is how the decoding/receiving computer would interact with the User:

- At installation of the unit, the User would provide a basic profile of what information is important; this profile would be updated regularly;
- The computer would be used to keep the User's appointment/travel calendar, address book, correspondence, and so forth;
- Computer monitors these files daily for cues as to what information the User needs on a temporary basis;
- Unit monitors the User's use of information and adjusts priorities of size and availability to match that use;
- Unit monitors cost of information used, warns the User if budgeted funds are being depleted too rapidly.

Such a decoding/receiving computer would lift that wonderful computerese term "user friendly" to a new level of definition.

CONTENT

An even greater challenge than the hardware and software, is the information itself; that is, how to manage the content of the New Medium. People are struggling with this challenge now. One of the promising developments is multimedia, although "integrated media" would be a more appropriate name. As stated above, it combines linear-logical information (primarily oral or written verbal information) with audio and video (nonverbal) information.

Another promising development is hypertext. Hypertext software goes beyond menus to allow the User multiple options for moving around in computer memory to retrieve information. Its goal is to account for every possible cross-indexing function instantaneously.

A more holistic view of information is at hand. At present, a librarian views information as what is in books, a journalist as stories (nonfiction), Hollywood as movies or segments of a TV series, the National Football League looks at information as games leading to and including the Super Bowl. Wall Street looks at it as stock tables. An artist looks at information as a painting or sculpture, a composer as a symphony.

The New Medium encompasses all of these and more. From the point of view of the audience member (the receiver, or User), information is what is easily available and interesting or useful.

Conceptualize the New Medium as a vast new continent. Its resources seem limitless. The potential for its being a sustaining and

David Kammerer and David MacFarland at Kansas State University instruct teachers on creating their own video, audio, and so forth, and combining them into multimedia presentations. Podium (out of MIT) is a software package that allows professors to begin with class notes and existing images, and so on, to produce multimedia lectures. The Illinois State School of Education requires teachers to have the computer skills needed in the educational process.

Melinda McAdams, a copy editor at the *Washington Post,* has predicted how hypertext will change the way information is presented: Highlighted portions of a story will indicate that a User can get background, the previous day's story, a completely separate article, a reference to another story in another database, maps, and graphics (new or archived). The interface, she warns, must be kept simple.

E-MAIL FROM MARIA

We can imagine that Maria Vasquez is sending an e-mail (electronic mail) message to a couple who are patrons of the El Paso News and Entertainment Company. She has interviewed them about updating their information needs and is replying to their requests. Ms. Vasquez has been retrained for her job. Formerly she worked for the El Paso *Times* circulation department on a delivery route. She moonlighted as a phone surveyor for a television rating service.

A MAJOR NATIONAL AND REGIONAL INTERCHANGE OF INFORMATION COULD TAKE PLACE IN THE EARLY HOURS OF THE MORNING WHEN COMMUNICATIONS LINES ARE THE LEAST BUSY, ALLOWING SPECIALIZED AND PAROCHIAL INFORMATION TO GO TO DISTANT USERS.

WHAT WE NOW CONSIDER SCHEDULED ENTERTAINMENT COULD GO TO REGIONAL DISTRIBUTERS EARLY IN THE DAY AND BE AVAILABLE ON DEMAND THROUGHOUT THE PRIME-TIME PERIOD.

Dear Mr. and Mrs. Jones,

I've followed up on our interview and am glad to note that we can make the changes in your EPNE services without an increase in your monthly rate.

Discontinued:

Multiple-listing and real estate transfers daily data. (Hope you enjoy your retirement, Jane, after a successful real estate career.)

Really Music. (Your son can pick this up once he's at his new job in South Anchorage, Antarctica.)

Commuter up-to-the-minute.

Added:

Detroit Arts High School Tatler. (Your granddaughter's high school news magazine will be available each Tuesday and Thursday.)

Fort Stockton Pioneer. (Glad you two are keeping up with your old Texas hometown.)

21st Century Explorer. (Let me know how you like this multimedia travel magazine.)

Pictures Unlimited. (Alfred, I loved your digital photos of Juarez at night. You're great!)

CBS Entertainment. (You already have TNN and NBC; does include "The Grandma Demi Moore Show.")

You are increasing your Pick and Choose option now that you have more time to browse.

Your morning lineup will include:

Weather, adding S. Anchorage report and forecast.
Sports (yes, Detroit Arts High is included).
Mutual Funds (use help button to add new ones).
El Paso/Jaurez Update; Good Morning North America;
The New York Times.

During the day, you'll continue to have updates on local weather, all the sports and news.

Remember the Big Update comes between 3:45 a.m. and 4:00 a.m. El Paso time, so save anything you don't want purged before that time.

Of course Ready Eye will be keeping you up with your travel bookings, appointments, and correspondence to provide additional information. If you need me:

Call by clicking here __or e-mail by clicking here__

Maria Vasquez

Box 3.1

Research reveals how people use media and computers. They like media they are accustomed to and use arbitrary categories (Gantz). Looking at news Users rather than providers gives consistent results; people will seek information they want (Martin). Users of financial information choose the Dow Jones Retrieval Service for specific information rather than the *Wall Street Journal*—and remember it better (Zerbinos). Upscale, younger farmers use videotex and teletext for perishable or volatile information (Abbott). Reading speed and comprehension are equivalent for high-quality screens and books, but lower for lower-quality screens (*Behavior and Information Technology*).

Note: References for research cited in this note are: Walter Gantz, *Journalism Quarterly*, Winter 1991; John L. Martin, *Annals of the American Academy of Political and Social Science*, September 1976; Eugenia Zerbinos, *Journalism Quarterly*, Spring 1990; Eric A. Abbott, *Journal of Communication*, Fall 1989.

"The competition . . . to become the universal interface between computer and user has been won by 'the object,' the visual symbol, not 'the word.'" Computer users are creating vocabularies of the visual.

—Robert Kahan

rewarding environment for countless people is matched by the opportunity for it to be wasted and spoiled, to be trivialized and misused. Those who create the content for the New Medium are the trail blazers of the twenty-first century. What they create will be "the world" perceived by the population, just as much as the land that lay before the eyes of the eighteenth- and nineteenth-century pioneers was their world.

These creators will be picking and choosing from among all the phenomena that stimulate the eye and the ear to provide the most succinct and compelling "stories" possible. They will be using trial and error, scientific sampling of audiences, focus groups, and every other tool they can find to discover how best to bring information to people that will be beneficial and rewarding. This can be an unparalleled creative opportunity for hundreds of thousands of information professionals in the decades ahead.

Think of it. Could Beethoven handle video? Could Shakespeare handle audio? Could Steven Spielberg handle a breaking news story? Geniuses in the twenty-first century may get a chance to try to handle the whole enchilada.

One creative person who has tackled multimedia is Rick Smolen. Smolen is well known in the world of photojournalism, particularly for his "Day in the Life of——" books (*A Day in the Life of Japan* was the first). The photojournalistic technique for these books is to dispatch a team of photographers to a location (such as Japan) and have them record what people are doing throughout that location on that day, then publish a photojournalistic book that gives a rich taste of the culture from a brief slice in time. Tiny maps and clock faces accompany each picture to show where and when the pictures were made.

In 1992 Smolen edited a work that was published in three forms, two of them multimedia. The work expanded upon an article in *National Geographic* describing a young woman's solo trek across the Australian Outback, entitled *From Alice to Ocean*, the work is in the form of a traditional photojournalism book. It also is published as a Kodak CD-ROM with an audiotape. Finally it is published as 3.5-inch computer disks for use with a Macintosh computer. The last version includes motion pictures, sound, still photography, and text in a single digital package, and allows the User leeway in what order and time frame he or she wishes to experience the work.

The opportunity the User has in the Macintosh version of *From Alice to Ocean* illustrates the most unusual dimension of creativity that the New Medium offers. It consists of the partnership between those who provide the information and those who use it. (Sometimes the Users may help provide information.) When all the information is digital and it is stored so that every item is easily available, one has the opportunity to expand one's informational horizons and to make one's own path through the information landscape.

A MULTIMEDIA HISTORY OF WORLD WAR II

A topic that cries out for multimedia publishing is the fiftieth anniversary of World War II (1939–1945). Records and artifacts of countless aspects of history's most extensive global conflict are available.

It is the topic of thousands of books, fictional movies, and documentary films. Historians have analyzed it. Museums are full of its weapons. A worldwide generation of its survivors is now in retirement. The war is the most vivid experience of many lives.

Multimedia would offer them and millions of others a chance to take individual walks down memory lane.

Using current resources one can, over the years, grasp something of the hideous enormity of the Holocaust, the systematic imprisonment and execution of more than 10 million people (6 million of them Jews) by the Nazis. Multimedia could allow one to gain an understanding quickly. At a single sitting, one might go through photographs taken at the death camps after liberation, hear survivors tell their stories, read the testimony given at the Adolph Eichmann trial, and sample excerpts from the day-to-day thoughts and experiences of a teenager in hiding from the *Diary of Anne Frank.*

SAMPLE EVENTS

- •INVASION OF POLAND
- •FALL OF FRANCE
- •DUNKIRK
- •BATTLE OF BRITAIN
- •INVASION OF RUSSIA
- •PEARL HARBOR
- •FALL OF THE PHILIPPINES AND SINGAPORE
- •BATTLE OF MIDWAY
- •BATTLE OF STALINGRAD
- •GUADALCANAL
- •EL ALAMEIN
- •D-DAY
- •LIBERATION OF PARIS
- •BATTLE OF THE BULGE
- •V-E DAY
- •HIROSHIMA

Examining a Battle

Or one could focus on a particular episode of the war, such as the Battle of Midway, where in 5 minutes naval superiority switched from the Japanese to the Americans.

One could concentrate on that momentous 5-minute period, reading what Japanese and Americans who had participated had written about it (including Ensign Gay's view while hiding under a life jacket, floating among the Japanese ships). Or one could examine pictures and diagrams of the American and Japanese aircraft

BOX 3.2

cont'd...

In reading an article or attending a movie, we have for centuries and decades repressed the questions that come to our minds as we go along, hoping that they will be answered later. Sometimes when they are not, we look elsewhere for the answers or express our frustration over the questions to our friends.

Consider a frivolous example: the Trekkies—those fanatics who explore every aspect of Gene Roddenberry's *Star Trek.* They know the geography of the Star Trek universe. They know the chronology of Star Trek history, from nineteenth and twentieth century adventures of the fictional crews of Kirk and Picard far into the future. They convene to interview the actors and hypothesize about motivations and deeper meanings. They truly go where no person has dared to go, and the kind of curiosity they exhibit indicates what the User of the new medium may expect of it.

From various news items:

[After the year 2000] "television won't be television anymore."

"Newspapers must develop new products or new competitors will."

"Information data bases are now an independent mass medium and their development shows similarities to that of radio and telephone."

A MULTIMEDIA HISTORY OF WORLD WAR II

cont'd...

carriers and gain an understanding of why timing was destructive to the Japanese craft and why fire control and suppression systems kept the battered USS *Yorktown* afloat and in action so long.

One could follow the action from its planning to its conclusion through animated maps. One could read details of how the ability to read the Japanese naval codes alerted the U. S. admirals and allowed them to surprise the enemy, and how the Japanese tactics and communications never allowed their full strength to be brought against smaller American forces.

Film clips could illustrate some of the historic events. Excerpts from Winston Churchill's *History of World War II* could put the battle in perspective from the view of its greatest strategist.

SAMPLE TOPICS
- HOME FRONTS
- PRISONERS OF WAR
- THE HOLOCAUST
- TECHNOLOGY AND WAR

SAMPLE SOURCES
- COMBAT PHOTOS
- COMBAT ARTISTS
- REPORTERS' STORIES
- SOLDIERS' LETTERS
- OFFICIAL REPORTS
- MEMOIRS
- HISTORIES
- WAR NOVELS
- WAR MOVIES
- RECOLLECTIONS OF SURVIVORS

Examining a Topic

The User would be free to examine these items in as brief or as great detail as he or she wished. Or one could examine a topic of the war, such as the development of electronics during the conflict: From British use of awkward radar towers during the Battle of Britain to radar on aircraft used to bomb targets below the clouds; the cumbersome precursors of computers housed in the bowels of battleships that aimed giant guns at speeding ships 15 miles away to the compact Central Fire Control systems aboard U. S. B-29 bombers at the end of the war, which eliminated the need to have men at defensive guns all over the plane.

Multimedia World War II would allow fanatics, scholars, or casual Users to go at the User's own pace and in the directions the User determined.

All would be in digital form. The use of icons, menus, buttons, and keywords would allow for quick searches and easy presentation.

Box 3.2

Dan Rather and R. W. Apple Jr. are chief correspondents for "The Vietnam War," a CD-ROM published in late 1994 by *The New York Times*, CBS, and Apple Computer, based on news archives, and containing video, audio, and written accounts. Smolen plans to deploy journalists to Vietnam in 1994 to assemble multimedia format information for a contemporary view of that nation.

With all the Star Trek lore available stored digitally, a New Medium Trekkie could ask questions the moment they came to mind, and receive answers (at least most of the time). There is a good possibility that this would stimulate long-repressed curiosity in many Users and would lead to new perspectives and interpretations, the breeding ground of new knowledge. The New Medium has the potential to provide all the information that anyone could possibly want.

SUMMARY

After centuries of using books, pens, and ink for gaining and distributing new knowledge, humanity is confronted by a new information age. Inevitably digital information is entering our lives at work, at play, and even at museums. The means to provide channels of communication are at hand; the organization of these channels is a current preoccupation. Two important challenges remain: (1) Providing a receiver/decoder device that is truly user-friendly; (2) creating the kinds of "stories" that take full advantage of the new possibilities.

PROJECTS, DISCUSSION TOPICS, AND EXERCISES

1. Create an information inventory of the class. Then match the inventory items with sources of information. Compare the many sources with what the New Medium system (described in this chapter) would make available in a single source.
2. Have a knowledgeable person demonstrate how the Internet is used for e-mail, bulletin boards, software and data transfer, and so forth. Find out from the class whether members use Prodigy, CompuServe, America Online, or other commercial services, and what they use them for.
3. Get access to a multimedia presentation of any kind. Rick Smolen's *From Alice to Ocean* would be ideal because students could write critiques and comparisons of the book version to the multimedia version.
4. Select a topic for preparation of a multimedia presentation: the obituary of a prominent or popular person would be an example. Create a multimedia bibliography of the material that is available on this topic. Consider various ways the information could be organized for the presentation.

SUGGESTED READINGS

Dennis, Everette, ed. *Media, Democracy and the Information Highway*. Proceedings of the Freedom Forum conference, 1992. The conference of government, media, business, and academic folk dealt with a broad spectrum of issues.

Koch, Tom. *Journalism for the 21st Century*. New York: Greenwood Press, 1991. How some of the new technologies are being used by journalists.

Krol, Ed. *The Whole Internet*. Sebastopol, Calif.: O'Reilly and Associates, 1992. A substantive guide to the international net.

Shaw, Donald L., ed. *Journalism Quarterly* 68: 4 (Winter 1991). Contains a section especially devoted to audience studies.

The Media Environment

Surveying the Effect of Media on the Environment—and the Environment the Media Have Created for Themselves

Editors are in the information business, not newspaper manufacturing. They should study consumers, start new ventures, get some staffers trained outside of conventional areas.

—John Lavine

A Sci-Fi Bedtime Story

When the arthritis twinged in his shoulder as he lifted his granddaughter, Isolde, up to the telescope, Eric reminded himself that he was getting old. Like his parents and grandparents, he had been born on the spaceship Endeavor, and so had his daughter and little Isolde. But Isolde, should she have children, would rear them on New World, the planet below. Tears salted his eyelids as he realized again that the dreams of generations were about to come true. People from Earth were going to populate a new planet in this distant galaxy. "Maybe we can do it right, or at least better, this time," he thought.

"Look, Isolde," he said, "See the orange lights on New World." The four-year-old's head nodded vigorously. Through the telescope the orange lights flickered on the blackness below. Beyond the horizon the stars sparkled.

"Those are what people back on Earth call campfires. Our pioneers who will be helping us land soon, use them when this side of

New World rotates away from its sun, and they have what is called night. The campfires warm them and give them light. They don't have to use their energy units so much."

"What's a campfire, Grandpa?" Isolde asked as she snuggled into his arms.

He began to rock, as he always did at her bedtime. "I've seen Earth videos of campfires, Isolde," he said. "For a long, long time big plants called trees have been growing on New World. Some die. They are like the old flowers we bring from our greenhouses, very dry and brittle. They can be broken up into smaller pieces. By applying heat to them, they begin to oxidize rapidly and give off heat and light. The pioneers have dragged some pieces of dead trees together and are sitting around the campfire."

"When we get to New World, can we have a campfire, Grandpa?"

"Yes, Isolde, we'll build a big campfire and dance around it," he said as he tucked the sleepy child into bed.

Eric stepped into the next compartment and switched on his Infomax. He had to make recommendations to the Futures Council on Information Policy in 10 hours and he wanted to review his notes. On the screen he read:

"The proposal to establish a paper mill and a printing plant, like so many other worthwhile ventures, must await our establishing ourselves as a self-sustaining population. The proposal is a valued part of our cultural heritage and when carried out will contribute greatly to the enrichment of the lives of our people. And it is true that the trees, ores, chemicals, and power potential are available to produce books and periodicals. But for the time being we must continue to store, process, and exchange information by the methods we and our forebears on Endeavor have become accustomed to.

"We will continue the production of the Infomax Systems' components and adapt them to long-range communication so they may be used on the surface of the planet. In the foreseeable future, the Endeavor in synchronous orbit above our habitations will serve as a communications satellite and major information- and storage-processing center. A high priority will be to establish centers on Earth that are not dependent on the Endeavor.

"The proposal to establish a paper and printing facility is not to lie dormant. In phase two of our settlement, pilot projects for production of presses and small amounts of paper and their use for art and certificatory purposes will be carried out."

Eric dimmed out the Infomax. He had often visited the museum and leafed through the books there. The tactile sensation of touching what another human had crafted excited him. The effort made to create the paper, and the ink and to bind the books told him a great deal about the Earth generations' struggles for learning.

"I'll see no new books in my lifetime," he thought. "But I will *dance around a campfire with Isolde."*

This is a chapter about campfires and books and things related to them. In our science-fiction vignette we can imagine Eric going to bed and sleeping the dreamless sleep of a child like Isolde because he felt he had made the right decision about the revolutionary changes facing his society.

The nature of the information/communication environment would change when the inhabitants of Endeavor moved to New World. Eric had a plan for that change. An organization existed to consider that plan and, if accepted, to implement it. Most importantly the Users of the information–communication system already were familiar with a similar system, and the techniques of creating the hardware, software, and content of the system were in use.

ENVIRONMENT OF CHANGE

Although we face radical changes in our communication environment, we have none of the benefits that Eric had as we try to cope with change. Even if a comprehensive plan for change were presented, there is no authoritative body that could act decisively to approve that plan and put it into motion. All the interested parties in our society would be in a position to have an influence on the decisions reached by our institutions. Further, there is no compelling evidence that radical change needs to take place now, as there was in Eric's situation. Expert and lay opinion would be divided on almost every facet of any proposal because there is no consensus that something must be done.

Finally, there is great commitment to the status quo, to the existing media, by both Users and providers. This commitment is a material one—major investments in production plants, transmitters, receivers, systems of distribution and of content creation, and all the rest. It is also a psychological commitment. I like my newspaper. Its owner likes the profits that have rolled in year after year, feels a responsibility to maximize the physical assets of the institution, and feels a responsibility toward all the employees who produce the newspaper. Change is threatening.

Lauren Seiler, a Queens College sociologist, has predicted that electronics will replace print because electronics is cost effective. Alfred Sikes, a former head of the FCC, has said that we can no longer assume that "Aunt Minnie" just wants plain old telephone service, noting that half the work force was using computers by 1992 and 30 million PCs were in use. "We're approaching critical mass if we haven't achieved it already."

Keep in mind, however, that all those things mentioned above were true in Gutenberg's time also. And, indeed, society was even more authoritarian and less accustomed to change than we are now. Evolutionary change has been a part of our society throughout our lives. We can plan and adapt in our pluralistic and sometimes chaotic institutions.

Like Eric, we need to understand the environment of our world and how the media are affecting it. Further, we need to understand the media environment that the *producers* of the media live in. We also need to understand the media environment that *Users* of the media live in. Then we need to consider the environment of change that we are part of and perhaps begin to make rational decisions about how to practice our professions in the midst of change.

That brings us back to campfires, books, and things related to them.

THE PAPER ENVIRONMENT

Did you know that the biggest use of forest products is for fuel? Half the wood harvested in the world today is used to cook food, heat habitations, and provide energy for other needs—a lot more than is used for printing, making containers, and building structures combined. That has been true for all the centuries of history and it still is true.

Is using all that wood for fuel good or bad? Most of us think of fuel as a product of coal mining in Wyoming, oil from underneath the North Sea or natural gas from we are not quite sure where (really it comes from Hugoton, Kansas). Wood for fuel causes a lot of trees to be cut down, but that's been going on for centuries and we still have trees. Burning wood causes substantial air pollution, but that can be controlled by limiting its use to sparsely populated areas. In fact, wood is a renewable resource; gas, oil, and coal are not. So perhaps we can give a provisional OK to the use of wood for fuel, especially since so many people are doing it anyway.

Now, let us consider paper.

In May 1992 paper suppliers scaled back increases in newsprint prices upon realizing their customers could not afford them. The *Washington Post* used 210,000 metric tons of newsprint in 1991 (off 14 percent from 1990), Knight-Ridder 610,000, Gannett 850,000. Newsprint companies said they were losing money.

The amount of wood used for paper is astonishing. United States newspapers alone lapped up 12.35 million metric tons of newsprint in 1989. (Paper costs $685 per metric ton. That figures to $8.46 billion.) Those tons and dollars represent trees that had to be cut down, hauled to the pulp mill, turned into paper, hauled to the newspaper, run through the press, hauled to the reader, read (more or less), and finally hauled to the landfill. A newspaper has a useful life of about 12 hours. Why turn such a transitory service into a manufactured product?

We can look at the use of trees to create wood pulp for paper and cardboard another way. In 1990, 130,000 people were employed in paper mills and the value of their product was $35 billion. In contrast, 53,000 people were employed in paperboard plants and the value of their product was $20 billion. However, the growth rate of paperboard production now exceeds that of paper production. Obviously processing pulpwood is a major industry. A final fact: less than 5 percent of U. S. virgin forests remain.

Most of the information above comes from *Grolier's Encyclopedia.* It was available at the Social Work branch library of the University of Washington. This branch library does not have on its shelves the many volumes that would make up a printed version of *Grolier's*

Encyclopedia, nor do any of the more than a dozen other branches of that library system. But on each of the scores of computer terminals linked to the library information system there is access to the computer database version of *Grolier's.*

So, at a computer terminal in Social Work branch library, one may look at the database dialogue box and click on "Grolier's Encyclopedia." When a new dialogue box appears, one may type "paper" after "Subject." A list of articles involving paper appears on the screen. One can select the basic article "Paper," and the entire text appears from which the above information was gleaned. (I did write my notes about "paper" on a 3-inch by 5-inch card; I don't have a laptop computer—yet.)

This is a convenient way to get information and it saves a lot of shelf space in the branch libraries, not to speak of the cost of producing all those volumes.

Having read thus far, take a look at the list below and place priorities on the different uses of forests and forest products in your own mind:

- Trees adequate to create the forests needed for oxygen-carbon dioxide exchange.
- Trees adequate to provide habitat for plants and animals.
- Trees for building houses and other structures and for furniture.
- Trees for climbing, for admiring and for providing shade on hot days.
- Wood for fuel, including campfires.
- Wood pulp for newspapers.
- Wood pulp for books.
- Wood pulp for artists to produce works in water color.
- Wood pulp for cereal boxes and cartons for new computers.
- Wood pulp to make paper to publish this book.

Selfishly, that last item is my top priority. I think this book is important, and there's no other way to get it to large numbers of people. The system for doing that routinely has not yet been established.

Objectively, and over the long run, the top five categories are most important. But don't forget those 185,000 people (most of whom have children at home who need food and shoes) who work in the paper and paperboard industries. Also, don't forget those struggling watercolor artists.

Remember there was a time when printing on paper was the only way to get information out to large numbers of people. Printing on paper has a long and honorable tradition and is going to be around for a long time. But as we all put our scarcely read newspapers into recycling boxes, isn't it time to think about cutting back?

Some new magazines have appeared that have audio and video mixed with conventional text and graphics. *Hyperbole, Verbum Interactive, HyperTexture,* and *CD-I World* have been distributed on floppy disks and/or CDs.

FIGURE 4.1

The print media and forest products are one example of how media interact with the environment. In earlier chapters the tendency to turn the provision of information, a service, into a manufacturing enterprise through the production of records and tapes, for example, was discussed. We need not quote a lot of statistics and cite a lot of examples to show that molecules are being used to move information when we could be using electrons to move it (as radio, television, and cable do).

That might mean some reduction in the need for building expensive new highways; it might reduce the demand on fuel supplies; it might mean those paper-mill workers could use that wood pulp to create more particle board, reducing the cost of building materials, stimulating the construction industry, and providing more opportunities for families to have a good house, without increasing the demand on our forest resources.

It could be a win–win situation.

THE ELECTRONIC ENVIRONMENT

Whichever mass medium one looks at, the problems of securing adequate revenue, fighting rising costs, and maintaining (not to speak of enlarging) audiences, are staggering. The usual complaint of owners and managers is "competition." Their astounding past successes have created an environment of high expectations. They produce in an environment of increased costs and market in an environment of intense competition. It is difficult for them to prosper. Are today's mass media obsolescent?

When we speak of *environment* we are usually talking about having a decent place to live. One that relieves stress rather than creates it. One that is constructive rather than destructive.

The electronic media have created a video and audio environment that is self-destructive. This self-destructiveness is bred by the success of the electronic media. They have captured an audience larger than ever conceived possible and are capable of holding people's attention longer than anyone has conceived of. Vast fortunes, reputations, and access to power have been created. Everyone it seems has jumped on the electronic bandwagon.

Now radio, television, and cable feed information down a media freeway jammed with traffic and interrupted every 6 to 12 minutes with a toll booth of commercials. Their executives expect audiences to assimilate the information as it goes past. When the networks were dominant, television was a 3-ring circus. Now with cable it's a 43-ring or 500-ring madhouse. Advertisers desperate to reach an audience can't be heard because the audience is so distracted.

TCI (TeleCommunications International), the giant cable television company, plans to provide 500-channel cable television service in Orlando sometime in 1994, describing it as "a full-service network."

Three recent peripherals to the video environment address this chaos: (1) the television set that provides a window on the screen so a second channel can be viewed simultaneously; (2) the remote device with easy channel selection and a mute button; and (3) the videocassette player. Let's examine each.

The window in the screen attempts to relieve the anxiety created by having so many choices and the frustration felt when a channel switches from something relevant to the viewer to something that is not relevant. However, having the two messages compete creates its own stress.

Turning to the remote device, the mute button does reduce stress by allowing the viewer to avoid unwanted audio. Since this is often done to eliminate the audio of an oft-repeated commercial, the practice may create stress among advertisers.

The remote channel-changing utility is a mixed blessing. It allows the viewer to switch between channels, each of which has something the viewer wants to see. But it has created a new phenomenon called channel surfing, in which the viewer with the remote switches through all forty channels, seeking the perfect wave. Measuring the stress this creates within the others viewing the same set and between them and the operator of the remote no doubt will provide data for a half-dozen doctoral dissertations and as many academic mass communication journal articles. A really challenging study would be to measure the disonance caused by switching continuously between two music video channels each of which is switching scenes every half-second.

The videocassette recorder (VCR) was conceived as a means of recording information scheduled for telecast when the User could not watch. The recording would be played at a later time and indeed VCRs are used that way. But unexpectedly the VCR created a whole new industry of videocassette sales and rentals. The convenience of being able to watch what one wishes to watch at a time one chooses outweighs the cost and inconvenience of securing yet another plastic box. The audience will go to substantial lengths to reduce the stress of the current system.

MULTICHANNEL NICHES

The executive director of the Investigative Reporters and Editors Association (IRE) has reported severe cutbacks in television investigative reporting. Networks and local television stations are tightening news budgets, reducing staffs, closing bureaus, and depending more and more on freelance and non-staff-produced material.

Multichannel television has created niche broadcasting. Two examples, CNN and the Weather Channel, illustrate other frustrations of a medium tied to the clock. One turns to the Weather Channel for the answers to questions like: What's tonight's forecast? or, What's the temperature in Boise? While waiting for the answer, the viewer probably sees a Michelin commercial, the European weather map, a sales pitch for a videocassette on volcano eruptions, and a promo on all the information the Weather Channel provides. Since Boise is not among the "Twenty Travel Cities," all one finds is the range of temperatures—20s, 30s, 40s—on a map, if one knows where Boise is on the map. It's still hard to get a quick, specific answer.

CNN represents two attempts to provide niche information, in this case, news. CNN attempts full-blown television broadcasting, with programs of news—world news, business news, entertainment news, and so forth—throughout the 24-hour period. The rationale is that the viewer will take time to find when to watch what he or she wants. Headline News takes the radio approach: brief summaries every half hour. The viewer must know that hard news comes on at the hour or half-hour, sports at 20 minutes after or 10-till, business news before that, and entertainment news just before the hard news. In addition CNN knows (and so do its advertisers) that everyone is going to watch when big news happens unexpectedly, but there is no way for advertisers to schedule their messages for the big audiences, so CNN has difficulty in taking advantage of its audience strength. More stress.

THE AUDIENCE FACTOR

Public debate has suffered because of televisions' shorter and shorter sound bites, says media critic Jay Rosen. One example: for years the public was unaware of the magnitude of the savings-and-loan scandal. The extensive coverage of the Persian Gulf War debate in Congress is an example of how television can relay the public stance of officials to the public.

The perceived need for advertisers to tie their messages to programming that attracts big audiences has historically created a drive by the traditional networks to aim at the largest audience and often the lowest cultural common denominator. It creates fads in programming, with networks emulating each others' most successful shows and for intense competition for the few hours when huge mass audiences are available. In an area like sports it leads to the promotions of the most spectacular athletes and events and virtual ignoring of unpopular or purely local amateur competition. In news and elsewhere the personality that will attract a following becomes as important as the content. The anchor is vital to survival.

Cable television has increased the competition for viewers. The FCC and broadcasters have responded by increasing the time devoted to revenue-producing messages and to self-promotion. Still further chaos.

Even the Public Broadcasting Service (PBS), the supposedly non-commercial public network, finds itself promoting its product and soliciting viewer support while increasingly acknowledging the support of corporate sponsors.

By contrast, there is C-SPAN, the cable channel supported by the cable industry as a way to feed the egos of Congress, which can regulate broadcasting through legislation. Turn to C-SPAN and one leisurely watches the Senate and House as they take up and dispose of legislation. It also points its cameras at the presidential debates, at conferences and speakers. Then it lets viewers call in and talk about what they've seen. For most viewers, most of the time it might be boring. But it's much more like the world most of us live in. We catch the anticipation and partisanship of the audience before a presidential debate. When C-SPAN reported all the debate on the Persian Gulf War resolution, watchers for a change saw their legislators struggle with their consciences and their vocabularies in trying to contribute to meaningful debate. It was fresh; it wasn't canned.

The proliferation of radio stations has brought about niche broadcasting that we can listen to while going about our daily activities. There is lots of music. There are people that talk about the music and moderate the listener-oriented talk shows, often with strong personalities. These people are used to capture audiences. This is an inane environment and, particularly on automobile radios, the scanner and the push button help the listener leap about the electronic spectrum, seeking something worth hearing.

THE PRINT ENVIRONMENT

The periodical print media, newspapers and magazines, face a different but equally unfavorable environment, partly created because they are manufacturing enterprises, partly because of the competition of the electronic media, and partly because the needs of their readers have changed.

Not so long ago in a monopoly newspaper town, printing the paper was a lot like printing money. The paper had the franchise to inform the public and to provide advertisers with an audience. It considered itself an omnibus institution, providing a broad spectrum of information, something to appeal to every reader in its community. It presented "all the news that's fit to print." That included everything from global events right on to the really important information: births, marriages, and deaths. ("Hatched, Matched and Dispatched" was the standing headline on one of these vital statistics columns.)

"We need to make a distinction between electronic publishing and journalism: electronic publishers, who have the profit motive foremost on their agenda, give us information. News has a social service foundation . . . This First Amendment protection journalists have flows from the social-service values practiced by many of our news organizations. Whether future electronic publishers will enjoy First Amendment protection could well hinge on whether they have a social-service foundation rather than just a profit motive."

—Frank Blethen, *Seattle Times* publisher

Almost very family in town got the paper, and it was a companion to turn to—by Mom when the housework was done, by the kids when they got home from school and wanted to read the funnies, and by Dad after work as he waited for the evening meal.

On a national scale, mass circulation magazines competed for dominance. *Time, Life, Saturday Evening Post,* and *Colliers* used to be the prime national advertising medium.

At one time newspapers and magazines prospered. Their advertisers were so diverse that the revenues from any one of them could not dominate their business decisions. The revenues were great enough that subscriptions and newsstand prices could be kept low enough to attract even marginal readers. The revenues were sufficient to meet the cost of production and still allow substantial space and resources for what was deemed good content.

During the 6-month period ending March 31, 1992, circulation of the nation's largest newspapers (with a few exceptions) continued to decline. Household penetration and readership lagged behind population and household growth. A readership study conducted in 1989–90 showed younger people reading less and continuing to refrain as they age. Non-working women were reading even less than working women, who read less than men.

Describing David Laventhal as the most powerful publisher in America in 1991, a trade publication reported him ready to spend $405 million on plant expansion at the *Los Angeles Times.* In December 1992, another trade magazine reported a trend by newspapers to upgrade technologically in order to produce traditional newspapers.

The advent of radio and television did more than increase competition. The two electronic media restructured what newspapers and magazines do and how advertisers spend their money. They attracted millions of people to spend more of their newly acquired leisure time with the media, but often at the expense of time spent with the print media. The great national magazines either went out of business or became slim and expensive to the reader.

Competition among newspapers decreased as the weaker paper in a given town disappeared. The surviving newspapers encouraged their staffs to practice "customer obsession," tighten newsholes, and brighten pages to stay profitable and attract readers. The motto is now "All the NEWS! that will fit."

Print media people feel stress as a smaller percentage of families get the paper, as readers spend less time with it, and as advertisers slip away too. They ask themselves, "What has happened to our franchise?"

Success attracts capital. Giant corporations now own large portions of the media. They and the smaller media companies too are justifiably committed to existing technology and techniques. This is a powerful status quo. Every media professional should rightfully be apprehensive about what lies ahead, and so should the public. Indeed all are fearful of change and at the same time afraid not to change.

THE MEDIA USER'S ENVIRONMENT

At the other end of the communication model, every User is surrounded by an array of media firing large-caliber and small-caliber, rapid-fire and sniper-fire messages. While under fire, the receiver must try to rationalize the image of the world presented, winnow out the information needed to survive (maybe even prosper), and perhaps find the desired cultural enrichment and entertainment along the way. It's a media war out there. No wonder readers, listeners, and viewers are disillusioned with the performance of the media.

Even if the media offered a more rational way to get information, the User would be less inclined to use it than earlier generations because the User has changed. Newspapers and radio were a great escape and a great educator in the days when manual labor for long hours was the norm for the typical American. Tired muscles and rested minds responded well to a newspaper or a radio show. Leisure time came in brief daily periods and the time after dinner (supper, we called it) was time for the news and *Amos 'n Andy*.

Now it is the mind that may be tired at the end of the work day. The body may be demanding a jog around the park. Long weekends combined with good highways and automobiles lure us to non-media activities. We want information, quickly, on how to take advantage of all the opportunities today offers us.

Or, if the User has a real interest in something—be it soap operas, operas, or soap—the User wants absorbing, detailed and relevant information—the complete experience.

Under these constraints the media tries to provide for those two disparate needs, and does a surprisingly good job. But the stress remains. And there is a better way.

One mass medium avoids two of the problems we have discussed above. Publishers of books still pay lots of money to put information on paper and ship it around to reach the Users. But they are not limited by scheduling, the way the electronic media are, and they are not dependent on advertisers for their revenue.

The motion-picture industry is in a similar situation and its links to television and videocassettes give it additional advantages.

Despite dramatic increases in the cost of a book and the price of a movie theater ticket and despite the competition for the attention of their potential Users, these media are doing quite well. Still, the New Medium offers them relief from some of their most expensive overhead.

Communication across racial, class, and cultural lines creates much-needed communities of interest, yet providing diverse groups with information that is easy for them to use is a challenge, and it is one we must face.
—Christy Bulkley, former Gannett newspaper publisher

THE NEW MEDIA ENVIRONMENT

There is no Eric to write a definitive report on what we should do about information policy and the environment. There is no all-powerful "Future Council on Information Policy" to act on Eric's report. And the people of Earth are not like the fictional Endeavor's occupants. Earth folk are accustomed to what we already have.

But we still face a wrenching adjustment to a new society that creates better information services and takes better care of our environment. What is needed is a medium that

- Is not constrained by having to manufacture products.
- Is not constrained by having to present information on a schedule.

- Is not constrained by having revenue-producing advertising messages tied directly to other content.
- Allows the User to get to the desired and important content efficiently.

Two prospects offered by the New Medium may move change along. One is the effect the New Medium would have on the environment itself. Another is the economies offered by the New Medium. It offers the print media (and music and video media) the opportunity to quit being manufacturers, allowing them to concentrate solely on service.

Here economies and environment go hand in hand, once the transition is accomplished.

The New Medium offers the electronic media new freedom from the clock. That is, radio, television, and cable institutions could quit running on a schedule, like a railroad, and start serving the consumer when the consumer has the opportunity to be served, like a restaurant.

SCHEDULED VS. MENU-DRIVEN INFORMATION

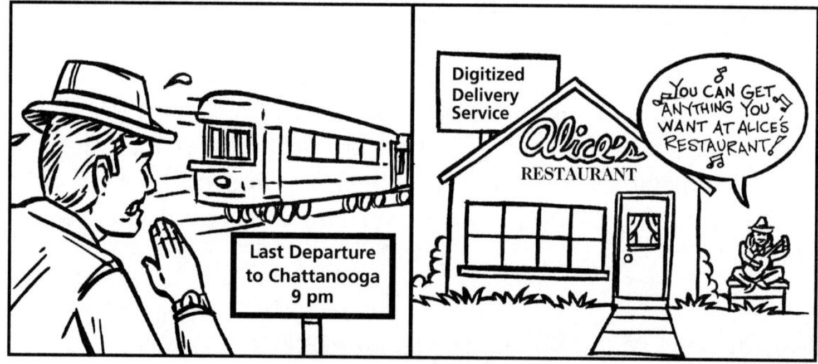

The largest capital investment millions of us will ever make is buying an automobile. Among the primary reasons we buy cars is the desire to go where we want *when* we want. That desire is a big reason for the infrequent use of public transportation. Consumers of information are equally independent. They want their information when it is convenient for them. They don't want to wait for someone to return a book to the library. They go out and buy it. The easy transmittal of digital information permits menu-driven rather than schedule-driven media.

FIGURE 4.2

Audio and video would be easily available when the User had time for them. For advertisers a new realm of creativity would be available: advertisements with the appeal of television commercials and the convenience of newspaper classifieds. An advertising message would be available to the consumer 24 hours a day. As a multimedia message it could take the consumer through details of the product or service or dazzle the consumer with all of its psychological advantages and lead the consumer to make a purchase decision, combining advertising with sales.

Within 15 years a wealth of interactive video services will be delivered into homes, according to the chairman of the FCC. Multimedia has come to children's video games, with one containing film strips of actual news events in QuickTime retailing at less than $50.

The New Medium would contribute to a cleaner environment and more convenient life style. The transportation system should not be carrying information; it should be carrying people, cans of tomatoes, pants, and lumber. The necessity for people to travel to get information (i.e., Cowboy Jim riding his horse to hear Jennie Lind) would continue to be reduced.

The New Medium could provide more information that is wanted and needed and could provide it in a better way. It would allow media professionals to concentrate on their primary responsibility: providing information. It would relieve stress.

SUMMARY

The mass media have been tremendously successful financially. The printing process has become obsolete for much of what the media do. Scheduling of radio and television programming becomes counterproductive when the number of channels available is so large. Changes are inevitable, but there is no orderly way to determine what the best changes would be nor a way to accomplish them. Goals do exist: reduce the amount of manufacturing by the media; change from scheduled presentation of information to menu-driven presentation; free advertising and non-commercial information from dependence on each other; help the User get the desired information.

PROJECTS, DISCUSSION TOPICS, AND EXERCISES

1. Investigate the cost of printing and distributing the campus newspaper. If possible, do the same for the major newspaper in your city.
2. Investigate how broad the computer network is on your campus and create a proposal for a text-and-graphics computerized newspaper. Create a sample issue and a proposed budget for operation.
3. Conduct brief interviews with radio station managers or program directors in your community. Report on their programming strategies. See if you can find out what the ratings are on the stations.

4. If you can find a newspaper that does computer pagination, schedule a field trip to see how the newspaper exists in a computer before it is printed.
5. Have a discussion on what the media environment is in your community and how it is likely to change.

SUGGESTED READINGS

Beniger, James R. *The Control Revolution*. Cambridge, Mass.: Harvard, 1986. Investigates how communication is used to control economic forces.

Izard, Ralph, ed. *Newspaper Research Journal* 14:2 (Spring 1993). A special issue on the newspaper of the future takes a hard look at the environment today's newspapers occupy.

Lardner, James. "The Anti-Network." *The New Yorker,* March 14, 1994, pp. 49–55. Examines how C-SPAN (the Cable Satellite Public Affairs Network) has gone about creating a media environment radically different from the presumption, rituals, and rhythms of commercial TV news.

Lavine, John. "We Can't Do Anything About the Economy." *Bulletin of the American Society of Newspaper Editors* 740 (April 1992), pp. 4–10. A publisher-turned-academic looks at the state of the media.

Mosco, Vincent. *The Pay-per Society*. Norwood, N.J.: Ablex, 1989. Beginning with a whimsical look at the impact of computers, this book confronts the problems of the information age.

Freedom in a New Information Environment

The Public's "Right to Know" Confronts the Business of Selling Information

Ye shall know the truth, and the truth shall make you free.

—John 8:32

When those words were written, the elders recognized as the wisest of all were pretty sure the Earth was flat and at the center of the universe. The smallest entity was a grain of mustard seed. Humans were the dominant and most important beings. It was a world full of unexplained mysteries and ignorant people.

Now we realize that the Earth is an orb, a planet in a relatively small solar system in one of a number of huge galaxies. We recognize that even a grain of mustard seed is a complex of thousands upon thousands of molecules and atoms made up of even smaller things. Are people the dominant and most important beings? Well, at least they are the only beings we know of who seem able to come to some understanding of the universe and to act on what they know in order to change things substantially. Now we know there is a whole universe full of unexplained mysteries and with every bit of knowledge we perceive, we also perceive greater gulfs of ignorance.

We will never encompass the whole truth, but its pursuit is indeed closely linked to our collective and individual freedom.

We know enough truth to destroy our civilization in an hour or two and perhaps make our planet uninhabitable. We know enough truth to end the millenia of subsistance living and create a consumer society in parts of the Earth. Food, warm clothing, shelter, and a lot of other things have become products and services that not only allow us to survive but provide the means to prosper. Now in recent years we have discovered what the ultimate product and service is: truth.

TRUTH: A NECESSITY

This is the information and communication age.

Do we face the best of times, the worst of times, or just hard times? The answer lies as much in how we deal with "truth" during these times as anything else.

A very down-to-earth definition of truth: accurate information. Perceiving accurate information and moving it about has become important, indeed essential, at every level of life. From the hand on the nuclear trigger to the hand that rocks the cradle, intelligent behavior depends on knowing what is going on. Computers and computer networks more and more provide that information more quickly and more accurately.

Yet, as was described in the previous chapter, the mass media are narrowly defining what truth to provide: only that which will snare the largest possible audience; only what the advertising revenue and cumbersome distribution systems will support. Less information means less power.

Walter B. Wriston, former chairman of Citicorp, sees a future in which control of information flow will be impossible, making such things as national boundaries and central banks obsolete.

The New Medium can reverse this trend. It can give citizens-consumers access to more of this power, and can make it easier for them to find the information they need. It can do this more quickly and less expensively than ever before. Since freedom depends in large part on knowing what one's options are, the New Medium should be a great boon.

Philosophically, our nation and indeed all enlightened people consider the informed individual the building block of society. Unstated but implicit in the First Amendment is the ideal of a free interchange of information and of a wide variety of informed opinions being freely expressed. To this end, the public must have access to the broadest range of information possible and each person must have the ability to seek out what he or she needs to know.

IMPEDIMENTS TO TRUTH

But for many the information age means that instead of buying and selling goods and traditional services, they will buy and sell information. Truth comes with a price tag on it. Economic and social influences tending to impede the freedom of access to information are

- The view that information is primarily a commodity to be bought and sold (or that may be withheld from the marketplace).
- The view that long-established institutions like telephone companies, newspaper chains, and networks should be protected by the government from change or that one or another of these institutions has a right to dissemination of certain kinds of information, or that ownership of the channel allows the owner to control the content.
- The idea that what individuals or institutions do, despite the fact that it has an impact on society, should remain private information. A doctrine must emerge that protects individuals and institutions in purely private matters but informs society in all matters influencing or involving the public. A broader concept is needed of what information the public must have access to.

These are controversial matters that should be considered in the light of the electorate—the public—needing to know. They are matters that should be high on the public agenda. The Disabilities Act of 1990 assures the disabled access to all buildings open to the public, whether publicly or privately owned. It also requires communications providers, like the telephone companies, to ensure that people who can't use telephones normally will be able to contact an operator who will then relay the information. This kind of thinking could be extended to access to information; persons handicapped physically or economically should still have fair access to information.

TRUTH: A MEANS TO WEALTH

The prevailing view, however, is that information—truth—is a commodity, a means to wealth.

A century ago the means to wealth was in the hands of the railroad magnates. For a time it was in the hands of the inventors and manufacturers. (Those pictures of Henry Ford and Thomas Edison motoring across the country in a Model T are quaint, aren't they?) Then we had John D. Rockefeller and J. Paul Getty; control of energy was their road to power and wealth. More recently, the wealthiest man was Sam Walton, who linked consumer goods to management and communication. Now in the middle of the 1990s we have Bill Gates, founder of Microsoft and creator of software that runs countless personal computers.

Symbolizing the conspicuous accumulators of wealth in the past have been giant locomotives, sleek automobiles, towering drilling rigs, and sprawling discount stores. What is a symbol for Bill Gates?

IDENTIFIERS: HENRY FORD AND BILL GATES

Henry Ford was the first entrepreneur to use a production line to build an inexpensive, easy-to-maintain automobile—the Model T. Everyone wanted a car, and many could afford the Model T. It ushered in the century of the automobile. Bill Gates pioneered a clumsy but usable disk operating system (MS-DOS) for personal computers. He recognized the value of and market for *software,* the programming that makes computers do things. MS-DOS uses a system of codes keyed into the computer to make it perform. If you can't remember the right command you have to ask a friend or dig through a book. The introduction of the Apple Macintosh computer popularized a more intuitive *operating system* employing recognizable *icons,* plus menus and dialog boxes that give users hints and options as to how to get the computer to perform. Gates' company, Microsoft, had a head start in market share, and soon responded with "Windows," a graphical user interface (GUI) that makes MS-DOS easier to work with. When in 1994 Apple introduced radical new hardware (the Power Mac) and upgraded the Macintosh's operating system to version 7.5, Microsoft strove to keep up by announcing a major overhaul of Windows code-named "Chicago."

The world still awaits the powerful but friendly Model T of computers uniting hardware and software, which will usher in the New Medium.

FIGURE 5.1

Microsoft's product is amorphous. Inside a box are some disks and booklets. But they are not the product. Until the information on the disks starts running around inside a computer, rearranging electrons at top speed, there is no product or service. It is so micro and so soft that a person cannot see it, hear it, taste it, smell it, or feel it. The alchemists tried to turn lead into gold. Bill Gates turns nothing into gold. The geniuses of the past used thought-power to manipulate *things.* Bill Gates and the other geniuses of our time use thought-power to allow our thought-power to do more than it has done in the past. Use their product and get truth more quickly, in greater quantity, and on demand.

Gates has described what he used to do as a lone software innovater and what he does now as head of Microsoft:

> Back then, I said "Hey, I know something that DEC (Digital Equipment Company) and IBM don't know. Either I'm really, really right or I'm really, really wrong. I can stay in at work three days in a row just to push forward and find out." And now I have 15,000 employees. . . . The big thing I do is write down in fairly crisp fashion what I believe the company should do, what I think the key problems are. . . . I let people know the basic framework we're in and then I review projects.

Gates gained prominance when IBM entered the personal-computer field. It adopted the Microsoft Disk Operating System (MS-DOS) as the software that would take IBM's inanimate personal computer, boot it in the behind, and get it going so that it could use other software to accomplish what you and I might want it to do. (It's pretty awkward, requiring the User to know a lot of mnemonic codes, and is being replaced by systems operating more intuitively.) Most of the other people who created software for word processing, databasing, spreadsheets, graphics, games, and so forth, used MS-DOS as the starting point for their work. Microsoft owns MS-DOS and gets a fee for licensing each computer owner who uses it.

Remember from Chapter One what the basis for digital computing is: binary mathematics. In other words, MS-DOS and other computer programs are mathematical formulas, almost infinitely complex mathematical formulas.

Now consider this: how rich would the descendants of Pythagoras be if we had to pay them a nickel each time we used the mathematical formula "the square of the hypotenuse of a right triangle is equal to the sum of the squares of the other two sides" (the Pythagorian Theorem)? The old Greek figured that out; he just failed to copyright it.

Of course there were no copyright laws in Pythagoras' lifetime and until computer software came along, mathematical formulas (certifiable facts, i.e., truth) could not be copyrighted. It's the *form* truth takes—a musical composition, a painting, a novel, a poem, a slogan, etc.—that can be copyrighted.

DIGITAL SURCHARGE

We can all agree that the creativity (indeed genius) and plain hard work necessary to produce computer software merits copyright protection. Indeed, copyright laws were created so that creators could be compensated for their time and effort. (I hope I get a couple of nickels for writing this book!) Let's not deny Bill Gates an honest day's wages for his efforts.

But the tendency is to magnify the cost every time something runs through a computer. Though it is less expensive to copy data from one computer to another (or onto another's floppy disk), "owners" of

The *Hartford Courant*'s FaxPaper costs $600 a year. One legal-size page is transmitted at 4:30 P.M. every business day to subscribers, previewing the next day's newspaper with emphasis on local and regional business news.

information often have a higher fee for data in digital form than for printed data.

- In more and more government offices, it costs more to get information in computer-readable form than it does to go read the paper records. Open records laws in most states require officials to make the records available to whoever wants to see them, free. Most of those laws require the government official to charge no more than the cost of copying for paper copies of the records. But for commercial purposes, some state offices are charging as much as $5 for a driver's license record.
- At the major nationally franchised copy center, the cost of a page produced from computer memory onto a laser printer is ten times the cost of copying a printed page on a conventional copier.
- Newspapers, for a fat fee, now fax to subscribing businesses reports from their afternoon conference of news executives a prediction of what the major stories in the next morning's paper will be.
- Periodicals offer their subscribers interim reports by fax for a fee much greater than their newsstand prices.

In short, it is now standard to seek a high fee from a select group of readers for "inside information." This is not new. That is what the hand-copied news letters produced in the fifteenth century were. Even today, publishers are reaping astonishing profits by producing scientific journals full of information gathered at taxpayer expense and selling them to academic libraries for subscriptions of $1,000 and more a year, again at taxpayer expense. The point is that, thanks to digital information processing and transmission, information is becoming a hot commodity. If it is viewed only as a commodity to be sold only to the top-dollar market, the ordinary citizen–consumer–human being is in trouble.

CONTROLLING THE CHANNEL

The biggest deals in today's business world are those involving corporations whose executives dream of making profitable breakthroughs into interactive, broadband consumer and business communications. Whoever does will control the channel. Those who tried in the 1980s did not have the success necessary to continue the effort, but others are entering the field.

Big communications organizations are creating joint ventures so that they can offer communications across political and geographic barriers. We are talking about who will control the communication channel worldwide, because a large part of the debate now under way is involved with breaking down national barriers to allow the global economy to operate efficiently.

Organizations currently producing very different products and services see themselves cooperating in the future: hardware people to provide the computers and peripherals; software people to link different systems together and make them work faster and produce more; communications companies to provide the channels; news and entertainment people to provide the content.

The competition is intense. Newspapers do not want the phone companies to compete with them by providing news services and classified ads to the public. Business interests have demanded that communication monopolies like the American Telephone and Telegraph Company (AT&T) and its family of Bell System regional providers be broken up. Both the broadcasting and telecommunications industries have been deregulated, by and large, to allow existing providers more latitude in how they carry out business and to allow others to compete with them.

It is assumed that the private enterprise system will compete and eventually provide the best possible service to all consumers. We can hope.

Two groups, for the most part, are left out of this debate. First, the people who present information—truth. Second, the people who consume what is presented.

In the first instance we are talking about journalists, librarians, advertising people, artists, playwrights, poets, novelists, musicians, actors, set designers, photographers, editors of videotape, designers of publications; in short, the people who know about messages, about presenting information, about truth. This group has a great deal of wisdom to apply to what the channel should be and do, who it should serve and how. It has the skills that are basic to creating the new kinds of communications, the new ways of presenting information, the better ways of getting at the truth.

Of the twenty members named to the National Information Infrastructure Advisory Council, which is charged with recommending policy for how the information superhighway of the future will operate, only one is a professional provider of information to the general public: Toni Bearman, dean of the School of Library and Information Science at the University of Pittsburgh.

In the second instance, by consumers we mean the public: all those people who need to use the content of the channel to determine the truth about their worlds for every kind of institutional purpose, for business, for family, and for purely personal purposes. They, ultimately, are going to pay the bill as they always have and they—we—deserve the best possible service for our money.

THE SOCIAL CONTRACT

My favorite American document is the Declaration of Independence because it spells out officially the concept of the social contract. It says that citizens should abide by the laws of king and government as long as king and government provide them with their inalienable rights—life, liberty, and the pursuit of happiness. It says that when king and government fail to do so, citizens should reject them by declaring their independence and establishing a new government. Revolutionary!

The social contract applies to every human endeavor, according to those who successfully promulgated it—men such as John Locke and Jean Jacques Rousseau. From a communication–information perspective the contract is stated pretty well in one section of the Communications Act of 1934, which says that there shall be made "available so far as possible, to all the people of the United States, a rapid, efficient, nation-wide and world-wide wire and radio communication service with adequate facilities at reasonable charges."

The view of Everett Parker, senior research associate at Fordham University, is that "it is the consumer and the public interest that have the most to lose or gain from communications policy . . . If we're going to have this [information] highway, then every household and small business should have open access to the system." He cites two pressing needs: adequate funding of a public communications service and protection of the interests of children in the communication system. He sees the Communications Act of 1934 as being broad enough to allow the FCC to do what is needed.

The United States is one of the few countries in which the public communication system is owned and operated by private companies.

Talking about the Bell companies–newspaper conflict, Frederick Williams wrote in 1991, "Do we really care who's going to provide such [information] services? Isn't it more important to know what services might be really valuable to the American public?"

Public policy as well as private enterprise have been instrumental in creating the institutions vital to our society. The Constitution says the national government will, among other things, "promote the general welfare." It assumes government will provide for national defense. While land was plentiful the government gave it to individuals as homesteads. It gave land to people who built railroads "to promote the general welfare." We have the public education system and tax-supported higher education. When rural areas were discriminated against by the electric-power industry, the government stepped in with Rural Electric Cooperatives.

The public, through our government, has had a vital role in communications and information dissemination. The postal service itself and its special rates for newspapers, periodicals, and books is the earliest example. The government authorized a virtual monopoly, AT&T, and required it to provide telephone service to all. For half a century AT&T and its subsidiaries dominated telephone communications in the United States, owning the channels, manufacturing and installing the equipment and adopting the technology it preferred. But the FCC and state regulatory agencies have always been there to prevent abuses. Radio and television stations are required to broadcast "in the public interest, convenience and necessity." This tradition is exponentially more important in the information age.

INFORMATION SUPERHIGHWAY

The communication and information channel of the future is often described in public discourse as "the information superhighway." The analogy this calls to mind is the establishment of the Interstate highway system in the 1950s. The Interstate system is patterned after the autobahns constructed in Germany during the 1930s. The Interstates avoid the problems of earlier highways that had evolved from wagon roads: intense congestion in every town and urban area; a single lane in each direction so that passing was hazardous; traffic going in different directions; and sharing the roadway at intersections. The Interstate system has at least two lanes in each direction and avoids congestion by having limited access and providing grade separations at intersections so that traffic may move from one roadway to another smoothly.

Signed into law by President Eisenhower and funded by congressional legislation in the late 1950s, the Interstate system now provides high-speed, safe roadways nationwide for everything from motorcycles to 18-wheelers. The last section of the original system, an engineering miracle on I-90 that winds through Glenwood Canyon, Colorado, was completed in 1993.

The Interstate highway system made long-distance truck and car transportation swift and problem free, compared to the old system of roads that sprang up ad hoc. The same problem-free system needs to replace the jury-rigged system of digital communications that we now have.

The "information superhighway" analogy is a good one. From it one can infer that the communication/information channels will be open to all, will be easy and efficient to use, and will have the proactive participation of the government in their creation, maintenance, and use.

Public policy took a step in that direction with the passage of the High-Performance Computing Act of 1991, which President Bush signed into law on December 9, 1991, hailing it as ensuring a new competitive edge for the nation in computing potential and as a great potential for future news and information services.

The law created the National Research and Education Network and delegated to a number of federal agencies, such as the National Aeronautics and Space Administration, the Department of Education, and the National Science Foundation, responsibilities to pursue supercomputer programs, develop networks, and establish channels, with a goal of being able to transmit one gigabit (a billion bits) per second by 1996.

The law, in its section on findings, concludes with:

> Such a program would provide American researchers and educators with the computer and information resources they need, and

> demonstrate how advanced computers, high-capacity and high-speed networks, and electronic data bases *can improve the national information infrastructure for use by all Americans* [emphasis added].

The primary sponsor of the bill was a senator from Tennessee, Al Gore Jr., who was elected vice-president in 1992. Gore compared Internet to the pre-Interstate road system. He predicted that establishment of a broad-channel, high-speed network could benefit all citizens, and he saw a multimedia approach to information as being important (see Figure 5.2).

Testimony before the committees that considered this legislation before its passage came from the president's science adviser, university presidents, and computer science experts. Only one of those testifying was a professional provider of information to the public: Paul M. Gherman of the Virginia Tech library faculty who represented the American Library Association and the Association of Research Librarians.

In testimony before Senate and House subcommittees on the High–Performance Computing Act, its most vocal supporter, Senator (but vice-president-to-be) Al Gore, used this illustration:

"This technology is an empowering technology, an enabling technology. This makes it possible [for] any schoolchild in this country to come home after school and, instead of playing Nintendo, to plug into the Library of Congress, not just to see the text, but to see color pictures of dinosaurs or whatever that child happens to be curious about at the moment, and to get access to exciting information configured and presented in a way that satisfies that curiosity and provokes more and makes it possible for individual children to learn at their own pace, driven by that curiosity."

FIGURE 5.2

For the channel to reach beyond the elite and benefit the public, in other words, for it to be a mass medium channel, more providers of information to the public need to be interested in it and involved in its creation.

OUR NARROW VIEW OF PUBLIC INFORMATION

In her autobiographical book *The Corpse Had a Familiar Face*, Edna Buchanan gives some reasons why she has worked so hard during the past three decades as a police reporter in Miami. The Pulitzer Prize-winner writes that she tries to get at least a mention of every homicide in Miami into the *Miami Herald*, despite her editors' views that "routine" murders are not news. She believes that there is one great thing of value that every person has: life. She believes that one person taking another person's life is a matter of great importance and should be noted.

This concept is venerated. The British poet and cleric John Donne wrote, "No man is an island . . . " and concluded his sermon with "Ask not for whom the bell tolls, it tolls for thee." Ernest Hemingway made *For Whom the Bell Tolls* the title of his most celebrated novel.

Sometimes mass media professionals forget that the population statistics now numbering in the billions worldwide consist of individuals. One person at a time lives or dies (a macabre example of binary mathematics). One person at a time reads, hears, sees. Each of those billions has unique information wants and needs.

Almost every year the bell tolls for some daily newspaper in the United States that has had a long and useful life. Executives of old networks and new satellite-programming enterprises wonder how long they will survive. Part of the cause for their apprehension is that by necessity they have had to ignore the fact that "no man is an island . . . "

In sophisticated circles people think it old-fashioned for weekly newspapers to print columns that tell who visited whom and who traveled to where. Yet these sophisticates are exposed to a daily media grind of aging models divorcing screen idols who are getting their faces lifted for the fifteenth time. We read these items for the brief tingle they provide, then move on to the next tingle.

The Hollywood gossip column is symptomatic of how the constraints of space and time in the contemporary media force them to focus on only what will appeal to as many Users as possible. For the most part, and despite their best efforts in many cases, contemporary media are out of touch with most of the things individual readers are interested in.

Only people who live in or near Council Grove, Kansas (or who once lived there) are likely to find the *Council Grove Republican* interesting. It is the smallest daily newspaper in Kansas. I found it interesting when I visited it because it goes against so many practices of bigger media. What Don and Craig McNeil do when they come to work every morning is to start typing everything they can find about Council Grove and Council Grove people into their computers, including advertisements. (What comes over on the Associated Press wire about Hollywood and Washington, D.C., is secondary.) They and their two or three employees do this until about 10:30 A.M. Then they hit the Print button and get all that information out of the laser printer. Then they trim it and paste it up into four pages, pretty much in the order it comes out of the printer. Then one of them jumps in a car with the four pages of pasteup and drives the 40 miles to Ag Press in Manhattan, eats lunch while the paper is run off the press, then drives back to Council Grove and delivers the paper. The next day they do the same thing over again.

They know that the major leagues aren't as important as the local swimming team because Craig is the team coach; that a presidential appointment is not as important as the new teacher at the local high school, because one of the typesetters is the spouse of the school principal. Most of all they realize the importance of putting all their effort into providing all the Council Grove information they can, perhaps to the detriment of appearance or sophistication. They are in touch.

Leo Bogart is a media observer of long standing who is pessimistic. He told those attending a Freedom Forum conference in 1992:

> As we move closer to the vision of the free-flowing, freely accessible electronic information stream, we see some concurrent trends, which are also the product of many complex social forces: (1) More information is acquired intentionally and less serendipitously as a result of a person's own editorial judgments. This means that there is less and less of a role for the professionals who package information; (2) There is a growing preference for entertainment over knowledge and (3) There is a widening polarization along social class lines of entertainment consumers and knowledge consumers . . . [Use of information has become more constricted] even as the database expands along with the opportunity for access . . . An information highway that's jammed with the likes of Jimmy Swaggart, Madonna, and Ice-T can easily be a road to nowhere.

Yet research indicates that children and old people, the poorly educated, and others will extend themselves to get information they are interested in. So does recent history: in small things, such as the proliferation of computer bulletin boards, niche periodicals, and e-mail, we see a kaleidescope of new uses of mass media; in large matters we have the phenomenon of CNN during the Panama and Persian Gulf conflicts, and of C-SPAN during the pre–Gulf War congressional debates; fax machines and e-mail again served as only ham radios have in the past to supplement and even replace the media in Eastern European, Chinese, and Soviet upheavals.

A Broader View of Public Information

Freed of the constraints described earlier, information providers face new opportunities despite Bogart's dire prediction. Once again the news will include what editors and news directors in urban centers have decided is no longer news: "routine" accidents, homicides, fires, school honors, garden club activities, service club speeches, sermons. Receiver computers can quickly isolate what is "important" news for the individual user.

Indeed, the whole gamut of information can again be available: real estate transfers, marriage licenses, new acquisitions at the library, bus schedules, any change in the price of bread.

The skills of the information provider—editor, reporter, filmmaker, and so forth—will be challenged at both ends of the spectrum. For information everyone is interested in, providers will have the maximum opportunity for complete exposure through multimedia. For information of specialized interest, providers can strive for the maximum in detail but also the perspective and background that gives the information meaning.

The New Medium will allow media professionals to fulfill the social contract. In 1948 the Commission on Freedom of the Press, headed by Robert Hutchins, issued a report that spells out the social responsibility of the media. What James Franklin called "tydings," the Hutchins Report called "news." We can substitute the word *information.*

Two of the goals of the media, according to the report, are:

- To provide a full and accurate account of the day's news.
- To give context to the news; the truth behind the facts.

For too long the media have had to scrimp in trying to fulfill their social contract. The New Medium provides a chance to expand instead of scrimp, to press for all the information of interest, to present it as completely and compellingly as possible, and to make sure it gets through the channel to the User.

Essentials of Freedom

My sister recently purchased and, at the age of 83 years, learned to use her first personal computer so as to communicate with her family via Prodigy e-mail. If this seems surprising, keep in mind that *people will pay for what helps them do what they want to do and will take the trouble to learn how to use tools that help them do it.* This principle worked with reading; it worked with automobiles; it will work with the New Medium.

This principle works with both the affluent and the deprived. In 1988 a study showed that the only group that had changed its spending habits appreciably because of the new technologies was the lowest-income group. The lowest-income consumers spend the largest percentage of their income on media and the largest percentage of time with it. Penetration of new technology into this market matched national levels: one-third have VCRs, 17 percent have computers.

"The new information age provides the opportunity for self-actualization."
—Frederick Williams

People are finding the personal computer is definitely a personal tool to do the things they need done. Many of these things are related to information, often personal information. As they hook their computers to fax machines and learn to deal with dozens of e-mail messages at work, as they write term papers and use computers for instructional purposes at school, they are becoming part of electronic networks and are participating in the information environment.

The old model of the public as audience must give way to the concept of individuals as providers of information "creators of small networks of information exchange," according to William Dutton of the University of Southern California.

Indications are that the Receiver wants the Encoder to get out of the way. People are disillusioned with the way information is being delivered to them and with the content of the information. Those with computer skills will figure a way to take control of their information environment. Those without the skills may be left behind.

Many media observers have a different concern: that computer users will be the elite and that the rest of us will be left behind. Mirabito and Morgenstern note: "Information can also be equated with power . . . a person who knows how to use a computer will potentially have access to a greater wealth of information than will a non-user. The information might give the first person either a political or economic edge in a variety of transactions."

Users of the Internet include a corps of "freedom fighters," according to author Steven Levy, who comprise communities "that blend instant access to hard information . . . with more informal means of acquiring 'soft' information . . . more in keeping with a village commons than the hard-and-fast transactions envisioned by futurists planning an information economy."

Other observers fear the information superhighway will be "an all-purpose, heavily traveled, automated toll road." The words come from a former head of NBC News, Lawrence K. Grossman. He sees a purely commercial information industry "converting every home and workplace into a computerized box office, shopping mall, video arcade and slot machine, open for business all day long, every day of the week."

Eric Roberts, president of Computer Professionals for Social Responsibility, expressed three similar concerns:

- If pricing structures do not cover universal service, the average person and the poor will be struggling to use the backroads of the information highway.
- If privacy isn't protected your TV could keep more detailed records of your finances than the IRS.
- And if the [information highway] is not designed to allow everyone to communicate freely and to publish their own contributions, it could become nothing more than a medium for delivering 500-channel television, with interactivity limited to home-shopping and trying to guess the next play during sporting events.

For broad public participation in the New Medium or, in other words, to maintain and expand citizen/consumer freedom, it is necessary to:

- Provide universal access to the channel.
- Provide universal access to the decoding process.
- Provide universal access to the information.

Achieving these three universals will require action on three fronts: policy, technology, and education.

Heather Hudson of San Francisco University notes that "access involves three factors: infrastructure or facilities, connectivity and cost." Infrastructure needs to be upgraded. Despite diverse delivery systems ("communications islands"), we must ensure that we can communicate with one another. Cost must be comparable to other types of service.

POLICY. Public policy is involved, to ensure creation of and access to a universal information highway and compatible systems. In September 1993, the Clinton administration issued a report, "The National Information Infrastructure: Agenda for Action." It said that the priorities for the national information infrastructure (NII) were getting government information on-line and accessible; developing (through private industry) applications and software allowing Users to access, manipulate, organize, and digest information; establishing network standards and transmission codes; ensuring the privacy of persons and security of information and networks; offering tax breaks and assistance in developing software and getting information online; and creating an interagency information infrastructure task force to propose policies and initiatives.

TECHNOLOGY. Technological development, production, and entrepreneurship is involved to create a usable channel and the decoding computers that will be inexpensive, easy to use, and profitable.

EDUCATION. Education is involved, not just in the use of computers but in the nature of information and channels, of news and entertainment of advertising and art. In a paper delivered at the 1991 Conference on Newspapers in Education, Barbara Shapley said students should be taught critical viewing skills—that is, to understand:

1. What mass media and popular culture mean.
2. How media shape attitudes and values.
3. The political and social implications of media.
4. Persuasion techniques.
5. Subliminal messages and bringing them to the surface.
6. How to read pictures.
7. How to compare various media and contrast intents and purposes.
8. That all media are constructions.
9. How each of the media is produced.

The United States is one of few developed countries where media literacy is not integrated into the curriculum, she noted.

New means of expression must emerge; new ways to assemble, organize, and turn information into messages may be the most important part of inventing the New Medium. There is a danger that Users will pay attention only to what is of immediate interest to them; that they will filter out information that is important but poorly presented.

Ideally the New Medium will contribute to a new environment of intellectual activity, an open environment that will diminish the constraints of time and space. People with handicaps will be able to work at home or in a care center. A ghetto graduate student can collaborate on a research project from his apartment with a professor on sabbatical in Australia. With one or both parents working from home, the two-income family will live together more of the time. And most valuable of all will be the ability to acquire, organize and contribute information freely. These things can happen if mass communications professionals play an active role in creating a truly free New Medium.

SUMMARY

From ancient times the search for truth has fascinated mankind. The democratic ideal requires an informed public. We face a time of increasing amounts of information and stringent limits on how much of it the mass media can conveniently make available. The New Medium promises a way to have easier access to information, but the information age is also heightening the perception of information as a commodity. Into public discourse has come the concept of a national "information highway" system. The public and mass communications professionals need to play a major role in shaping this system so that all may benefit.

PROJECTS, DISCUSSION TOPICS, AND EXERCISES

1. Examine various brands of personal computers and report on the operating systems. Compare what system commands format new floppy disks and what commands end the use of one program (application) and initiate the use of another kind. Discuss the advantages of each operating system. Discuss the ease of learning, the speed at which each works, and the potential for use by ordinary citizens.
2. Does the campus have a printed student–faculty directory? How much does it cost? Is the directory available on a computer network? Which is most convenient?
3. How much information does your school's catalog give on each course taught and on each member of the faculty? Is

any of this information available on a computer network? Would students like to see the syllabus for a course before they enroll in it? Would they read the entire vita (résumé) of a teacher they might have a course with? How important is getting more information to students about things that affect each student?

4. If your campus computer network has one or more bulletin boards, or a "news" outlet, apply professional standards of accuracy, language use, news values, and so forth, to the content. Is there a role for professional mass media people in determining what computerized mass media will produce?

SUGGESTED READINGS

Buchanan, Edna. *The Corpse Had a Familiar Face*. New York: Random House, 1987. A veteran big-city reporter who has not lost touch with ordinary people describes her work.

Commission on Freedom of the Press. *A Free and Responsible Press*. Chicago: University of Chicago, 1947. This little book, also called "The Hutchins Report," is a primer on social responsibility theory.

"High-Performance Computing Act of 1991." Public Law 102–194 (S.272), 15 USC 5501 . . . When technology and the legislative process intersect, a document like this emerges.

Williams, Frederick. *The Communications Revolution*. Beverly Hills, California: Sage, 1982. A pioneering work on freedom of information in the new technological era.

The Media in Transition

Incorporating Digital Communication into Existing Media

Technology must be seen as socially shaped and its consequences as indeterminate.

—Robin Fincham

The transition to digital computerized mass communication—the New Medium—is under way. Where will it take us? Sociologist Robin Fincham indicates that we can't know. Another sociologist, David Lyon, urges an "interactive model of the relations between technology and society." So, while the thesis of this book is similar to Lyon's (that is, we can use models to make some predictions), it has already been acknowledged that in a revolutionary situation it is difficult to predict what people are likely to do with a new technological tool. This chapter will look at the brief history of digital computerized mass communication and then take up in some detail its status in the mid-1990s.

Alfred C. Sikes compares our view of the information future to that of the February gardener: "full of uncertainty and obstacles. We will need to have universally accessible networks—networks that offer the public the same capacity or bandwith that major corporate Users today take for granted."

Early Efforts

Throughout the 1980s and into the 1990s serious efforts have been made to establish mass media based on computerized information traveling in electronic channels, both in North America and in Europe. They have either failed or achieved varying levels of success.

A disappointing example is Prestel, inaugurated by the British telephone system. Through a telephone line and using either a conventional television set or a special set, a User can get access to information by keying in symbols. Menus and a cataloging system allow Users

The *Birmingham Post and Mail* Prestel videotex service has had as many as 400,000 accesses in a singlé month.

to get pages of text and rough graphics quickly. The User pays a fee to information providers who participate in the system through a network of computers. Users may send messages to other Users on the system and it provides gateways to databases not accessible otherwise. Prestel was inaugurated in 1979.

In summary, Prestel encodes by turning information contained in numerous databases into pages accessible through easy-to-use menus. It uses telephone lines as a channel and either a conventional keyboard or a keypad plus a television set as a decoder. The other systems are similar in concept.

Gateway (established by the Times-Mirror Company), Venture One (by CBS and American Bell), and Viewtron (by Knight-Ridder) were enterprises in the United States that failed. All used telephone lines and television sets and permitted User interaction.

Venture One served subscribers in the Ridgewood, New Jersey, area. It offered news, information, home-shopping, and home-banking services. Advertising on the system provided for either direct contact with the advertiser by phone for additional information and a possible sale or no direct contact, but a purchase form on the screen that could be completed (including a bank card number) to make a purchase.

Viewtron was more broadly based in southern Florida and offered a broader set of services. It was designed to serve many community information and consumer needs. A User paid for a "wand" (small keyboard) and a monthly fee, using a standard television to read text and graphics. In addition it provided news and local information as well as gateways to an encyclopedia, the Associated Press, *The New York Times,* and other databases. Business transactions included receipts filed in the User's electronic mailbox.

Rather than being a general service, Telidon is a system established by the Canadian Department of Communications to allow groups such as farmers and the tourist industry to have videotex services. It has been successful and links its services through gateways. A major contribution of Telidon is in establishing a video standard that provides higher-quality graphics than Prestel. The standard has been refined and adopted by the American National Standards Institute as the North American Presentation Level Protocol Syntax (NAPLPS).

Online Videotex Service in the San Francisco area provided 300-350 videotex Associated Press news stories daily. Each User paid a $50 deposit, a $20 enrollment fee, and $9.95 a month for an online terminal connected to a phone jack and a power plug.

These interactive services were preceded in the 1970s by one-way teletex and audiotex services. These services provide pages of text on a television screen, or audio messages on a telephone. A viewer tunes in or dials and receives prerecorded messages. In audiotex, particularly, the systems approach interactive status by providing a tremendous number of prerecorded messages, updated regularly, and a long directory of telephone numbers used to reach the messages.

ANALYZING THE '80S

The experience of the 1970s and 1980s is valuable. Standards like NAPLPS provide a pattern for the future. Cooperative ventures were tested and are being pursued avidly. Most important, knowledge about Users is accruing. What information are they interested in? What will they do and pay to get that information? In what form do they want it?

The experience gained also indicated that problems remain on the technological level. For many purposes, paper records are still cost effective. The lack of standards hampers efforts to broaden digital systems. The systems are dependent on the reliability of channels and equipment. The economies of scale that would make them financially attractive to both Users and providers have not been obtained. But these systems do offer enhanced storage and retrieval, easy revision, and relief from schedule-driven, product-driven media.

Problems exist on an institutional level. The private enterprise system fosters multiple standards, hampering broad systems. Entrepreneurship is a volatile way to develop a broad system. Advertising methods must be adapted to a consumer-controlled medium, or a different source for mass media revenue must be sought.

A critical appraisal of the failed systems indicates that they concentrated heavily on creating communication systems, but neglected information systems. They required the User to spend a lot of time and effort getting to the information itself, and the information by and large was recycled from other media.

TECHNOLOGY OF THE '90S

A multitude of technological changes have taken place since Prestel, Viewtron, and so forth, were created. Personal computers are much more common. Desktop publishing has revolutionized graphics and design in digital media. Multimedia is a practice rather than a concept. Digital video has been accepted as the standard of the future. Digital audio is a reality with the burgeoning of the compact disk. CDs are coming into their own as an interim multimedia product and a personal computing tool. Fiber optics, satellite enhancement, and digital compression are broadening channel options.

At this point it is sufficient to note that the digital environment is much more compatible to interactive communication now than it was in 1979. Using the Shannon–Weaver model, we will proceed to discuss these developments.

DIGITAL ENCODING

The history of computing is largely the history of encoding because what a computer does depends on how its operator programs

ENCODING TRANSITIONS

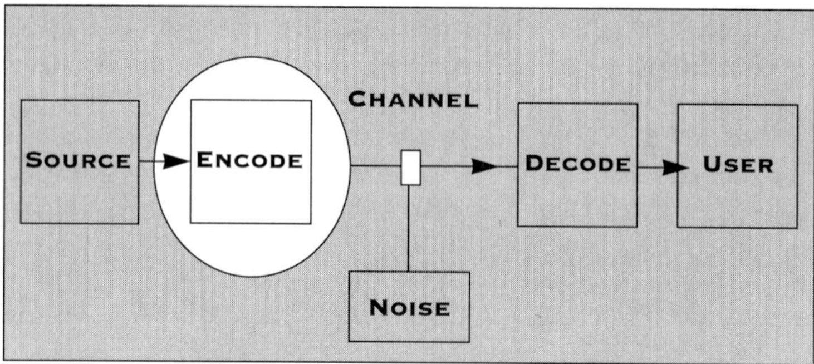

Encoding of information is at the heart of computer science.
Digitization of all kinds of mass media information is a reality.
Storage, organization, and retrieval of this information is a reality and is called *archiving*.
Techniques of combining text, graphics, and audio in single documents is a reality and is called *multimedia*.
The technique of cross-indexing all kinds of information is called *hypertext*.
Gateways permit disparate software systems to get information from one another.

FIGURE 6.1

it (see Figure 6.1). In almost every aspect of the mass media, tremendous amounts of programming have been done.

For example, a single issue of the *Seattle Times* in 1993 reported, not one, not two, but three separate encoding entrepreneurship efforts.

Three groups of companies plan to produce high-definition televisions in time for the 1996 Olympics: General Instrument Corporation and Massachusetts Institute of Technology, Zenith and AT&T, and a consortium composed of Philips Electronics (Netherlands), Thomson Consumer Electronics of France, and David Sarnoff Research Center in Princeton and NBC.

- Microsoft had secured the cooperation of more than a dozen Seattle businesses to test inexpensive software that would link all their office equipment, fax, copying machines, e-mail, and so forth. (Tomorrow computers will coordinate offices; the next day they will coordinate dwellings.)
- Microsoft and Time-Warner were joining to establish standards for interactive cable television allowing Users to select the entertainment they wanted when they wanted it.
- High-definition television was on its way to making existing television sets and VCRs obsolete because it would operate on digital signals, and that because it will be digital, it could be integrated with home computer information.

We want to focus on three kinds of software programming.

UNIVERSAL DIGITIZING. First, as indicated in Chapter One, many newspapers exist in digital form before they are printed. The software to create text, graphics, and photographs is phenomenal and getting more so. When television goes high definition, all television will be digital. The compact disk has turned music into digital form. That takes care of print, audio, and video—the basics of mass media communication. (Will we have digital odors and taste? A synonym for fingers and toes is digits. Virtual Reality technology has provided feely gloves—digital digits?) The software needed for encoding for the New Medium is a reality.

ORGANIZATION AND RETRIEVAL. Second, and just as important as digitizing information, is the computerized organization and retrieval of information. The key-word search has made it easy for anyone to seek out information nuggets from mountains of data. This has revolutionized the way businesses, government, and libraries operate. Hypertext, whereby "buttons" allow Users quick access to cross-indexed multimedia content, is a reality. Developing easy-to-use processing and retrieval systems is a challenge.

COMPUTER SELF-MONITORING. Third, and equally important, is the programming a computer itself can do by monitoring how it is used. We will discuss this one in the Decoding section later.

The great digital breakthrough of the 1990s has been multimedia. In the early years of the decade it was an awkward and cumbersome process carried out only by near-fanatics or those far-sighted communicators who saw its possibilities. However, the introduction of QuickTime software brought digital video to almost any Macintosh computer and made multimedia a desktop possibility. The meshing of text, graphics, audio, and video into an integrated medium is the major digital contribution to content thus far. HyperCard and other hypermedia software has made moving about in a multimedia context possible.

Staff members of *Publish* (a magazine for desktop publishers) decided to produce their own multimedia promotional video and learned a lot about multimedia in early 1991. They found that print people are not used to working with video and that the technology at that time made integrating sound, text, and video a challenge.

ORGANIZING DIGITAL INFORMATION

Digital words, sounds, and pictures are ubiquitously stealing into our lives. So is data processing, something that is pretty heavy sounding. However, at the grocery store checkout stand or the department store cash register, data processing takes place every time you buy an item. The item goes off the inventory, the sale goes into gross receipts, into your charge card account, and possibly to the commission account of the salesperson.

Not too long ago stores would be closed for an afternoon or a day in the middle of January for inventory, so the owners could see what merchandise they actually had. Inventories operate differently now. The creative owner of Beneton, an Italian manufacturer of women's

Allsport is an agency specializing in sports pictures. By creating a computerized database—an archive—of all its pictures, and allowing clients to browse, it has dramatically increased sales. Development of software, like Mosaic, makes this kind of archiving possible.

sports wear, has been quoted regarding his success. A contributing factor, he said, was knowing within a day or two what colors of what garment were selling best all across Europe and the Americas. By knowing, he pointed out, more garments of that color could be produced, increasing sales. And when sales slow, manufacturing and distribution stop. Only rapid transfer of digital information could give him that information.

Mass media applications of data processing are not currently as apparent as the cash-register scanning wand, but in the area of text particularly they are just as useful. Newspaper libraries (morgues, they were called) used to be a collection of reference books plus drawers full of miniature manila folders stuffed with clippings on various subjects. Now the computerized newspaper each day is dumped into memory and often any staff member can key-word for any information needed from his or her own desk terminal. In addition, commercial databases such as NEXIS provide instantaneous access to the contents of dozens of publications going back for a decade or more. Finally, advertising and news people are going directly to governmental and institutional records for demographic, marketing, and investigative-reporting data.

"We usually buy books now as much for the pictures as for the text; we can get textual information on-line (through computer searches) but our artists need to refer to pictures," the librarian of the *St. Petersburg Times* told me some years ago.

However, on the same visit to that newspaper, I saw color photographs that had been transmitted digitally to the newspaper by the Associated Press being cropped and scaled on a computer terminal. The archiving of digitized audio, video, and still pictures is an active area of encoding now. Large amounts of memory are needed to store them, and words appended to each item are used to catalog and retrieve them. But every utterance and image has a distinct pattern. Will we some day search for sounds and pictures the way the FBI matches fingerprints?

Systems of digitizing information and of storing and retrieving it exist in many forms. That brings us to one of the great problems faced by those who would create a universal New Medium: standardization. The term *gateway* has been used in describing some of the early attempts at digital mass communication. A gateway allows a system using one kind of hardware and software to enter a system using different computers and programs, and retrieve information from it.

In the mid-1980s, the National Science Foundation established EXPRES to facilitate transfer of long scientific articles electronically between sites using different kinds of computers and software.

One of the phenomenal things about Internet, the government and educational network used by millions across the planet, has been the ability to cross many of those lines. Digital Equipment Corporation has been a commercial leader in this area. However, these links are as much channel matters as encoding matters. Channels are the next topic (see Figure 6.2).

CHANNEL TRANSITIONS

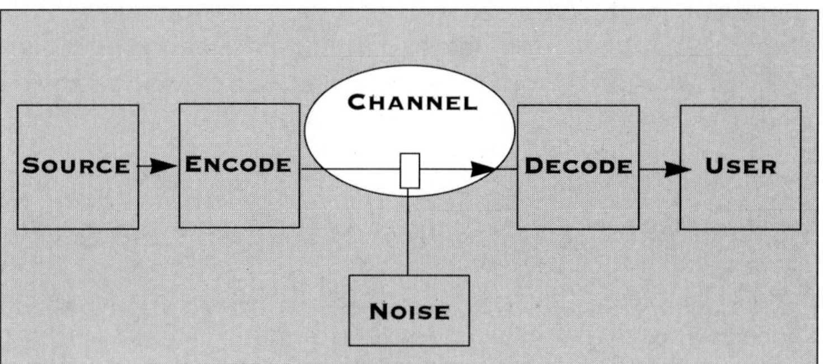

Building the channel leads to controlling its use.
The channel will be a global network.
Computer, telephone, cable, entertainment, and publishing companies are forming alliances and partnerships to compete for channel control.
The FCC represents the governmental and the public interest; legislation seeks public access.
Satellites, fiber optics, and other technology make the channel possible at a cost of $400 billion in the United States.

FIGURE 6.2

DIGITAL CHANNELS

One of the most stable institutions in American life for the first three-quarters of the twentieth century was the "phone company." As reported in a previous chapter, in order to provide telephone service for all at a high standard, the government gave AT&T a virtual monopoly on phone service in the United States. The parent company handled long-distance services. Its subsidiaries included a manufacturing entity, Western Electric, which produced those sturdy black phones; a research entity, Bell Laboratories (which invented among many other things, the transistor); and regional companies that handled local service: New York Bell, Southern Bell, Southwestern Bell, and so forth. The employees of this all-encompassing organization referred to it as "Ma Bell." Individual Users called it "the phone company." (There were also many local independent companies tied into the AT&T long-distance net.)

"The phone company" provided the television and radio networks with the essential electronic hookups, as they were called. It provided businesses with inter-office systems, and it provided everything else used on the system. Its copper wires held the nation together in a communications context. Like the U.S. Post Office it was a "common carrier," taking anyone's messages and delivering them to whomever they were addressed to.

If AT&T's monopoly still existed, the government, the public, and providers of information would all be trying to tell the company what kind of universal channel of information we need in this computer/information age.

Technology made the production and installation of communication equipment easier and less expensive. That and the desire of others to participate in the communication enterprise led to a strong push for an end to the virtual monopoly. In the few years since the courts ordered AT&T to divest itself of its subsidiaries, competition has burgeoned so that operating electronic communications channels has become one of the most competitive businesses in the world. The new technologies making it possible included microwave and communications satellites. Entrepreneurs correctly surmised that the information age was an opportunity to build giant new enterprises.

One such enterprise, Sprint, was a $23-million-a-year business in 1983. In 1992 it was a $6-billion-a-year business. Here is a paraphrase of what William Esrey, chief executive officer of Sprint, told a group of college students in 1992:

> Technical and design people are setting the strategic paths for the future. The telecommunications organizations are moving from being utilities to providing value-added services. Computers and competition have brought this on and have turned the world upside down in two decades. The world is all tied together in what will be an integrated world-wide communications system. It will look like a global mind and indeed it will be putting minds together. This will break down traditional organizational barriers and will include providing personal communication services. No business can ignore it. Nations must support the needed infrastructure. The company is planning to establish Sprintnet, a data network. Sprint must be flexible, able to seize opportunities and capable of creating alliances and partnerships.

Here is some support for what he said:

ALLIANCES AND PARTNERSHIPS. Continental Cablevision made plans to link to the Internet in 1994, allowing customers to plug PCs and a special modem directly into their cable television channels, bypassing the phone company. Microsoft, Time-Warner, and Tele-Communications Inc. (TCI) plan a company to be called Cablesoft. They are the largest companies in software, entertainment, and cable television, respectively.

SEIZE OPPORTUNITIES. The joint effort by the three companies would be to establish a standard for the transmission of interactive programs. The group establishing the standard will create the standard that best fits its goals. Southwestern Bell is already involved in cable television in Israel and England. The companies have applied for permission to operate video and information services in the United States.

GLOBAL NETWORKS. British Telecommunications PLC, Britain's major phone company and the fourth largest in the world, is buying 20 percent of MCI for $4.3 billion. This will provide a British presence in the United States and give MCI, the sixth largest phone company, cash to expand and opportunities outside the United States. They plan a global net, with MCI handling the Western Hemisphere and British Telecom the Eastern.

This is evidence of a giant battle for control of the communications channel of the future. It is a channel as vitally important to the ordinary people and small organizations of our society as to the giants who are waging the battle and who would like to control the channel.

THE GOVERNMENT AND THE CHANNEL

The arbiter of various interests in this competition is the government, most often represented in communications matters by the FCC. The biggest proposed merger involved TCI and Atlantic Bell—a cable television company and one of the "baby" Bells. When the FCC acted in the public's interest on a law placing a limit on profits for cable companies, the merger fell through.

The FCC also has played a major role in encouraging computer, cable television, and telephone companies to work together and to seek broader roles for themselves. Here are some examples:

- The FCC has worked to encourage emerging technologies such as low earth-orbiting satellites and pocket telephones. It has also eliminated barriers, speeding availability of video dial-tone (a network offering customers images, text and voice on demand).
- Another FCC ruling opens the same opportunities to telephone companies that cable television companies now have. At the time of the ruling the telephone companies were prohibited from owning the programming and they probably won't enter until that changes.
- Still another FCC ruling makes possible interactive video networks using phone lines. It could speed the installation of fiber-optic networks and allow newspapers and phone companies to cooperate.

However there is concern that the public interest may be in second priority on the FCC's agenda after the encouragement of economic activity.

Eli Noam, of Columbia University's Institute for Tele-Information, has noted that competition in the information arena is "more of a political competition before governmental bodies, rather than a competition in the marketplace." The role for government, he believes, is to develop a national communications grid that would interconnect many existing and future networks and include everyone. It must overcome barriers of separate network systems: cable television, alternative local exchange companies and other businesses as well as the phone companies. At present there are more than 12,000 electronic information providers.

In 1992 Congress passed the first telecommunications policy legislation since the Communications Act of 1934: the Television Consumer Protection and Competition Act that limits the rate-raising options of cable television companies. It was passed over the opposition of the industry and despite a presidential veto, serving notice that the government will act on the public's behalf. Only in 1994 was the law enforced by the FCC, which claimed it did not have enough resources for enforcement. It was enforcement of this law that resulted in the breakup of the proposed TCI–Bell Atlantic merger.

Howard University's school of government is creating a database for current research on policy issues related to electronic networks and information in digital form.

A government report reveals that in recent years, U.S. companies have invested more than $50 billion annually in telecommunications infrastructure.

The communications channel of the future ranks along with other great projects that government has turned into realities on behalf of "the general welfare." The Erie Canal, the Interstate Highway system, the Postal Service, the Tennessee Valley Authority, the Panama Canal, and NASA are but a few examples.

The channel will be expensive, costing an estimated $400 billion for a comprehensive fiber-optics network. Each artificial earth satellite costs tens of millions and has a limited useful life. However as a percentage of gross national product most of the projects listed above were just as expensive. Refinements of the channel technologies continue.

SATELLITES. The first communications satellite (Intelsat) provided one television channel or twenty-four voice channels. Intelsat VI has 48 transponders, providing three television channels and 100,000 telephone voice channels. In the future is the Advanced Communications Technology Satellite that would carry out a lot of the switching and processing now done on the ground. Its footprint(s) would use "hopping spot beam" technology to go to the portion of the earth's surface below it where the communication traffic is. Projected further in the future is the space platform that would provide a location for multiple satellite uses, allowing for updating and expansion of facilities without individual orbits.

ADAPTATIONS. High-tech adaptations of low-tech channel technology are under way as existing voice-band (copper-pair) circuits are used for slow-scan television. Compression of all kinds of digital data allows for storage and transmission using substantially reduced capacity.

The momentum of communication technology and entrepreneurship leads to the relatively safe prediction that the information superhighway is on its way.

DIGITAL DECODING

Digital decoding is the most exciting part of the New Medium. Through technology it establishes a closer relationship, a partnership, between the provider of information and the User of information. Its success will also depend upon using computer technologies in ways that they have just begun to be used. What is needed is a Model T computer: low cost, low price, easy operation, gets the job done. (See Figure 6.3.)

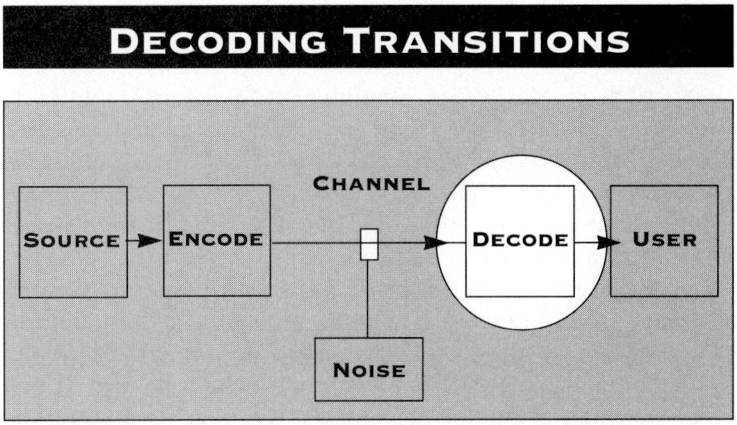

DECODING TRANSITIONS

SOURCE → ENCODE → CHANNEL → DECODE → USER

NOISE

Components for decoding exist. The device itself is still to be perfected. It will provide a partnership between the User and the Sender. It must be:

- Easy to use
- Powerful
- Responsive
- Adaptable

FIGURE 6.3

The interactive systems of the 1980s emphasized the transmission end of the operation and settled for using telephone keypads or early personal computer software at the receiving end. Users had to spend a lot of time doing awkward things for relatively little information.

EASY TO USE. Operation of the computer-software package should be intuitive (perhaps with the capability for key-code shortcuts as the User becomes more accustomed to it). Universal icons, menus and screen display formats would assist all in learning to "read" the New Medium. Remember, the availability of lots of printed matter encouraged millions to become literate in a relatively short period of time.

HEAVY-DUTY. But the performance of the package should be powerful. It must be able to store lots of digital information, to receive it and purge it automatically. It should be fast, allowing the User to get information in the flick of an eyelid.

RESPONSIVE. The computer and software should automatically respond to the perceived needs of the User, providing more information of the kind the User has demonstrated an interest in, and at the same time cuing the User toward important new information the User is unaware of.

ADAPTABLE. Ideally the computer and software would be adaptable to all the needs a User might have at home or in a job. The goal would be to offer a computer-software package the User couldn't afford to refuse.

This remarkable device would seem to be a distinct possibility both from the standpoint of its production and of its acceptance. Alan Haber of the Electronic Industries Association points to these statistics: personal computers are now in 33 percent of 94.6 million households and are expected to be in 50 percent by the end of the decade. The precipitous decline in computer prices shows no sign of tapering off. "The personal computer has entered the mainstream market," he concludes.

At the same time personal computers are becoming more powerful. The introduction of PowerPC and Pentium chips in 1994 is allowing desktop computers to act like Macs or IBMs more interchangeably, for one thing. At the introduction of the new RISC (Reduced Instruction Set Computing) chips, predictions were made that these devices, designed with PCs in mind, will also be at the core of the largest computers constructed in the future.

In 1993 for the first time more computers were purchased for the home than for corporate use. It is estimated that as of 1995 one in four homes nationwide has a personal computer. Already 21 percent of households have *more* than one PC.

The kinds of messages, how they are organized, and how well they mesh with the perceptions and desires of the Users are as important to the decoding process as the computer and its software.

EFFECTIVE MESSAGES. Information presented in the form of effective messages will do more than anything else to make the New Medium a service the User cannot afford to be without. More than ever before the message will be presented to the User on its own merits, free of the constraints of scheduling, of space in the manufactured product, and of having to be adjacent to other messages. Executives and creators will have an opportunity to spend more of their time, effort, and creativity on the message itself. Multimedia and hypertext will allow information contained in a message to be presented in the most appropriate form and allow the User to pursue it according to the User's priorities.

ORGANIZATION OF MESSAGES. In traditional media, both print and electronic, messages are forced to intrude on each other, distracting the User. Advertising is placed adjacent to other content in an attempt to assure the advertiser of maximum return on the cost of advertising. If the New Medium Users are freed from being confronted by messages that interrupt their flow of thought and that they may have no interest in, it will enhance the New Medium's usefulness and desirability.

ADVERTISING. At the same time, the New Medium would offer advertisers new opportunities.

- It would allow advertisers to pinpoint those Users their messages are directed to (and who are most interested in their messages), and to update the messages momentarily.
- It would free advertisers of the time and/or space constraints of presenting their messages. An advertising message could have the appeal of a television commercial, the detail of direct-mail, and the convenience of a want ad all at the same time.
- It would allow the advertiser to make an individual contact with the User.

With these and other advantages, the New Medium would offer advertisers a service they cannot afford to be without.

USER PARTICIPATION. Each User has different interests. Every weekly newspaper editor knows this and takes that fact into account. For example, learning the correct spelling of every family name in the circulation area is vital. The giant media also strive for accuracy but until recently were little concerned with individual interests. For maximum effectiveness the New Medium should actively seek to discover the interests and characteristics of individual Users, to the extent of interviewing each, teaching each to use the decoding computer, monitoring the individual's use of the New Medium and following up with more person-to-person dialogue. It would be impossible for an organization to custom-tailor content for each User. But by providing great masses of information plus a decoding device programmed to meet the individual User's needs, the same result can be accomplished.

Establishing the New Medium so that it does these things is a challenge, a very exciting challenge, for tomorrow's media professionals. Already through formal education and interim technologies the groundwork for establishing the New Medium is under way.

TRANSITIONS FOR PROFESSIONALS

I'm pretty old. I can remember when my sister (the one who is in her eighties and recently bought a computer) would bring her portable wind-up recordplayer home from college. She and my brothers would play those old Victor 78 rpm records, the ones with the dog on the label and the words *Fox Trot* to describe the music. The player head was heavy, the steel needles were sharp (they wore out quickly and cost money to replace), and the records were very vulnerable to wear. So, to save money and wear and tear on the records, my brothers would go out to a West Texas mesquite tree, harvest some thorns with their pocket knives, and use the thorns in place of the steel needles. The music wasn't as loud, but it worked!

People are doing things today that will seem equally quaint 50 years in the future, but those things will help in the transition to the New Medium.

The story above came to mind after I read that a compact disk is now available with the following things on it: Microsoft Word software, a *Hammond Atlas, American Heritage Dictionary, Roget's II Thesaurus, Columbia Concise Encyclopedia, World Almanac,* and *Bartlett's* and *Columbia* dictionaries of quotations. The encyclopedia includes audio and video information about various things as well as text.

I expressed to my wife my astonishment at this cornucopia of information in such a small package. My wife was born well after the mesquite-thorn phonograph needle era and, as a librarian, is a constant User of CD-ROMs. She replied, "What's so odd about that?"

But for me it's a miracle. I could call all that out of my own little computer if I had a CD-ROM drive. Then I read that in 1994 most Apple Macintosh computers had started coming equipped with CD players, standard. I'll have to get one.

TRANSITORY CDs

The compact disk system is one of the transitional devices that will make the New Medium possible. CDs are inexpensive, transportable, and easy to manufacture, and each stores a large amount of any kind of digital information.

Media professionals already are using CDs for all kinds of things. Soon multimedia presentations (Publications? Recordings? No word quite describes it; maybe we'll just call them multimedias or multis or medias, you name it) will become common, perhaps a popular product. If so, Users will experience a new kind of participation (Reading? Viewing? Listening?). Each User will experience the presentation in a different way because the presentation will not be linear or in a single medium but it will be easy to use. I'll close my eyes and listen to the music; you'll want to see the video first; someone else will read text and ignore the rest until later; even the order in which the text is read will not be the same for each User. Users will find themselves participating in the presentation as never before.

Creators of these presentations will find their creativity challenged as never before. Instead of carefully compromising on what to put in and what to leave out and of crafting a linear presentation, the creator will be trying to include everything any User would want and in a coherent but conveniently serendipitous form.

Creators of effective CD presentations will fit right into the New Medium environment. They'll forget about manufacturing the CDs and send the presentations right out over the digital information superhighway to the Users' computers.

So, multimedia and hypermedia are the topics to consider to see how professional media people are transforming themselves into New Medium people.

MULTIMEDIA/HYPERMEDIA EDUCATION

University-level curricula in multimedia exist, specifically at Columbia College (Chicago), Georgia Tech, MIT Media Lab, New York University, San Francisco State, and San Jose State. There may be others.

The trend in this direction is endorsed by mass communication educators. Robert Blanchard of Trinity University, who has opposed "green eyeshade" training of reporters and editors for a long time, urges media cross-training and getting away from traditional media forms.

Joan Conner is dean of the Graduate School of Journalism, Columbia University, a program specifically oriented toward preparing people for work in the existing media. In her 1992 newsletter she reported that the school was beginning to educate "journalists who are equally at home in the language of print or video." The school expected 48 print students to sign up for the video course; more than 100 enrolled.

Those attending the 1992 Broadcast Educators Association convention were told that journalism education must stress fundamental skills (think, decide, create); faculty must stay on top of changes; computers will play an increasing role; and that digital formats and high-definition television are making radical changes in the media.

In a move that reflects the interdisciplinary trend caused by the information age, Rutgers University has combined communication, librarianship, and journalism into a School of Communication, Information and Library Studies.

The use of multimedia/hypermedia techniques on university campuses is widespread. Alert faculty members are adapting it to the classroom and designing courses allowing students to pursue subjects at their own rate of learning and in individually determined directions.

Campuses with their computer nets and populations who own PCs and are computer literate, are fertile fields for embryonic digital mass media, some of which include video and audio with text. An example is *Medialink,* which is available on 8,000 personal computers at Stanford.

JOURNALS ON THE NET

Although it is not yet multimedia, traditional academic publishing is changing in the direction of the New Media. Librarians Molly Royse and Ellie Marsh reported in 1991 the existence of ten refereed electronic academic journals and predicted that by the year 2000, 20 percent of academic journals would be published electronically.

Ann Okerson of the Association of Research Libraries (ARL) recalled at a 1994 University of Washington library convocation a late 1991 meeting at which all the editors of electronic academic journals were in the same room—twelve people. Each year ARL issues a directory of electronic academic newsletters and journals. The May 1994 directory listed between 400 and 500 titles; of these, fifty or so, in Okerson's words, "are really good refereed journals."

NorthWestNet NodeNews for December 1993, is a typical online journal for a particular interest group: members of a regional network. Its thirteen articles occupying twenty pages single-spaced when printed out included such topics as government policies on communication technology, convergence of media, expanding Internet access in North Dakota, and the future of NorthWestNet. Production costs are minimal since it is keyboarded into the NorthWestNet PC and distributed on the Internet; there are no printing or mailing costs to the producer and there are few restrictions on length of articles.

Just as the electronic mass media changed the nature of newspapers and magazines, the use of e-mail and electronic data transfer is changing the nature of academic publication. Formerly scholars in a discipline learned of like-minded scholars and their research by reading journals and attending conventions; now the first contact may well be through a bulletin board, also known as a discussion list. Okerson estimates that there are some ten thousand discussion lists on the Internet and that, of these, 1,800 have scholarly and academic value.

TRADITIONAL MEDIA TRANSITIONS

The contemporary media have energetically undertaken enterprises that can be considered transitions to the New Medium.

Down through the years when people would get into an argument, one of the arbiters they have turned to has been the local newspaper. "Was George Brett's best batting average .380 or .390?" may enter the ear of a sportswriter from the telephone. The sportswriter is likely to know the answer or have his handy stats book nearby and be able to settle the argument (.390). In times of international crisis newspapers have traditionally offered to readers for a small fee maps of the crisis area so they can better keep up with what is going on. These kinds of things have expanded dramatically as the media have turned proactive in offering services to Users.

Many media outlets offer voice services, publishing long lists of four-digit telephone extension numbers, each of which gives a different recorded message about everything from when and where movies are showing to stock prices.

AN AUDIOTEX CASE STUDY

The *Kansas City Star* calls its service, appropriately, *StarTouch.* On a snowy schoolday morning as many as 24,000 calls may be received from parents who dial the *StarTouch* number associated with a child's school to see if it is closed. This service has replaced interminable waiting by a radio or busy signals at the school's phone. It is a convenience.

The *Star* often gives its reporters tape recorders to take on assignments. From the raw tape of a speech or meeting, *StarTouch* will offer excerpts to callers who find out about the excerpts in a promotional box that accompanies the reporter's story in the paper. It's a way to let the User get closer to the story and perhaps decide how sincere or intelligent the speaker was.

When Kansas City Royal Brett got his three-thousandth hit late one night in a game played in California, the *Star* retrieved the radio announcer's account of the historic event, put it on *StarTouch,* and promoted it on its sports pages. The first day 85,000 calls were received, 15,000 got through. At the time Brett retired, years later, the record-hit number was still receiving 3,000 calls a month, allowing fans to relive the magic moment.

Stories are developed from reader response to *StarTouch* initiatives. When the anniversary of an important event nears, readers who were present or participated are asked to telephone the newsroom. They then become sources for traditional news stories. Or readers may be asked to give their opinions regarding an issue via a *StarTouch* number, and what they have to say is the stuff for a reaction story.

David Zeeck, a *Kansas City Star* executive, says *StarTouch* draws newspaper and readers closer together, provides an added dimension to the *Star*'s coverage, and allows it to provide more of the information it has to interested readers.

The *Star* also offers its readers helpful information by fax or mail as do other newspapers, such as the *Lansing* (Michigan) *State Journal* (70,000 circulation), which usually gets a dozen requests on things like day-care center lists and texts of speeches. A hot sheet on mortgage refinancing brought 340 requests in 3 days when interest rates began to come down.

ONE NEWSPAPER'S INITIATIVES IN NEW TECHNOLOGY

WHO: In the late 1980s former *Kansas City Star* publisher Jim Hale recognized a young executive, Scott Whiteside, as an innovative thinker, and named him to head a committee on technology innovation. *StarTouch,* an audiotext system, was the result. Nancy Tracewell is now director of electronic media, and Fred Schecker was brought into the organization two years ago to provide liaison with the newsroom. They, with a computer specialist and a sales manager, are the basic staff. Whiteside now is an executive with Times-Mirror Corp.

WHAT: Through 72 lines, persons may telephone *StarTouch* and by "touching" four digits on their phones, receive information on arts, business, community calendars, news, promotions, sports, weather, and more (over 300 categories). *StarTouch* gets 15,000 calls a day; over 9,000 are for business information.

WHEN: 24 hours a day.

WHERE: *StarTouch* is in a corner of the very big *Star* newsroom. It consists of personal computers, a sound booth, and telephones.

WHY: "Our goal is to enhance the newspaper," Schecker said. It allows the *Star* to break the broadcast and cable monopoly on instant news. Routine information important to even a modest number of Kansas Citians can be made available, reestablishing the newspaper as a source of information. Where a source tape (e.g., an audio "clip" or live quote) enhances the information, that can be added.

HOW: Some services (such as Dow Jones) are purchased. Some reporters take tape recorders on their newspaper assignments for *StarTouch*. The newspaper promotes *StarTouch* in its columns, urging readers to call in with responses or to seek additional information. Schools cooperate with homework hotlines, and other institutions provide information free in return for audio credit for providing it (a local business news service; an alternative school that provides a "writing line" and a reader of stories). Reporters for the paper provide tidbits that don't make the paper for a "weird news" number. A one-minute story is about the right length.

WHO CARES: Kansas Citians do. The service was operating in the black after a year, using a brief "sponsorship" message with phoned items. When "Achy, Breaky Heart" topped the country music charts, 15,000 persons called in to hear a taped excerpt. A call-in *StarTouch* box was included with an expose on a phony fundraiser for fire fighters killed in an explosion, resulting in a caller (who had accidentally recorded the high-pressure sales pitch on his answering machine) providing audio support for the story; the reporter got hundreds of calls from readers who were outraged by the scam. In north Kansas City *StarTouch* provided a homework hotline to each school and a mailbox for each teacher. Parents loved it. Schecker (who has a master's degree in education and helped set up the lines) received an award at a testimonial dinner. The *Star* has bucked the national trend and shown a slight increase in circulation; *StarTouch* staffers think they helped.

WHAT'S NEXT: The *Star* already offers a fax service on everything from how to use Thanksgiving turkey leftovers to the form for extending the deadline on filing an income tax form. Now being beta tested is *StarView:* the *Kansas City Star* online to personal computers using Windows. The *Star* will not use an existing communication service such as CompuServe or America Online because it wants to preserve its identity.

Box 6.1

The radical change in newspaper appearance since *USA Today* entered the market is related to multimedia. *USA Today* brought graphics and color to American newspapers. At the same time newspapers turned to graphic design as a means of attracting readers. One of newspaperdom's most active organizations is the Society of Newspaper Design, which publishes a stimulating bulletin and conducts numerous short courses across the country. The designers have assumed the responsibility of deciding what information is best presented in what form: maps, diagrams, charts, graphs, photographs, text, and so forth. Traditional newspapers were highly text oriented. Contemporary newspapers are aware of nonlinear methods of presenting information.

AUDIO AND VIDEO TRANSITIONS

Whereas newspapers have been exploiting nonverbal communication, radio has discovered User participation. The radio call-in show is related to the personal computer with a modem bulletin-board phenomenon. Announce a topic or create a bulletin board and they (the Users) will come with opinions. As indicated previously, the success of stores renting movies recorded on VCR cassettes is the entertainment industry's response to the User's desire to control his or her own television screen.

Will CD-ROM multimedia be the next big transitional step, as suggested earlier? We will have to wait and see. How long will the transition take? We will have to wait and see for that too, maybe a long time. But what is approaching is a critical mass of Users who are eager to get their information in new ways and a critical mass of creators who can provide the content for the New Medium. Then it is likely to take off with the curiosity factor that always accompanies something new and different, giving it a big initial boost.

SUMMARY

The transition toward all-digital, all-computerized mass media is under way. Encoding computers and software have made the most progress. The possibilities for a powerful and comprehensive information channel, an information superhighway, look good. Decoding hardware and software are possible but are not yet realities. Lagging farthest behind in the transition are the creation of communication messages appropriate to the New Medium.

PROJECTS, DISCUSSION TOPICS, AND EXERCISES

1. Find a subject you are interested in and offer an outline or chart for a multimedia CD on that subject. Use the World

War II proposal in Chapter Three as a sample starting point. Create a chart of hypertext links to the content.

2. Discover which newspaper in your area has an audiotex service. Test how effective it is. Interview the director of the service on how it is working and where it is going; does the newspaper have fax service to the public?
3. Pick out your favorite advertisements as starting points for New Medium advertisements. How would you attract people to the advertisement; provide people with an opportunity to go into greater detail on the advertising message; close the sale?
4. Look through newspaper microfilm to retrieve advertisements of personal computers for the years 1987, 1989, 1991 and 1993. Compare prices and power of computers. What is the trend?

SUGGESTED READINGS

Fincham, Robin, and David Lyon. "From 'Post-Industrialism' to 'Information Society.'" *Sociology* 21:3 (August 1987), pp. 463–465. Two diametrically opposed theoretical approaches to technological change.

Finnegan, Ruth, Graeme Salaman, and Kenneth Thompson, eds. *Information Technology: Social Issues*. Nineteen papers cover varied aspects of the subject from North–South divergences to technology in banking.

Bjorn-Anderson, Niels, Michael Earl, Olav Holst, and Enid Mumford, eds. *Information Society for Richer for Poorer.* A look at a European attempt at bringing order to information technology transition.

Shaw, Donald L., ed. *Journalism Quarterly* 69:2 (Summer 1992). Six articles deal with "America in a Visual Century." Good background on the changes leading up to the current transition.

Practical Models

Learning How to Build the Medium of the Future from the Internet, the Associated Press, CDs, and So Forth

Rather than fewer editors, we will very likely need more and better managers to make sense of the swelling flood of information.

—**Roger Fidler**

Back in 1991 I read a story about an American who caught a German spying on U. S. military installations and selling the information to the Soviet Union. Fairly typical spy novel? No. The American was an astronomer in California. The German never left Germany to do his spying. The American did all his detective work on a computer in Berkeley. And it wasn't a novel. It is a true story (with lots of suspense and even romantic interest!).

To begin to understand the transition now under way in information handling, one should read Clifford Stoll's *The Cuckoo's Egg* (New York: Doubleday, 1989, 323 pp.) and then get some knowledge about the Internet, the fantastic information processor that allowed the events the book relates to happen.

The Internet Model

Here is the extent of the transition, measured by the Internet. In January 1993, the *Boston Globe* reported that the Internet was logging 20 billion transmissions a month. It has 4 million individual persons using its resources from more than three dozen countries. For the most part the individual Users get to use it free. Since those figures appeared, the Seattle Public Library announced a grant allowing it (and therefore all its patrons) access to the Internet. No doubt many other institutions hooked up at the same time. The Internet's size was expected to double by the end of 1993.

Supporting that estimate were figures released in January 1994, by the Domain Survey of the Network Information Systems Center indicating that the number of Internet "hosts" had grown by 69 percent in the previous year to a total of 2.2 million hosts (with from three to ten Users per host). What would P. T. Barnum, Cecil B. DeMille, Joseph Pulitzer, or Robert Sarnoff do with a medium that could reach 4 million affluent, educated people in three dozen countries?

Research shows that use of personal computers is based on social norms and three components of expected consequences: complexity of use, fit between the job and PC capabilities, and long-term consequences.

It's too bad the late Sam Goldwyn isn't around to give us a succinct description of the Internet. In 1945, right after the bombing of Hiroshima, he was quoted as saying: "That atomic bomb is dynamite!"

More millions of Americans are using CompuServe, Prodigy, America Online, or any of the other commercial computerized information services. But the Internet is the broadest and the busiest. Here is what the Internet can do:

When I'm at my office in Manhattan, Kansas, and want to communicate with my wife in her office in Seattle, Washington, I click on my computer's Internet e-mail icon. A form appears. I type my wife's first name. I type the message. I click on a box labeled "Send." It's there in minutes (competing with several dozen other e-mail messages on her cue). If she wants to reply, she types a message at the bottom of mine and clicks on "Return." That's it.

- Exchange files (including huge amounts of information) between host computers. (The Internet has a million host computers. It links 10,000 computer networks.)
- Provide remote log-on, which means one computer can go use another computer's software to process information contained in the other computer.
- Provide e-mail service between any Internet User and any other Internet User, plus e-mail gateways to Users on other networks.
- Provide bulletin boards, including such things as newsgroups, discussion lists, and electronic serial publications.

Time magazine credits the Internet concept to Paul Baran, of the RAND Corporation, who wanted a way to communicate in case of nuclear attack, so he envisioned "a computer-communications network that had no hub, no central switching station, no governing authority, and that assumed that the links connecting any city to any other were totally unreliable."

A strange conglomoration of soldiers, bureaucrats, and scientists (interestingly, no private-enterprise entrepreneurs) created the Internet. It grew out of ARPANET, a Defense Department research network linking government installations with university, industrial, and research organizations. The defense establishment moved its military operations off the Internet in the mid-1980s. It is now primarily for educational and research use (very broadly defined), under the aegis of the National Science Foundation through NSFNFT.

No single organization manages the entire Internet. NSFNFT is overseen by Advanced Network & Services Inc. (created by a consortium of Michigan universities, IBM, and MCI). Some groups that strongly influence it are the Internet Society and its Internet Architecture Board and Internet Engineering and Research Task Forces.

The real miracle of the Internet is that so many different networks have been linked in a system that really works on such a voluntary basis. The reason for the miracle? The academic-scientific community (as well as many other Users) find it so valuable they just can't afford not to have the information it provides. The Internet is dynamite! (See Figure 7.1.) Interestingly, its tremendous development corresponds to the period during which the contemporary mass media have experienced increasing stress.

Charles Radin, writing in the *Boston Globe,* linked the Internet to the High Performance Computing Act of 1991 and to the proposed

INTERSTATE AND INTERNET

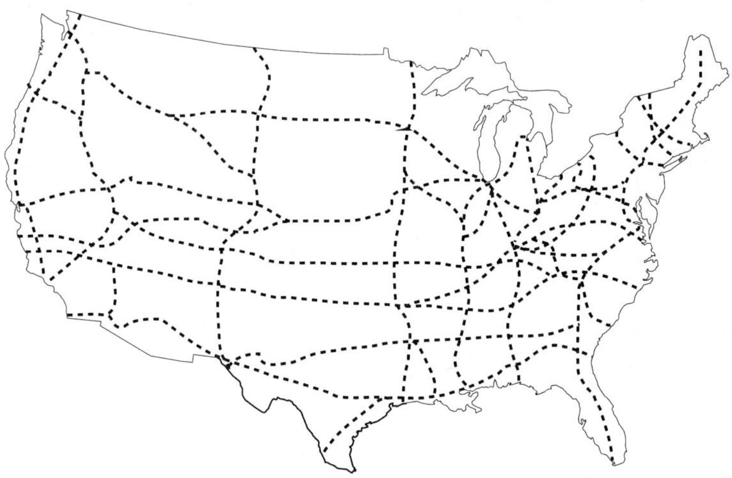

To travel the interstate highway system one needs a map (more accurate and detailed than the one above) to select a route and estimate a time of arrival. Not so with the information highway called the Internet. In fact, Federal Express discovered several decades ago that it was quicker and less expensive to fly packages from cities all over North America to Memphis, reorganize them by destination, and send the right packages by all those planes back to the originating cities than it was to have an origin-to-destination system. A straight line was no longer the quickest route between two points. The Internet deals with digital information. Somewhere there must be a map with all the alternative routes an Internet message could take. But Users do not need it. Messages are launched and if they have difficulty taking one route they take another, arriving at their destination not eventually, but instantaneously.

FIGURE 7.1

national information superhighway. As a transitional model for the New Medium it is appropriate to consider that the Internet

- Exists and grows because it is so valuable.
- Is free to individual Users.
- Is effective; it works.
- Is personal.
- Is also institutional.
- Moves humongous amounts of information as well as tiny messages.
- Links all kinds of computers and networks.

A Super Internet?

However, the Internet is not a full-fledged mass medium. Instead it is full of specialized information. The medium that we are discussing in this book would be proactive in addressing the information needs and desires of, well, everyone. A super Internet could have the capacity and capability to reach everyone, but would only reach the goal we have set for the New Medium if it offered everyone "access to the day's events," and "the meaning behind the facts" and the cultural and artistic opportunities that undergird our society.

New York City is not the only distant place I am interested in. I have also lived in Fort Stockton, Texas; Greenville, Mississippi; and Fayetteville, Arkansas. My wife's home is Fayetteville, North Carolina. Since the *Fort Stockton Pioneer*, the *Delta Democrat-Times* (of Greenville), the *Northwest Arkansas Times*, and the *Fayetteville* (N.C.) *Observer* all exist in those newspapers' computers, it would not be difficult for the New Medium to zap data from them right into my computer. I would be able to keep up with Joe Alexander, Mary Sferuzza, the Belzung family, and Aunt Ruth! How nice! Notice that the whole concept of the information we get has changed. Reporters and editors would no longer limit themselves to information they believe *everyone* wants; now they send along all the information *anyone* wants. My computer would screen out information of little interest to me and put what I most want where I can read it, hear it, see it at once.

Indeed, one of the fears expressed about the information society is that it will fall short of the goals expressed above. Leo Bogart's three trends concurrent to the information era were cited earlier and express these apprehensions well:

- More information is acquired intentionally and less serendipitously as a result of a person's own editorial judgments.
- There is a growing preference for entertainment over knowledge.
- There is a widening polarization along social class lines of entertainment consumers and knowledge consumers.

The new technologies that make the New Medium a possibility also provide an opportunity to reduce the polarization Bogart has identified by offering knowledge in a compelling and convenient form and alongside the entertainment. This was a technique used by Joseph Pulitzer, who pioneered the truly popular press at the turn of this century. His tactic was to wrap serious commentary and reportage in a package of bright and entertaining journalism.

The New Medium might well succeed if the next generation takes a lesson from Pulitzer. Just what is it that the Joseph Pulitzers, P. T. Barnums, and David Sarnoffs have done to be great mass communicators? We will return to our Shannon–Weaver communication model in examining that question.

A Mass Communication Model

I used to live in Manhattan, New York. Now I live in Manhattan, Kansas. They are quite different. I like them both and when I am at one Manhattan I always miss the other one. Perhaps you have noticed that quite a few movies are made on location in New York. So, when I am watching a New York movie, I pay attention to the background scenes. How is my New York of years past different from today's New York depicted in the movies? As a result I was not surprised in the late 1980s upon visiting New York to discover open-air Vietnamese vegetable-and-flower shops, rap artists on the sidewalks, and a

Adding Content and Feedback to the Shannon Model

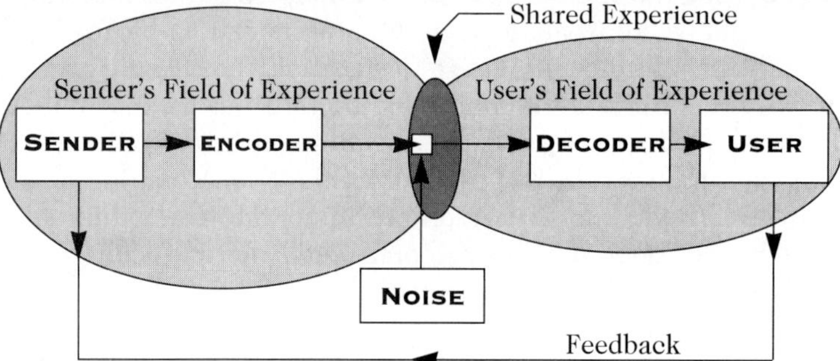

The concepts established by Schramm and DeFleur when they added fields of experience and feedback to the Shannon model are the most important concepts for mass communications professionals to consider as they create the New Medium.

Content comes from the vast field of information available. Users find the content compelling if they can relate to it. By understanding their shared field of experience, the professional establishes that relationship with the User.

In the New Medium, feedback is much more than reaction to what the New Medium provides the User. Feedback from the User:

- enhances the shared experience.
- contributes to the content, with the professional recognizing the value of feedback as content, verifying and enhancing its credibility and disseminating it to those Users who find it important.

Figure 7.2

skyscraper with its top cut off at an angle; they weren't there when I lived in New York.

That's the way we use the mass media. We compare our experiences to what the media tell us, draw conclusions, and learn from the experience. In Figure 7.2, an enhanced Shannon–Weaver Model demonstrates this activity.

Some things have been added to the model, thanks to two noted communication theorists, Wilbur Schramm and Melvin DeFleur. Schramm suggested that communication required content or information, which comes from experience. So he created a "sender's field of experience" representing the information the sender had, and a "receiver's field of experience," representing the information the receiver already had.

Notice that the sender's field of experience is bigger than the receiver's (User's). Actually in a mass media context it should be much bigger, theoretically encompassing all of human experience, knowledge, art, and culture.

Notice that the two fields of experience overlap into shared experience. There has to be shared experience (both sender and receiver need to be using the same language, for example; and we measure what is new by what we know about something similar).

Notice the "feedback" line at the bottom. That is DeFleur's contribution. He realized that as communication takes place, the responses (or feedback) from the receiver affect the continued communication from the sender. You need to let the New Medium know what you want to know so the New Medium can provide you with that information. The New Medium can respond much more quickly and more efficiently than can contemporary media.

The role of the mass media professional begins to emerge as we examine the model. The professional is aware of the User's field of experience and, with that in mind, looks into that vast universe of information the User is unfamiliar with, selects what is important or interesting, and presents it in a way that fascinates the User.

Russian scholars before the demise of the Soviet Union noted the growing demand for books and asked where will all the paper come from to print them. They predicted that books would be translated into another information carrier.

FOCUS ON THE USER

As professionals have looked to the future of the news media in particular, they have recognized the need to keep the User in mind when preparing the content. Jon Franklin has deplored the lack of attention to the importance of creating "stories." Content will be all-important in the future, the two-time Pulitzer Prize-winner said. People will pay for information they want, but it must be useful. He noted how book publishing is booming, and concluded by expressing the need for studies on how the mind reacts to narrative and other presentation techniques. On the bright side, it is his view that there will be more reporting jobs and more quality reporting jobs in the future.

The roles of editors are changing in many contexts. For example, communication researcher Dimitri Weiss has noted that house journal (internal public relations media) editors are becoming corporate communicators, information managers, and future facilitators of communication.

Roger Fidler, who has been commissioned by Knight-Ridder to examine the potentialities of a digital newspaper, is in agreement with Franklin. Fidler sees the digital newspaper as something quite different from a database. He notes that databases are passive; newspapers are not: "The newspaper model is one in which it sells you information. It actively involves you in the process of getting information and exposes you to information that you didn't know you were interested in at the time." The electronic newspaper will not ignore browsing.

International communications scholar Johannes Johansen has summarized the requirements for use of a digital medium: while efforts are made to ease access in order to attract more Users, Users demand that systems should be of good quality: systematic, precise, and reliable.

Electronic newspaper functions will continue to have reader-friendly design, organization of sections, high-quality editorial content, and useful advertising, according to Fidler. Still pictures could become video snippets. A voice-activated component would allow the paper to be read to you. It would scan abstracts and have the computer read stories to you while you drive to work.

THE JANUS MODEL

One institution from the contemporary mass media world could serve as a useful model for the New Medium as a provider of information. Here are some of the institution's attributes: pays close attention to Users' information use; gathers information from a vast universe; efficiently stores, processes, and communicates information, tailors information to Users' needs, stays abreast of latest technology, is not burdened by the use of a manufactured product as a distribution device; and deals effectively with the transmission of information to meet Users' time schedules.

The institution is the worldwide wire service as developed in the United States: the Associated Press in particular. The Associated Press (AP) is a century and a half old in concept. A group of New York newspaper publishers realized that it would be economical to share the expense of a single boat and reporter who would meet all ships coming into New York Harbor to get the latest information from abroad. Prior to the agreement each publisher sent out his own boat. Most of the information was routine. The new system, a cooperative, worked well. When the telegraph was introduced, AP and competing organizations became "wire services," although they now depend on satellite transmission, rather than copper wires, for most of their heavy-duty communications.

So it is appropriate that AP still has its headquarters in New York, across the street from the RCA Building, home of NBC, and within walking distances of a great number of the nation's broadcasting companies, advertising agencies, and publishing houses. However, the AP operates quite differently from them. It could be called the Janus of the information world. Janus in mythology is a god with a face on the back of his head as well as the front. He is equally cognizant of what is happening behind him as what is in front. AP gets information from Users and provides information for Users; it provides the media in Buenos

Aires, Argentina, with news from all over the world, and it sends news from Buenos Aires all over the world. It looks both ways all the time. This is the gatekeeping function of the mass media, and the gate needs to swing both ways.

The New York headquarters of a wire service will have a foreign desk, receiving news from outside the United States. It will also have a world desk, taking news from all over the world and sending it to clients all over the world.

New York is not the only place where information is processed. AP has bureaus located all across the world. The bureau is a smaller Janus. For instance, the Kansas City bureau serves clients in Missouri, Nebraska, Kansas, and maybe another state or two. AP members in those states are required to make their information available to the AP, which also staffs in person or by telephone many stories in the area. If an AP member is interested in information from beyond the bureau's reach, that interest is relayed to the bureau chief in Kansas City, who passes on the word to New York and tries to make sure the request is met.

The bureau chief has diverse responsibilities, among them the routine of keeping the bureau operating, and overseeing both the communications equipment and the information processing. This executive also makes sure AP headquarters policy is carried out. In addition, a very major responsibility is to make sure the Users, the members of AP, in the chief's territory are served properly. This requires travel, telephoning, and mainly a lot of listening. Then there's the budget, payroll, and other clerical tasks.

AP tailors its services to the needs of the Users. A small radio station will get a smorgasbord of regional, national, and international news, features, entertainment information, weather, sports, and business. A great metropolitan daily newspaper will get the "A" wire of nothing but national and international news, plus regional wires from all the states it cares to pay attention to, plus an all-sports wire, business wire, and features wire.

Information for newspapers is written in newspaper style and is delivered on the newspaper's cycle: all morning long for afternoon papers and all afternoon and evening for morning papers. Information for radio stations is recycled every hour with briefs, 5-minute newscasts, sportscasts, and so forth, ready for the announcer.

AP has an audio service for radio stations and a video service for television. The wire services have been leaders in technology, particularly for newspapers, including the telegraph, teletypewriter, wirephoto, teletypesetter, and digital high-speed text, graphics, and photo transmission.

Wire services are inclusive rather than exclusive in what they provide their Users, knowing that the User would prefer to choose from a large menu of information rather than having to make do with a skeleton amount of information.

Forty years ago AP faced intense competition from United Press and the International News Service. Because of its success at doing the things mentioned above and its strong foundation as a cooperative owned by the media, it is the preeminent information-gathering organization today.

LOCAL "WIRE SERVICES"

One possible way for news operations, print and broadcast, to prosper in the future is to emulate on a local scale what AP does worldwide. The New Medium will allow individual Users to "edit" their own news in the future, with the help of effective local bureau chiefs. These local information specialists would sensitize themselves to community and individual needs, would pass on from the larger world much more than any individual would want, and would delve into the records, archives, and goings-on of the community to provide a complete information pantry for the individual to select from.

This development of a possible information strategy is taken from a news context. Would it also apply to culture, entertainment, continuing education—the total information picture? The emancipation from strict scheduling and product-oriented information would help make it so.

Modeled after AP, a New Medium organization in a community, large or small, might find itself organized as follows:

- Local information services
  entertainment and culture
  reference
  news
  bulletin boards
- Imported/exported information services
  entertainment and culture
  reference
  news
  data transfer
- User services
  new Users
  continuing relations
  promotion and development
  advertising
- Technical services
  local network
  import–export network
  central office equipment
  User equipment
- Clerical services

This organization puts a heavy emphasis on the User and on information. At the same time it is freed of the manufacturing, distribution and tight scheduling responsibilities of the contemporary media. The New Medium would need the resources now devoted to manufacturing, distribution, and scheduling to do a good job.

THE INFORMATION-PROCESSING MODEL

Dumping raw data, barely organized, into a User's computer will overwhelm the User in about two minutes. In fact that is what the mass media tend to do now in spite of themselves. They tell us something is rotten in Denmark, show pictures of people in Denmark holding their noses and piles of sagging cheeses. Then they switch to a commercial (not cheese). The reaction is "Who cares?" or "Is that my favorite Danish cheese?"

If I am a "Who cares?" User, I should be able to zip on to something interesting. If I am a cheese person, I should be able to find out more about the situation.

Librarians, statisticians, and reporters are very good at processing information now. The reporters unfortunately don't have the space or time to be as complete as they could be. As a before-and-after New Medium example, let's look at a sample story about a state law changing the fees for auto license tags.

Today's medium would tell you that the cost of an auto license tag is going up (of course) effective next January 1. It would tell you how much the increase would be for an inexpensive car and for a very expensive car. It would tell you that the increase will be less for old cars than for new cars. It might tell you that for the first time people registering cars in urban areas will pay more than those registering cars in rural areas. Then it might start telling you the reasons the politicians have decided to raise the fees and give you some distressed reaction from car dealers and taxi cab operators. It might quote an economist on the effect of increased fees on sales of durable goods, and a government official on where the additional revenue will be used.

However, the first thing you really want to know is how much is the increase going to be on your 1994 Ferrari (or 1983 Escort, as the case may be). Every news professional knows the impact on the individual User is the biggest news of all.

Today the newspaper would have to publish a full-page chart and you would have to search through it with a magnifying glass after reading lots of small print directions to find the answer. Radio and television couldn't hope to help you.

The New Medium would be able to include high in the story a fill-in-the-blanks formula. You type in make of car, model, year, county, or city of registration. Zap. The answer appears right there on your screen: $139.50 this year; $187.25 next year. If you can't spell the name of the model, the screen will spell-check it and if that fails, it will tell you to go out to the car and copy the model name down correctly. If you can't remember the model year, the computer will refer you to the auto registration database and you will see a copy of your current registration with model year highlighted on the screen.

Would you use this service? It depends on who pays the registration fee on your car. If you do, you bet your checkbook you would.

The techniques described above represent the use of spreadsheet and database information processing. The New Medium will require media professionals to be proficient with these kinds of skills. Some other skills needed by New Medium professionals: using indexes, using keywords, using public records.

INDEXES. I use an index every morning: socks in upper-right-hand drawer, T-shirts second drawer, shirts on right side of closet, and so forth. Categorizing things and placing them where they are easily accessible, then being able to use that organizational system to retrieve them is indexing. Librarians are highly skilled at indexing information and at retrieving information by using indexes—card catalogs, the *Reader's Guide to Periodical Literature,* and so on. (Until the computer came along with key-word searching that was about the only way to deal with a few million books and periodicals.)

Back in Chapter Three is an imaginary e-mail letter from Maria Vasquez to Mr. and Mrs. Jones reporting on an interview she had with them and a subsequent order of information services that their New Medium computer would bring to them. What Maria did was take the interview and create an index of the kinds of information the Jones couple was interested in. Then she delved into gigantic indexes of information services and matched their needs to what was available.

Librarians do this thousands of times daily. A patron outlines a research project. The librarian takes that information and matches it to appropriate databases provided by an information service such as Dialog. Then the librarian and a computer get the appropriate database on a phone line and retrieve either bibliographic references or entire texts of information that the patron may use.

Hypertext is a new way of using cross-indexing. It lets the computer "turn the pages." Instead of telling the User, "Turn to page 23 for the complete text of President's speech," it tells the reader, "Click here," and the speech will appear. Ideally every related item of information in a hypertext file would be instantly accessible from any item related to it.

Prior to the demise of the Soviet regime and its centrally organized systems, a group of Russian scholars expressed concern about library technology and the rapid increase in the amount of information. They proposed syndicates for scientific and technical information that would encompass all available information resources in a fully automated system with subsidiary regional branches, and ultimately connected with the All Union Office of Information.

KEYWORDS. Information is indexed usually at the time it is created according to practical but arbitrarily established categories. For instance, a directory of radio and television stations will list them geographically and include the names of top executives at each station along with address, phone, power, and so forth. The index allows easy access to information about stations. But how about information about news directors? How many news directors are named Bob? How many are named Mary? (A new category has been created: first names of news directors.)

If the directory is stored digitally, it is a simple matter to search your new category. First, create a subdirectory of news directors. Then, use the keyword Bob for one search and the keyword Mary for a second. The result may give you an idea whether more males than females are news directors.

The New Medium will allow Users to conduct keyword searches of all kinds of information. A User would be able to examine the text provided during a given time period to see if the New Medium was paying any attention to Albania, stamp collecting, or gays, for example. In fact, the User could check to see if any reference is made to gay Albanian stamp collectors.

Most important, the User and provider could program the decoding computer so that it searches all incoming information for keywords the User is interested in. Then the decoding computer could display this priority information as soon as the User turns it on. Beyond that, the computer itself could pick up on new words in the User's frequently used information categories and add them to the keywords without prompting by the User or the provider.

RECORDS. Birth, baptism, school enrollment, graduation, marriage, military discharge, property purchase, auto registration, hunting license, business incorporation. These events and hundreds of others are reflected in records kept in every community. Many of these records are public, available to anyone who cares to look at them and often created and maintained at taxpayer expense. The New Medium should make them as near as a User's decoding computer.

All kinds of business and professional people use public records for all kinds of purposes. Mass media professionals use them to keep public officials on the straight and narrow, to develop advertising strategies, to decide whether to expand operations. Now that public records are kept in computer memory, these people are using them as never before. With the New Medium, we can go back to making the raw records available directly to Users. In the past, train schedules, marriage licenses, and real estate transfers were all published. Now, often, there isn't room. That can change.

DATABASES. The records referred to above are databases, provided that they are in a form to be searched using database tools. The New Medium in each community should use those databases and its own resources to establish additional useful databases. One that comes to mind is a database on each person in the community: when he or she was born, moved to town, moved away, died, and all other pertinent public information.

At present if we don't know how to spell a person's name we are likely to go to the telephone directory. City directories provide additional information but it still is sketchy. The powerful and the privileged are able to find out almost anything they wish to about a person, whether it be through a credit check, a private investigator, or just by being nosy. While knowing a lot about a person is against the current trend of privacy, the information society dictates that more information on each individual will be available in the future than has been in the past. In the nineteenth century John DeLayne, editor of the *Times* of London, pointed out that "the press lives by disclosure." For ordinary Users, the question is not, "Can anyone find out about me?" Those with resources can. The question should be, "Do I have access to the same information everyone else does?"

Here is what one business writer had to say about snooping around: Monitoring a competitor's activities can be easy, inexpensive, and legal. Subscribe to information sources such as clipping services, the *Wall Street Transcript,* the *Official Gazette,* and computerized information services. Require feedback from sales personnel, cultivate relationships with securities analysts and stockbrockers, and determine how competitors market products. Small companies don't have to reveal information that big public companies do.

Accurate information about individuals who make up society is the basis of good general information. The public through the New Medium should have access to it.

Other appropriate databases the New Medium might maintain: real estate history, background on every community institution. meteorological information, a record of economic trends, and so forth.

RELATIONAL DATABASES. When Elliott Jaspin was a reporter, a story about a school bus accident piqued his interest. The driver's license of the bus driver had been suspended months earlier. How many other school bus drivers had suspended licenses or had been convicted of crimes like selling illegal drugs? Jaspin asked one public-record database for the identities of all the school bus drivers in the state. Using the resulting list, he searched another database—the driver's license and court records of the state—to discover that indeed some dozens of undesirable school bus drivers were responsible for the safety of school children every day. The state tightened up surveillance of school bus drivers, and Jaspin got a new career: teaching reporters how to use public records and computers to develop important news stories.

Businesses compare census data to ZIP code zones to find the most lucrative potential customers for their direct-mail advertising. That is another use of a relational database.

By looking at county census data, women in one of my classes discovered with some satisfaction that Riley County, where Kansas State University is located, had the highest ratio of males (ages 15 to 35) to females of any county in the state.

Once familiar with these kinds of techniques, Users of the New Medium can make their own decisions about many things based on hard data, if the information and the tools to process it are provided.

USERS AS PROVIDERS. During the 1989–1990 U. S. invasion of Panama, CNN used a new technique. As a worldwide satellite television news service, it had discovered that people all over the world tuned in when things erupted. So it put a graphic of its toll-free 800 telephone number on the screen and asked people in Panama to call in and tell what was happening. The CNN announcer couldn't get much out of one caller. He was understandably reluctant to go to his window high in a downtown hotel because of all the shooting. However, he was pleased to know that the hotel was providing a safe haven for its guests in the basement. He asked the CNN announcer if he thought it was safe for him to go downstairs.

That's User participation.

The mass media have a tradition of turning to authorities as well as ordinary citizens for their opinions, knowledge, wit, and artistry. The New Medium could allow unprecedented opportunities for User participation. Audio and text bulletin boards can provide these opportunities.

One of the most interesting jobs I ever had was handling letters to the editor of the *New York Herald Tribune*. Every day I would have forty to fifty pieces of information that no other journalist had; sometimes there would be hundreds. From them I could produce a fascinating column of information, acid commentary, and humor.

The New Medium should offer new opportunities to media professionals to create bulletin boards on every topic. Move over, Larry King.

MULTIMEDIA. The multimedia model for presentation of information has been discussed at length in Chapter Three and elsewhere. It boils down to presenting information in whatever form provides the most effective cognition: sometimes a written description or narrative; sometimes a chart or map; sometimes a drawing or cartoon; sometimes a photo or video; sometimes a voice and other sounds; sometimes a combination of all.

The other aspect of multimedia is that the User is allowed to pursue the available information at the pace he or she chooses and by and large in the order of his or her own choice. Together, these models open the way to an unprecedented way of communicating that will challenge the creativity and ingenuity of the next generation of communicators.

Brad Templeton of ClariNet Corporation, which has been distributing a digital newspaper on the Internet since 1989, predicts that through the use of multimedia, Users will be able to "read the lead coverage, but follow links to sidebars, read the actual press release from the White House, read the response writen by those covered, skip to a video of a live interview, or to the coverage of the story by one or all major television networks."

Let us return to the phrase that opened this textbook: we must think anew and act anew. The New Medium offers media professionals new opportunities requiring a fresh viewpoint and new techniques. More important, the New Medium could compel its Users to consider their world differently and allow them to act more effectively in society. That is our hope.

SUMMARY

By becoming familiar with Users' fields of experience, New Medium professionals could provide them with what they want and need from the information galaxy now available. The Internet model provides the technology. The wire service model provides the organization. Data-processing techniques add new ways of gathering and presenting information. The bulletin board model enhances User participation. The multimedia model provides the professional with compelling means of presentation.

PROJECTS. DISCUSSION TOPICS, AND EXERCISES

1. Visit an AP bureau, interviewing the bureau chief, the head of technical services, and a correspondent to discover how they work with members and with AP headquarters. What technologies are they using?
2. With a librarian, become familiar with the Dialog guidebook that librarians use to assist them in on-line searches. Read the descriptions of a dozen or more different databases to get an idea of the variety of information available and the differences in the way the databases work.
3. Through the Internet, CompuServe, Prodigy, or America Online, get access to at least three bulletin boards. What kind of information is on each? Which is the best from your point of view, and why?
4. With other students, prepare a guide for getting access to the Internet at your location. Can public-access PCs be used? Can an individual's personal PC at home get access? What services are available on Internet? Who is available to show you how to use it and what documents (books, etc.) are available to help you use it?

SUGGESTED READINGS

Hanson, Janice. *Connections, Technologies of Communication*. New York: HarperCollins, 1994. An up-to-date review of technology as it relates to communications, including its relationships to contemporary society.

Lane, Elizabeth, and Craig Summerhill. *Internet Primer for Information Professionals*. Westport, Conn.: Meckler, 1993. Gives the basics of the Internet in 169 pages.

Rieder, Rem, ed. *WJR* (*Washington Journalism Review*, now *AJR* for *American Journalism Review*), October 1992. The articles by Jon Franklin and Roger Fidler in particular provide insights to the future.

Schramm, Wilbur. "How Communication Works." *Process and Effects of Mass Communication*. Champaign: University of Illinois Press, 1971. The discussion on feedback and fields of experience are relevant, as are many other seminal articles in this classic text.

Users of the Media

Capitalizing on the Advantages of the New Medium to Meet the Needs of Busy Users

When it comes to the marketplace for information and culture, the population as a whole is quite satisfied. Widespread cultural frustration and unmet demands for new ideas and new media are, for the most part, favored fantasies of a small artistic elite and wishful thinkers.

—W. Russell Neuman

If the above statement is true, why bother with the New Medium? Instead shouldn't we as professional media people continue to try to improve, refine, and extend the existing media? The answer is: yes and no.

"Yes" to Neuman's statement. The population as a whole is quite satisfied. In his book *The Future of the Mass Audience,* and in other reports on the extensive studies that have been made of the public's relationship to the mass media, it is clear that the public as a whole spends a lot of time with and money on the media. It is also clear that the public feels no desire to add more media.

"No" to the inference just made that the New Medium is not needed. Neuman provides a comprehensive description of the contemporary mass media "audience" (including readers and listeners) based on his own research and that of dozens of other social scientists/scholars. It indicates that the interfaces between the public (particularly individual members of the public) and the media are flawed. This chapter addresses the ramifications of these flaws.

Up to this point the book has focused on technology and its relationship to existing and future media. We have made observations about individuals who produce and use the media. And we have made observations about mass readership and audience.

But it is more important to understand readers, listeners, and viewers than it is to understand the machines that produce media. Thus we now focus our attention specifically on readers, listeners, and viewers. The Users are more important than the technology for a couple of reasons.

The first reason is fundamental to our profession as mass commication professionals. The mass media are the tools we use to provide individuals with information they want and need. We succeed when the public is composed of people who are informed, educated, entertained, and intelligent participants in society. We use the technology to empower them.

Second, the transition to the New Medium is a revolutionary change. It will not take place until there is a critical mass of Users committed to the New Medium as their source of all kinds of important, interesting, and entertaining information.

The concept of a critical mass is borrowed from physics. When a critical mass of certain radioactive elements is achieved, the elements experience rapid nuclear fission, causing a nuclear explosion—truly a revolutionary happening. When a critical mass of New Medium Users is attained, the demand for the New Medium will result in revolutionary change in the use of mass media.

The self-destructive nature of the current mass media environment has been described in earlier chapters, but public attitudes toward and acceptance of the New Medium are fundamentally essential if a better way is to emerge. So let us examine the contemporary mass media "audience."

THE CONTEMPORARY AUDIENCE

Distraction and information-overload stress are quick, easy, and accurate descriptions of the emotions felt by contemporary media Users, who either work or go to school. Great amounts of time are consumed by these activities. Work is mentally demanding now. School should be too.

Not many generations ago, heavy manual labor rather than intense mental effort was the norm. After work people rested their muscles and exercised their minds by reading, attending lectures and theatricals, and discussing matters they considered interesting and important. Cultivating the mind was a social activity and a great way to meet people

After hard days of thinking on the job or at school, today's citizens spend a lot of their nonwork, nonstudy time in nonmental activities: sports, hanging out in malls, stores, clubs, coffee houses, restaurants, and bars. Clothing, pampering, and cultivating the body is a social activity and a great way to meet people. People today aren't particularly looking for things to occupy their minds. They cook, sew, chop wood, garden, paint, and polish for fun and consider it personal development in the same way their great-grandparents esteemed debates, lectures, and reading. Often mental activity is stimulated by their interpersonal relationships rather than by the media—at church, at a club, or in the homes of friends and family.

The mass media have to fit into a busy social and personal matrix. So when do people use media?

- They do turn to the media for specific information, for absorbing information of substantial interest and for escape.

Cable's Weather Channel and newspaper market reports are examples of specific information. PBS's *The Civil War* and the *Philadelphia Inquirer*'s *What Went Wrong With America* series are examples of serious and substantial content. *Roseanne* and *Garfield* are examples of pure escape. These examples constitute a gross oversimplification of media content, but they do indicate both the range of information and the range of motivations people have for seeking information.

- They have media access whenever they want it.
- They want the media to provide instant gratification.
- They would like to get more of what each really wants but have to settle for what is offered.

Because they have access to all these media, people want instant gratification and really don't like to settle for just what is offered. They are channel surfers and headline readers.

- They have gadgets for almost every possible activity. They don't mind spending money on gadgets that offer them some reward.
- They learn sophisticated skills.

People drive complicated automobiles between home and work and at both places operate dozens of different kinds of devices. Many of them like to tinker or develop skills that appeal to them.

- They want things but they hate to deal with clutter.
- They want information that has value: something that fascinates them; something that helps them do something they want to do. They want it now. They don't want to spend a lot of effort getting it.
- They are value conscious. The opportunities for spending their disposable income seem infinite. They want to get their money's worth.
- They use computers, but in narrow ways.

Some are anticomputer. (Some are techno-nuts.) Once they find a use for computers, they reject going back to old methods of accomplishing the same task. They like to use computers, but most of them hate to go through the trouble of digging into a manual to develop new computer skills or upgrading the skills they already have. If someone is available at the moment when they need a new skill and shows them the computer techniques to accomplish something they want to do or how to get some information they want, they quickly adopt the technique and are gratified.

As we look deeper into the nature of those who use existing media, we find a number of interesting traits.

LOW SALIENCE

"Media use is active and selective but casual, habitual and only semi-attentive," notes Neuman. Multiple activities are possible for individuals—that is, they may be paying some attention to one medium while paying attention to another medium or carrying out some other activity. This is borne out by a comparison of quantitative studies: one study on media use indicates that the typical individual spends 6+ hours daily with the media; another study of leisure time indicates the typical individual has only 5+ hours of leisure time daily. Is everyone sneaking time off from work or necessary home responsibilities to use the media? No, they combine activities, reading the paper on the bus to work or listening to the car radio while picking up the kids after music lessons.

A survey of 200 families that had computers in the home showed that 88 percent subscribed to a newspaper and 36 percent subscribed to two, indicating that computer owners are information junkies.

In a 1976 study on recall of network news stories Neuman found that 5 percent of the stories were recalled unaided and another 45 percent with prompting, but on only half of those could details be related. Jacoby and Hoyer in 1982 found that only 4 percent of their sample could get all 12 questions about content of a commercial correct; only 17 percent could get as many as six questions correct.

Of course, such Users must divide their attention or they will miss their bus stop or run a red light. This divided attention is termed "low salience"; Users of the media often do not pay much attention to them or understand and retain much of the information that is offered.

Today's media encourage low salience by interrupting the audience's train of thought with slam-bam advertisements and chaff. When I was a child listening to the radio, three tones and an announcer saying "This is N-B-C" used to be the network's identification. Now a surrealistic peacock changes colors like a chameleon, does back flips and then metamorphizes into something entirely different, while I lose the continuity of the show I was watching.

THE COMFORT FACTOR

Users are lazy. (Or to be more polite and use Neuman's words: "For knowledge acquisition in general and for public affairs knowledge in particular, people are not inclined to give such matters a great deal of effort.") They prefer preconceived notions to information that challenges their biases. They are also lazy in their media habits, choosing a "sure thing" that they know will provide some gratification rather than risking substantial time on something new and different. Users also prefer the medium they are most accustomed to. Communicator, message, channel, and audience member characteristics may each contribute to the "comfort" factor.

As each medium (movies, radio, television) has been introduced, it has been seen as a new educational medium that would encourage learning and make it easier. Each was more "vivid" than its predecessor either through sensory stimuli or immediacy. However, vividness of content, research has shown, attracts attention but does not contribute to comprehension or retention.

Two attributes that contribute to acquisition of knowledge are diametrically opposed to the previously described characteristic of low salience. They are concentration and participation in the process (interaction).

HOMOGENIZATION AND DIVERSITY

Creators of today's media content would agree almost universally that two attributes that will attract great masses of people are action and humor. Columnists such as Mike Royko are read as much for their wit as their insight. The McLaughlin Gang's collective decibel level is more impressive than their collective intellectual contributions. Quiz shows use spinning wheels, flashing lights, and graceful hosts. Beer commercials seldom linger on heavy consumers, focusing instead on people with amazing physical attributes in a heightened level of activity.

I cite the lively examples above, hoping to keep you interested in the abstract concept of homogenization, of the tendency of all media to dwell on the same kind of content, in this case action and humor. Using these and other known producers of "vividness," the media copy each other's successes *ad nauseam*.

Yet none of the creative people in the media can infallibly predict success. Book publishers and producers of motion pictures and television programs create relatively large numbers of books, movies, and shows, all using the known ingredients for success, with the hope (usually rewarded) that a few of them will be extremely successful, thus covering the losses and disappointments of the many that have little success.

The media go beyond using these known qualities that will attract an audience. They copy the formats of successful productions. Thus the media create a surfeit of similar content and a homogenized audience. This homogeneity is User driven (demand side) and producer driven (supply side). It is User driven because the creators are aware of low salience as a detractor from media content and of vividness as an attractor. They use one to offset the other. It is producer driven because of the economies of scale and scope the existing media must adhere to and because of the special nature of current advertising support.

Advertisers want their messages close to widely consumed content for maximum exposure to the public. Over-the-air and cable networks want large audiences and periodical publishers want large circulations to attract advertisers. Thus they seek the homogeneous audience.

Author Stephen Levy notes how the Internet and other computerized information services allow people with similar interests, freed from geographical and time constraints, to exchange information in a many-to-many setting quite different from the few-to-many mass media environment. He cites User protests to Prodigy's ill-fated attempt to reduce e-mail and enhance commercial operations. It created a public relations nightmare.

Yet, there is a strong resistance to homogenization among contemporary Americans. Individuals identify themselves as being members of distinctive groups, and even as being unique persons. The expanding service/information enterprises of our time appeal to these distinctions, some of which are affluence, educational level, ethnicity, gender, age, occupation, political/philosophical/religious orientation. Even the older "major" television networks recognize it. For example, Arsenio Hall in the early 1990s carved out a late-night audience of young, somewhat hip viewers on Fox television. Then CBS and NBC fought to position late-night shows featuring Jay Leno and David Letterman to include the same audience, and Hall's show expired.

INFORMATION OVERLOAD

In my community of less than 60,000 population, four daily newspapers circulate. More than twenty movie theater screens are in use. Cable television offers thirty-seven channels. Ten radio stations are on the air. Five bookstores are open. Periodicals and paperbacks are available at another dozen locations. Videotapes can be rented at yet another dozen locations. A similar number of locations sell audiocassettes and CDs. Two libraries are open. Every week the mail brings to my home a foot-high stack of printed material I have subscribed to or that is unsolicited. Even more mail comes into my office. My computer is linked to the Internet, and I must spend a couple of hours a week attending to the interest-area User lists I subscribe to or I'll have hundreds of unread messages before I know it. E-mail keeps me in touch with colleagues. My family wants me to hook up to Prodigy so we can stay closer in touch.

There is no way I can attend to all the information that all these various channels offer. There is no way I can avoid having to deal with vast amounts of information of no value to me at any given moment. My friends tell me about books, movies, television programs, and journal articles that I should not have missed. I keep a box in my office where I put documents that I must read later. At the end of the semester I throw away all the unread documents so I can use the box for next semester's documents that I must read but don't. Newspapers compose (or decompose) the largest bulk in my recycling bins.

I don't feel like a User of the media. I feel used by the media.

Critics cite information overload as a potential curse of the New Medium, but information overload is already here and what the critics say applies to the present:

- They cite as a future danger the effect of information overload on the human psyche, yet many people already cancel their newspapers because they feel guilt over stacks of unread material.
- "There's a real danger here of getting saturated with the entertainment stuff so that you cannot find your way to the good stuff," notes Tad Pinkerton of the University of Wisconsin in Madison.
- Dr. Don Rosen of the Menninger Clinic in Topeka, Kansas, has observed: "I am not at all sure that reams and reams of information is effective communication at all."

Having easy access to lots of information would lead to a splintering of media Users into narrow interest groups, critics claim. Individuals would pay attention only to what they chose rather than being exposed to what is necessary for a person to be well-rounded. Unity within the community, the nation, and the world would diminish.

"For the last forty years television has helped Americans share experiences," said Matt James of the Kaiser Family Foundation in California. He cited *All in the Family, Roots,* and *The Smothers Brothers Comedy Show* as crossing generational, cultural, educational, and class lines. Having three commercial networks and PBS provided a national sounding board for ideas, news, and information. Videocassettes and cable television are changing this and, he said, the information superhighway would change it even more.

These experts predict that the New Medium will make the problem worse rather than providing a means of dealing with information overload.

INTERACTIVITY

Contemporary Users of the media indicate that they want interactivity, yet they shrink from using it actively. The most common form of interactivity with the mass media occurs in social situations. People with shared interests discuss the media and how they have used it. This human filtering process leads to increased media use as John returns to the media to sample what Mary has recommended. Individuals interact with the media for the same purpose, buying *TV Guide* for suggestions on what to seek out on the tube, or paying attention to commercials and critics on television who give information about what is coming to movie theaters.

This is positive interaction, and in the contemporary media environment it is largely casual and haphazard. Substantial negative interaction also takes place. People "volunteer" and "resign" from media use at will. This kind of interactivity has always existed. A study of readers who had "resigned" from taking a newspaper say they have done so because of parochialism, superficiality, redundance, and bush-league reporting. Newspapers, because their circulations are confined to a geographical area, tend to emphasize the interests of that area and are viewed as being "narrow" or "boosters" by many of their readers. Newspapers publish every day or every week so the day's news or the week's news is their product. Often the long view, the truth behind the facts, is neglected, leading to the charges of superficiality and redundancy. Bush-league reporting is described as lacking in depth and as inexpert and inaccurate coverage.

Other studies of readers who "resigned" disclose a guilt or economic motivation. Unread papers pile up. The subscriber finally admits that no time is available for the paper or that it is a waste of money.

The cable television industry is confronted by a phenomenon known as churn. Viewers drop the service or portions of it such as movie channels that require a premium payment for a time, and then come back to it.

Channel surfing, that is, using a television remote-control device to flip from channel to channel, has been referred to as an example of low salience, a lack of close attention to what is being offered. It is also an example of interaction between User and medium.

Users interact with the contemporary media in a haphazard and reactive way, rather than proactively and methodically. For example: movie critics on television determine which movies they will talk about and viewers are required to consider their views passively. Suppose the viewer designated which category of movies he or she was interested in, monitored the current releases for movies in that category and then asked for the reviews of each critic on those movies only. Or suppose the viewer checked each day to see if Dan Rather, MacNeil–Lehrer, Tom Brokaw, and Peter Jennings all agreed on what the most important news was and then considered what each had to report on that story, rather than having to choose one or the other newscasts *in toto.* Interaction may be more than an opportunity to select a narrow menu from a vast smorgasbord of information.

This consideration of the contemporary use of the mass media leads to a somber list of attributes: alienation, overload, homogenization, unrequited diversity, laziness, and a lack of proactive interaction. At mid-century George Orwell in his novel *1984* predicted that by that year people would feel like individuals adrift in an uncaring urban society dominated by a monolithic government information system. The monolithic information system is not a reality, but confronted by the haphazard and mass-society-oriented information system we do have, many individuals may well feel adrift. However, adopting the new technology will not necessarily solve the problems. It certainly will not solve them all and it will certainly create some more. But it does provide an opportunity to take these existing problems into account and, one would hope, to improve the relation of people to media.

A NEW DEFINITION

Throughout this book the word *Users* has been capitalized, because the concept of "using" the media is at the core of the New Medium. The New Medium is a medium of Users as defined in the equation below:

Readers + Audience + Viewers = Users

Since none of the terms on the left side of the equation adequately describes the people who will have access to a medium that combines text, audio, video, and graphics, a new term is needed. The term *Users* is appropriate to the way media professionals should look at those they serve. It is appropriate in two ways.

First, those of us who watch television, listen to the radio, and read publications already "use" those media. I get the weather report off the television Weather Channel, the school closing report from a local radio station, and the quotation on my little mutual fund from the newspaper every day. For escape I watch mindless situation comedies, listen to mindless music, and work mindless crossword puzzles.

Second, the New Medium is a participatory medium. We already are willing to work pretty hard to get information we want. If the New Medium makes it easier for us to get more of what we want, we will use it more than we use contemporary media.

So, we consider Users.

USERS, TIME, AND SPACE

The creatures that use the media—us—have invented the media largely in an effort to conquer time and space. Publishers of books hope the books will go to many people all over the world and remain in use for many years. Letter mail conquers space at the expense of time and has a permanence. A telephone conquers space and time but is impermanent.

Mass media are specialized efforts to conquer time and space, with the space concept represented by the numbers of persons using each medium. In 1980 a Japanese commuications scholar, Tetsuro Tomita, placed the various media on a time–space grid that indicates the specialized nature of each by showing the time required for the sender's message to reach the receiver and the number of receivers it could reach. Each medium occupies a different portion of the time–space grid indicating its specialized nature and its communication function.

> "Traditionally, print media occupied the space domain; the broadcast media occupied the time domain." Those distinctions are dissolving.
> –W. Russell Neuman

What Tomita's grid revealed was a "media gap." Swift communication of information to limited numbers of Users is relatively neglected. Logically, this kind of communication does not take advantage of the economies of scale and scope that contemporary media rely on for economic survival and profitability.

The media gap is something like a black hole in space. Since we can't see into it, we have difficulty comprehending it. What have been the social, economic, cultural, intellectual, and psychological effects of not being able to communicate in certain areas of the grid? We can speculate, but we have not been able to have a very clear understanding until recently. Personal computers and big computer networks are providing means to fill the media gap—notably, e-mail, bulletin boards, and databases.

E-mail is practically instantaneous by Postal Service standards. Only the telephone is more instantaneous. Like conventional mail, e-mail does not require the simultaneous attention of sender and receiver, as conversation in person or on the telephone does.

Bulletin boards may reach hundreds or thousands of persons and by periodical standards are almost instantaneous. Unlike broadcast, bulletin board communications have a permanence.

In Figure 8.1, "databases" occupies a small square within the Media Gap. In reality computerized databases can occupy almost the entire horizontal axis of the grid, since databases can be personal (used by only the creator) or available to all. This is a blurring of the Tomita grid itself.

These new methods of communicating have sprung into being from the grassroots up. Their popularity indicates that a demand for this kind of communication existed which the contemporary media did not provide.

Successful innovation on the Internet contrasts with the experience of Prestel in Great Britain. Prestel tried to introduce an unwanted product directly to the masses. Erik Arnold of Sussex University notes that "innovation [quoting Mowery and Rosenberg 1979] 'walks on two legs': they couple demand-side needs with technological opportunity."

In all likelihood the advent of the New Medium will make the Tomita model obsolete. Personal computers in a universal network will do much more than fill the Media Gap. They will fill the entire grid, making time and space—as well as the contemporary media created to cover a limited area of the grid—all but irrelevant.

Many of the characteristics Users of the contemporary mass media exhibit are reactions to the way each medium fits into the Tomita space–time grid. Having access to information without the space–time constraints of discrete contemporary media may well automatically increase attention to and comprehension of the information available.

USERS AND CONTENT

When different contemporary media are placed on the Tomita grid, the advantages and shortcomings of the kind of content they contain become apparent. Big audience = universal content. One-on-one communication = very selective and personal content.

All of this content, whether universal, personal, or somewhere in between, comprises the Field of Experience (the vast amount of information available) that was referred to in Chapter Seven. At that

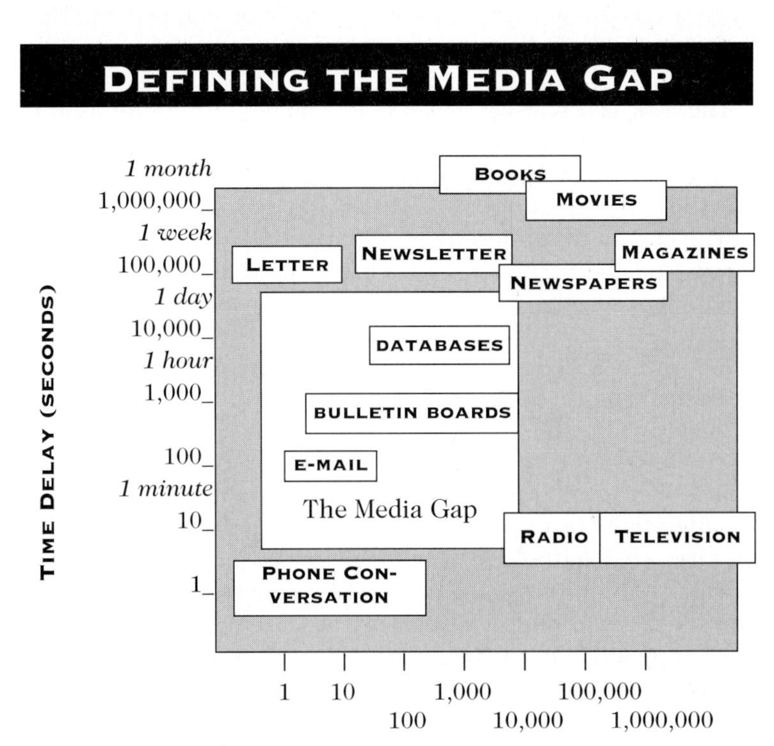

Tetsuro Tomita of Japan's Ministry of Posts and Telecommunication in 1980 placed mass media and some kinds of interpersonal communications on a time–audience grid. The grid revealed a "media gap," an area where it was difficult for people to communicate in a convenient period of time. Now electronic forms of mass communication and interpersonal communication such as e-mail, bulletin boards, and databases are filling the media gap.
(Tomita's model of 1980 adapted.)

FIGURE 8.1

point we said it was the responsibility of the mass media professional to select from the whole universe of information the particular information the User wanted or needed. As the professional does this selecting, some information easily fits into the category of being universally interesting, other information is overwhelmingly interesting to fewer people and some information is interesting to only a very few.

The contemporary media tailor themselves to these categories in two ways: they aim at a narrow group of Users, providing every detail on those few subjects that will please this group; or they aim at a broad group of Users, providing the most interesting information they can

"Selective, pinpoint newsgathering" by reporters and editors provides information that fails to see beyond "the predefined horizons of the newsroom team," according to Canadian computer executive Steve Bonisteel, a former news editor. He said he misses being able to see all the news that comes into the newsroom and is not published.

find about those few things that everyone finds compelling. The contemporary media are having a tougher and tougher time trying to do both.

The New Medium will have as its channel an information superhighway that can carry a much higher percentage of the total available information to every User. The digital processing and storage capabilities of the New Medium can identify and put onto the information superhighway all that information. What is lacking are the convenient off-ramps and the easy-to-open packaging so that Mary Smith can get information about the Challenger Explosion, which everyone is interested in, and can also get information about a new kind of ceramic kiln that she and a few thousand other producers of collector dolls are tremendously interested in.

This concept of intense interest by the many in some information that everyone wants, and intense interest by the few in certain information, is vitally important to creating the New Medium. Both kinds of information must be expedited in very usable form to as many of those as are interested and can be accommodated.

Mass media professionals who have become experts in paring the amount of information to an economy of scarce channel space need to adapt to providing for an economy of plenty. This attitude of an economy of plenty fits the models offered by the Associated Press, the book industry, and the motion picture industry. The latter two in particular try for the highest possible production values on all the potentially successful products they can afford to produce. They gamble that some will hit the bullseye of the Media User Target (see Figure 8.2), that some will fall near enough the center to break even and that those falling far enough from the center to be unprofitable will be few in number.

Users of information now found in niche publications and the parochial press will have the same access to that information as they have to the universally sought information, and the production values used in creating the niche information can be increased because of the ease with which it reaches all those interested.

The off-ramps of the information superhighway comprise the remaining bottlenecks to the New Medium's success.

ACCOMMODATING USERS

Creating easy-to-use off-ramps and usable information to travel the information superhighway are primary responsibilities of the mass media leaders of the future.

Contemporary media leaders view the attributes of the public that relate to the media as being carved in stone. Users are lazy, their attention to the media has low salience, they are easily distracted, and they have a limited number of things they are interested in.

THE MEDIA USER TARGET

A CONTENT BULLSEYE CAPTURES EVERYONE.
A HIT IN THE OUTER AREA STILL CAPTURES SOME USERS.

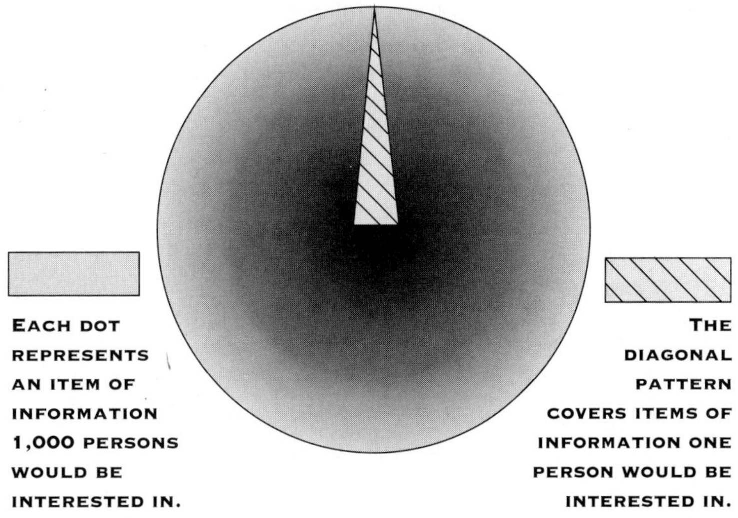
EACH DOT REPRESENTS AN ITEM OF INFORMATION 1,000 PERSONS WOULD BE INTERESTED IN.
THE DIAGONAL PATTERN COVERS ITEMS OF INFORMATION ONE PERSON WOULD BE INTERESTED IN.

The target above represents all the information that could possibly be communicated by the New Medium. The bullseye represents the kind of information that is extremely interesting or important to almost every User (*Gone With the Wind* in 1936 or the Kennedy assassination in 1963). The area near the bullseye represents information that is of substantial interest to a substantial number of Users (important news, popular entertainment, new products and services). The outer areas represent information of interest to fewer and fewer Users. An individual will be interested in everything in the black area, in quite a bit of what is in the adjacent areas, and will be just as intensely interested in some of the information in the outside area.

Since the New Medium eliminates most of the constraints of how much information can be offered, and eases geographical and scheduling constraints on distribution, it offers the possibility of easy access to any information by any User.

The theoretical possibility is that much more information can be made available to everyone, and since the widely scattered persons interested in an item on the periphery of the circle can all have access to it, it will be possible not only to offer the information but, just as important, to invest in presenting that information completely and compellingly.

FIGURE 8.2

"The [newspaper] industry's response to the readership problem . . . is your basic MTA response. Like the bus company of the '50s, your local information monopoly interprets the current decline in demand not as a signal about the quality of the service but as evidence of some trend that is beyond control. As the newspaper leadership laments this trend, it balances the books and boosts profits by cutting services . . . Realistically, the question is less what will happen to newspapers than what will happen to the audience—and what does that mean for journalists? I would argue that we should try to separate our profession, which has a real market and role in the information age, from the newspaper industry, which by all evidence does not. We need to figure out how to sell information directly."

—Pulitzer Prize-winning reporter Jon Franklin

The attributes of stress, short attention span, and information overload described thus far will continue to be with us. Users of the media have no "required reading lists," nor do they have to take examinations on the content of the media they consume. They voluntarily expand or limit their use of the media.

However, the contemporary media exacerbate many of these User tendencies. The New Medium offers the opportunity to accommodate the User by reducing the impediments to media use.

Some ways to improve User environments:

PROVIDE ALL THE INFORMATION POSSIBLE. The two things to keep in mind on this topic are:

- Mass media have had to pare (often to the bone) the information they present because of their time or space limitations. That view is obsolete.
- User interests span the gamut of available information. If only a few people broadly scattered across the globe are interested in a topic, they will find a medium that provides that information very valuable.

When the information superhighway is built and the information services that will feed traffic onto the highway are organized, the developers need to think inclusively rather than exclusively: always more information, always to more Users, and always at the least possible cost.

This is a reversal of some current media trends and of the cost policies of many current information providers. If information costs are high, the public will be discouraged from seeking information and the spectre of an information elite will be realized. Sam Walton did not get the reputation of being the richest man in America by selling yachts to millionaires. He got rich by putting a Wal-Mart everywhere people congregated and filling it with merchandise they wanted at the lowest possible cost. The New Medium needs a Sam Walton.

PROVIDE FOR EASY ACCESS. Make the information easy to get to. I know where the molasses is in the supermarket where I shop regularly. It's not with the sugar or near the flour I use for baking. It's with the honey, syrup, and jellies. I hate to go to a different supermarket because the products rarely purchased are so hard to find. I have to search for them.

Going a long way toward providing easy access to information in the New Medium will be the development of computer hardware and software that respond to spoken language, that use intuitive devices, and that are aware of the kinds of information the User desires. Then information will be easy to find.

Libraries are institutions that epitomize easy access. Librarians acquire information according to the needs of library patrons. They catalog and shelve it in an orderly fashion. They publicize the way the information is organized. They personally assist patrons in getting the information they want, and the really good ones alert patrons to new information they know the patron will be interested in. Mass media professionals of the future will also exhibit these attributes.

> "Given that speaking is generally faster and more convenient than typing, speech is likely to become the typical input to written communications. Given that reading text is faster and more flexible than listening to speech, electronically displayed text is likely to remain the typical output . . . any combination of sound and visual modalities might be chosen."
>
> —W. Russell Neuman

REDUCE DISTRACTION. When I become absorbed in a good mystery novel, I don't want to be disturbed: not by the telephone, not by conversation I would normally be interested in, not by an invitation to come eat lunch. I want to find out who the despicable character was who bumped off the gentle nanny in the park.

The ability to concentrate—to follow a narrative line or a logical explanation, to analyze and to imagine—is a trait that seems to be unique to human beings. It is basic to efficient use of information. It is the key to learning. Constant interruption of thought processes produces disorientation. Let's be blunt: it drives you crazy.

Some movies and books allow us to concentrate. Most of the rest of the contemporary mass media spend most of their time trying to attract our attention rather than trying to protect our concentration.

The New Medium has the flexibility to leave us alone as we explore information and at the same time to provide us with pathways and road signs that can lead us to related information or to new worlds of information at any time we wish to move on.

ENCOURAGE PARTICIPATION. Concentration is basic to understanding information. Participation in acquiring and using information is the key to maximizing the amount of information understood and used.

Effective teaching involves the learner in the process. A student may be required to read the work of outstanding reporters, to listen to lectures on reporting techniques and to do in-class writing exercises, but until the student gets an assignment from an editor, interviews some sources, completes writing a story before a deadline, sees a byline in print, and takes the flack from readers, sources, and editors for any mistakes made, that student has not truly assimilated the knowledge necessary to be a reporter.

The historian and novelist Shelby Foote in his youth signed a contract to write "a short history of the Civil War." Twenty-five years later the history was published in four volumes. He gained even broader fame for his perceptive on-camera commentary in the PBS production of *The Civil War,* which consisted of information—letters, pictures, reminiscences—from the war itself.

As Foote did research for his "short history," he became more and more involved in the project. His hair had begun to gray and the documents had piled up. But, he said, he never understood what it meant to be a lad drawn into the war until a visit to Shiloh battleground. He said he picked up a branch and pretended that it was a musket with a bayonet on its end and that bullets were whistling about his ears. Then he dashed up a hill screaming a Rebel yell. Then he knew. Participation in assembling the material for his book led Foote far beyond where he intended to go.

By capitalizing on the flexibility of the New Medium, the Shelby Footes of tomorrow can enrich the intellects and imaginations of its Users by allowing them to participate in the way the information is used.

SUMMARY

Alienation, overload, homogenization, frustrated diversity, laziness, and a lack of proactive interaction are some of the labels placed on the people who use the contemporary media. Although these traits will remain in the future, many of them are exacerbated by the nature of the contemporary media, which aim for mass audiences, limit the amount of information offered, and distract their Users. In the creation of the New Medium, mass communications professionals should adopt the goals of providing as much information as possible in easy-to-use forms offering the User opportunity to participate in the process and without distracting the User.

PROJECTS, DISCUSSION TOPICS, AND EXERCISES

1. Monitor an hour of commercial television. How many times did the channel intentionally attempt to break the concentration of the viewer, and what was the nature of each break in the continuity of information: station breaks, commercials, promotional messages. Analyze subjectively how these interruptions affect viewer behavior (channel surfing, getting up for a drink of water) and state of mind.
2. High school and college activities often involve people in participatory information use. From your experience, indicate an activity and recall how information was used to develop skills in such things as sports, music, forensics, art, 4–H, and club leadership responsibilities. To assist you, create a form on which the type of activity, the nature of the information necessary to carry out the activity, and the effectiveness of the learning experience is described and compared.
3. Inventory your own information overloads: total pages of textbooks for current courses; total pages of notes, workbooks, handouts and library material required thus far in the term; information required to register for classes, secure and maintain housing, meals, and clothing; information related to organizations you are involved in; mass media information for personal use; personal information such as

letters, telephone calls, e-mail. Get a subjective comment from your fellow students on whether they experience information overload and how they deal with it.

4. Create a survey instrument on the concepts of information overload, media distraction, and homogenized content, with the goal of finding whether Users of the media are aware of these constraints. Apply the instrument to a sample of a population and interpret the results.

SUGGESTED READINGS

Bradbury, Ray. *Fahrenheit 451.* New York: Ballantine Books 1991. (First published 1953.) A prophetic novel about a society in which books are an illegal substance and televised interactive infotainment has taken the place of personal relationships.

Cronbach, L. J., and R. E. Snow. *Aptitudes and Instructional Methods.* New York: Irvington, 1977. Discusses the effectiveness of participatory learning.

Frank, Ronald E., and Marshall G. Greenberg. *The Public's Use of Television: Who Watches and Why.* Beverly Hills, Calif.: Sage, 1980. Delves into viewer habits.

Mowery, David, and Nathan Rosenberg. "The Influence of Market Demand Upon Innovation: A Critical Review of Some Recent Empirical Studies." *Research Policy* 8:2, April 1979. An early exposition of the innovation–push, demand–pull theories about the introduction of new technology.

Neuman, W. Russell. *The Future of the Mass Audience.* New York: Cambridge University Press, 1991. Currently the definitive work on media Users.

Orwell, George. *1984.* New York: Signet Books, 1949. The novel that first brought to public attention the potential effects of a universal mass medium.

Rosengren, Karl Erik, Lawrence A. Wenner, and Philip Palmgreen, eds. *Media Gratifications Research: Current Perspectives*. Beverly Hills, California: Sage, 1985. Studies of why people use the media.

Tomita, Tetsuro. "The New Electronic Media and Their Place in the Electronic Marketplace of the Future." In Anthony Smith, ed., *Newspapers and Democracy: International Essays on a Changing Medium.* Cambridge, Mass.: MIT Press, 1980. The study demonstrates how communication media are related to one another.

The Content of Tomorrow's Medium

Telling Stories in a Digital, Multimedia, Hypertext Environment

Once upon a time. . . . They lived happily ever after.

—Mother Goose

Our discussion of the emerging digital mass medium comes down to one final step in the communication process. Using the Shannon–Weaver model of communication we have discussed senders, encoders, channels, noise, fields of experience, and feedback. In the chapter just before this one we discussed receivers, or Users, as we identified them. Earlier we identified and described the important characteristics of decoders (the devices that interpret the message so the User's mind can understand it). What remains to be discussed is the short jump from decoder to receiver—the jump from medium to mind.

The jump is short, but it is a jump into the unknown. Brilliant people have done their best to explore the mind. Novelists following James Joyce have used a literary technique called "stream of consciousness" to get at what minds think and why. Doctors following Sigmund Freud have used psychoanalysis to get people to tell them what their minds are thinking that the patients for the most part are unaware of.

We know our minds are sensitive to stimuli received by way of the five senses. We are able to remember things. We are able to learn from the stimuli we receive and to act upon what we know. We know that internal human communication involves every cell in our bodies, that our minds are integral parts of our bodies, that our mental processes react to substances secreted within our bodies, or introduced from outside our bodies and that our mental processes require oxygen and nutrients provided through the circulatory system.

We know that our bodies respond to what our conscious and unconscious thinking processes tell them, whether it be tears of joy or sorrow, nervous or amused laughter, reflexes to protect us from harm, and so on.

We know that a break from heavy mental work, some exercise and—most of all—some sleep are necessary if our minds are to function comfortably.

Indeed, scientists probe the mind and examine its primary manifestations—our communication and behavior—in every humane way they can think of to try to understand what may be the last great unexplored frontier: the human mind. They have discovered a great deal. Still the mind remains uncharted territory. There is no grammar or vocabulary of the mind. There is no mathematical formula to explain the mind's own logic.

The New Medium and the Mind

So how does one use the resources that the New Medium offers to make the final jump into the mind of the User? That is the question this chapter discusses and the topic can be summed up in one word: content. (See Figure 9.1.)

The CBS television program *Good Morning America* for a long time had the slogan "Breakfast for your head." That's a concept easy to understand if you are a morning person, a big-breakfast person. Breakfast is a chance to get some warmth into one's stomach, some nutrients coursing through one's bloodstream, something yummy onto one's tastebuds. As the program's slogan indicates, the mass media feed stimuli into the mind. Doing that effectively makes a mass medium successful.

The onset of a new medium attracts Users because they are curious about it. Over time Users adapt it into their daily environment and then the content becomes crucial. If the content is not accepted as vital by the User, boredom sets in. Bearing witness to this phenomenon is Bruce Springsteen's 1992 song "57 Channels (and Nothin' On)." On the other hand, when the content is compelling, the User finds paying attention to be time well spent. Give me Mr. Springsteen himself, or Pavarotti; *Hallmark Hall of Fame* or *Night Court;* the Dallas Cowboys or the skating team of Torvill and Dean; columnists Molly Ivins or George Will; *Star Wars* or *Schindler's List; The New York Times* or my hometown paper, the *Manhattan Mercury,* and you have engaged my

THE IMPORTANCE OF CONTENT

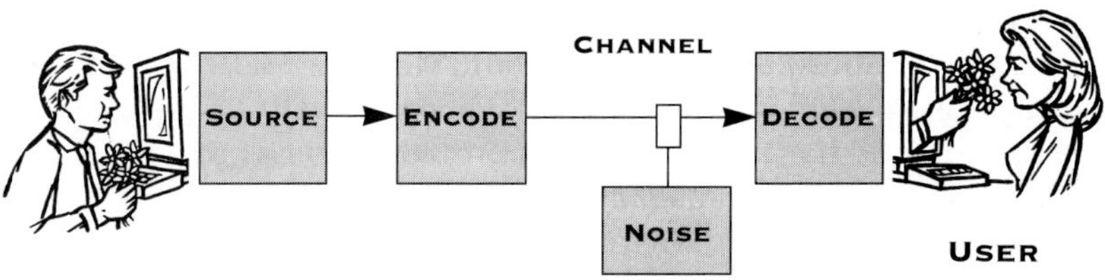

The professional communicator is all-important to the New Medium. No matter how efficient the New Medium is in providing information, unless the content is compelling, the User will be reluctant to pay attention to it. It is the professional communicator who turns data into compelling content.

FIGURE 9.1

mind. The challenge of the New Medium is to provide its Users with content that engages their minds, and to provide it conveniently so that they can partake and still have time to do all the other engaging things that beckon.

Who is to preside over this intellectual feast, to drive the New Medium in an informative and stimulating way? The answer: mass media professionals.

Mass media professionals for centuries have been observing the chaotic world we live in and, using the tools of whatever medium lay at hand, have been trying to describe our world in an accurate and compelling way for those who expose themselves to the medium. This basic function will not change. The existing techniques will provide a basis for developing the content of the New Medium.

An editor of *The American Prospect* magazine, Tony Bogar, notes that in an environment of expanded content, "synthesis and analysis will become even more important. There's so much information out there, but so little of it is in usable form for the average person."

To develop the content of the New Medium, one must consider the strengths and weaknesses of existing media content, plus the apparent strengths and weaknesses of the New Medium, and then proceed to modify the former to conform to the latter.

STRENGTHS OF THE EXISTING MEDIA

Social responsibility, credibility, and familiarity are characteristics of the media that we must take into account.

Warning attendees at the 1994 Interactive Newspapers Conference to protect the integrity of the information they provide, Donald Brazeal, editor of the *Washington Post's Digital Ink,* said: "We must avoid those who want to rent us a hotdog stand in their electronic shopping mall . . . Our greatest risk is letting others define us."

SOCIAL RESPONSIBILITY. Users of the mass media do not hesitate to complain when they feel an information provider has let them down. Often complaints involve mistakes or insensitivity. Some providers get the reputation of never providing any meaningful information about controversial topics; others are criticized for overemphasizing the negative aspects of society. These criticisms are related to the concept of social responsibility. Our society operates through informal (sometimes very formal) social contracts. We expect the Burger King Whopper we buy when we visit San Diego to be at least as good as the one we get down the street in our hometown. We want the providers of a product or service to deliver as promised.

The New Medium as described herein makes an all-encompassing promise regarding information. It promises a near-universal spectrum of visual and aural stimuli that will provide the User with a near-universal spectrum of information.

Quality content is the measure of social responsibility. Providers of the content of the New Medium will determine how well it serves the information needs of society.

CREDIBILITY. Existing media have credibility, and it is related to the next topic, familiarity, as well as to social responsibility. CBS, NBC, and ABC have established their credibility and social responsibility over the years, so much so that when they err (as when NBC "helped" a pickup truck to catch fire on one of its news programs), it is a news event. *The New York Times* is credible. Your hometown sports announcer is credible. Even those supermarket tabloids are credible in the sense that we all know that they are going to stretch the truth beyond what we can believe. They can be depended on to be incredible, a perverse form of credibilty. Having the CBS logo or the nameplate of an established newspaper on content gives it credibility.

Moving into the New Medium requires that content be related to those that produce it so that Users may attach an appropriate level of credibility to it. As existing media adapt to the New Medium they will bring with them whatever credibility they have accrued. One of the responsibilities that new providers of content will have is to establish themselves as credible sources of information. Media professionals in a local setting can depend on the information they provide as a measure of their credibility, since it is easily tested by local Users. Users must depend on media competition to give them a measure of the credibility of information from beyond the individual User's horizon.

Answers to the following questions help determine the credibility of an information provider: Is the provider responsive to User needs and requests, consistent in providing information, frank about mistakes that are made, prompt in correcting mistakes, diligent in pursuing all the kinds of information the User wants, up front about operations of the providing service and about its personnel, not guilty of bias or prejudice and careful to avoid conflicts of interest in business or political matters that would give the appearance of bias?

FAMILIARITY. The familiarity factor is the greatest strength of the existing media. We know that a premium channel is the best way to watch a movie at home; that the newspaper is a quick reference for where to eat (or what's on TV); that a late night sports roundup will give us all the scores and some taped highlights of that day's action. We interact with the media out of habit and comfortably. Stress accompanies any change in these habits. But, over time, we do change when we find that a different set of habits suits us better or when forced to by arbitrary decisions from those who produce the media.

The stress of adapting to the New Medium will be great if it seems to be primarily arbitrary. It will be lessened if it occurs over time, as it will, and as the advantages become obvious. Providing content advantageous to the User is basic to the transition. The motion picture *Field of Dreams* is convincing. If indeed someone built a baseball diamond at the edge of a cornfield where I could see Shoeless Joe Jackson, Babe Ruth, and Ty Cobb all playing in the same game, that would be the greatest sports medium ever. Build it (and provide the content—that pantheon of players) and "they will come."

The quality and quantity of content that the New Medium offers (accompanied by ease of access) will determine the rate at which the New Medium is accepted. Accomplishing this task requires taking advantage of as many of the content strengths of the existing media as possible. What are these individual strengths?

STRENGTHS OF THE PRINT MEDIA

Creators of newspapers, magazines, and books thrive on the ability to acquire and synthesize information and direct it to a niche of the public.

The niche for most newspapers is geographical. The niche for most magazines is by interest area. The ability to identify and establish rapport with Users in those niches is a quality to be carried forward.

While announcing the *Raleigh News and Observer*'s online newspaper, *NandO*, publisher Frank Daniels III said the new service would meet the newspaper's goal: "We're in the business of helping people within the community find out about the community. And we'll do whatever it takes to accomplish that," noting that printing on paper is "an environmentally unsound way to deliver information."

ACQUIRING INFORMATION. Newspapers more than other mass media cooperate with each other in the acquisition of information. Although the editor of a small weekly newspaper may not be a member of the Associated Press, in all likelihood that editor has the phone number of the nearest AP bureau tucked away so that if a news event of interest beyond the weekly's circulation area takes place, the editor can inform the AP, provide the facts, and get a check in the mail. In fact, the worldwide network of reporters and editors, cooperating through news services like the Associated Press and through information syndicates, remains the information backbone of all the news media, including the broadcast media. This content has moved easily into the databases and other information services already available in digital form. Maintaining, refining, and expanding the information-gathering nets is important to the New Medium.

SYNTHESIZING INFORMATION. Other media also synthesize, but at the same time they stay closer to the original occurrence (real or imagined). The producer of a movie or television drama attempts to create a setting in a studio or on location and have characters create the illusion of real events. Sometimes television points its cameras (and radio its microphones) at reality and lets us see and hear sounds and images unmodified by human minds and hands. Remember this as a strength of these media to be discussed later.

By its very nature, though, print media must synthesize. The great writers can create near-reality in our minds but they do it with words in text. For hundreds of years text interspersed with drawings was the only mass medium. Through those centuries words put together in text have become languages within their respective languages. Besides being able to state facts and reflect emotions, words in text serve effectively to make information concise, to provide transitions from one medium to another, to point the way in communications and to serve wherever a flexible informational tool is needed. The ability to create and adapt textual matter is at the center of creating appropriate content for the New Medium.

The print media, particularly in recent years, have found it important to synthesize by combining verbal and nonverbal information. A contemporary newspaper or magazine is likely to present textual matter in a table, data in a graph or a complicated device in a cutaway drawing. It will use pictorial logos to indicate the information is on a continuing topic, and boxes to point the User to related material elsewhere, even in another medium like audiotext.

"The ability to piece together seemingly disparate pieces of information—what we commonly know as editing—to create a news product is still going to be a treasured art," notes David M. Cole in the *Cole Papers*, a publishing technology newsletter.

ENTRY POINTS. Use of these various devices has led to the concept of entry points, whereby the User has opportunities to begin considering a body of information at several different places: through a table, a summary, a picture, or a story referred to elsewhere. The New Medium will expand upon this concept of entry points since it is similar to multimedia (the ability to present audio, video, text, and still graphics seamlessly) and hypertext (the ability to move among these different forms of information easily).

PACKAGING. The discipline required to fit information onto a printed page has contributed to the print media practitioner's skill in packaging information. From stringing unrelated items together in vertical columns, the print media moved on to using headlines to summarize information and attract attention, to the creation of the photo essay and to the information package boxed over most of the page, with a main story, sidebar, map, photos and graph. Expanding these techniques to include video and audio is an imperative to create the New Medium.

Jonathon Seybold at the 1993 Seybold Conference asked, "Is the implication . . . that people who come from a print background may actually be better positioned and trained to deal with interactive media than people who come from film?" Michael Sullivan, former photographer with degrees in design and computer science, answered, "They don't know it, that's all; I'm trying to clobber them over the head."

ORGANIZATION. The regular production of a newspaper or magazine as a manufactured product, provides a tangible record of how well information is organized. Editors use last week's publication to improve on next week's and they steal ideas from other editors' newspapers. Many publications organize information to match the needs of their readers, their advertisers, or their own production requirements. *The Wall Street Journal* presents topics in the same spot in the paper each day (or in the same place on a particular day of the week). Newspapers and magazines departmentalize content for easy access and provide indexes to specific, often-used information. *Playboy* recognized that a magazine production reality (that its two innermost pages are on one side of a single sheet of paper) could be combined with a marketing strategem (the Playmate of the Month) and created the highly successful centerfold. A fashion magazine presents page after page of those advertisements that cost the most at the front of each issue and almost hides its editorial content so that readers are coerced into spending time with the ads.

PERMANENCE. Permanence has always been a positive attribute of the print media, and this is particularly true in the area of advertising. Whether the advertisement is a two-line classified or a full-page display ad, it's there in ink on paper—the price, the product description, the location, the discount coupon, the headline, and the selling message. The consumer can cut it out and keep it. It even serves as a pseudo contract between the provider and the consumer. Print is a great advertising medium.

NARROWEST BANDWIDTH. Text presented digitally uses a minimum of electronic capacity. That makes text appropriate for modifying or enhancing content in the New Medium. A multimedia presentation can easily offer duplicate text in multiple languages. Or text can be added that duplicates audio for the benefit of the deaf.

Print media offer many (but far from all) the kinds of content needed to organize information in accordance with the traits of the New Medium.

STRENGTHS OF THE AUDIO MEDIA

Information ceased to be at the mercy of time and space with the introduction of electronic media—telegraphy, telephony and radio. Electronics transformed all communication including mass communication. In 1950 Edward R. Murrow and Fred Friendly produced and narrated a CBS program with the title "Hear It Now." Use that title as a description of the major strength of audio media.

ORAL TRADITION. The introduction of audio mass media also meant going back to the oral tradition. *Homo sapiens* talked long before he wrote. Even today some illiterate people can speak eloquently and hear perceptively. Audio media reach a wider audience than print media.

THE FAMILIAR VOICE. Compare two examples of electronic communication: a telegram from your best friend when you have a problem, compared to a telephone message from your best friend. Even if one ignores the two-way nature of telephony, the words you hear from your friend carry more information. You hear the concern and support behind the words. Just as important, you hear the familiar sound of your friend's voice. Audio offers the familiar and trusted voice and the feeling behind the words. Some listeners have become adept at identifying the voices of actors when they are employed for commercial purposes (James Earl Jones saying "This Is CNN" and Robert Mitchum saying "Beef—It's what's for dinner.")

THE FIRESIDE CHAT. Audio can create the seeming intimacy that President Franklin Roosevelt achieved with his fireside chats to the American people, or reflect the indignation of all Americans as Roosevelt did when asking a joint session of Congress for a declaration of war against Japan following their sneak attack on Pearl Harbor on December 7, 1941. "A day that will live in infamy," he said, and all of us who heard it remember it. Audio professionals can produce almost any other ambience as well.

WRITING FOR THE EAR. Radio changed writing. Only playwrights and those few people who wrote out their speeches learned the techniques of writing for the ear before the introduction of radio. Traditional writers over the centuries had for the most part sought ways to simplify the text itself and create messages the eyes could examine efficiently. Most text is not tied to time as the spoken word is. We can examine printed text in detail or scan rapidly. Redundancy, simplicity, word order, abbreviations, and complicated words are dealt with differently depending on whether one is writing a story for print or a script for broadcast. Writers for radio have developed the ability to put words on paper (or screen) so that an announcer or actor can present them orally with ease and with meaning.

THE MAKE-BELIEVE BALLROOM. For the most part text engages our minds. The esthetics of reading are quite different from the esthetics of hearing. We read a poem and make it our own by interpreting. Audio is much more adept at enthralling our minds. We hear the poet read a work and take the poet and the poem into our minds. In a different way audio media have changed the experience we have with music. It is now both a solitary experience and a group experience, and we can experience it at almost any time and place, alone on a mountaintop, walking down a crowded sidewalk, or traditionally at a concert hall. By the same token, through radio we join the crowd at the ballpark and share "the thrill of victory and the agony of defeat" (as the ABC Sports tagline phrased it) in real time, or we rent an audio book to listen to while traveling the highways.

PRIMAL AND VERBAL SOUNDS. The bat strikes the ball. The crowd roars. The announcer tells us that the star of our team has just hit a grand-slam home run. Our most primitive ancestor would have recognized the sound of a club striking another hard object; the classical Greeks and Romans would have understood the oral outburst of thousands. We await the words of the announcer to tell us what our ears could not see. The sounds of nature and the noises we produce can be combined with the spoken word in audio.

CONVERSATION. Two people batting a topic back and forth, whether it be neighborhood gossip or the threat of nuclear war, stimulates further thought and conversation. The audio media have used the telephone as a feedback and participatory device to create dialogues and debates for the ear.

COMPANION ALONG THE WAY. While our hand-eye coordination is occupied with driving or folding up the laundry, our ears can be keeping up with the ball game or be pleasantly entertained by music; meanwhile, if a news or weather bulletin needs our attention, our ears are alerted and we can stop less important activities.

NARROW BANDWIDTH. Just as text can be added or modified using a minimum of digital memory, audio can be added or modified economically.

Audio content can be a primary source of our attention, an adjunct to other sensory stimuli, or a diversion while other activities are in progress.

STRENGTHS OF TELEVISION

In 1951 when Murrow and Friendly adapted their CBS Radio program to television, the name became *See It Now.* That could be a definition for the content of the mass medium that in the last half of the twentieth century has laid siege upon and indeed captured the population of the world. *See It Now* only scratches the surface of the content of television, because television has as its heritage the basic fascination of people with themselves and with others, with the invention of sport and games and of spectator sport, with role playing and drama, with news and education. Literature, art, music, dance, and cinema are integral parts of television's heritage. As the powerful and ubiquitous medium that it is, television has spawned new kinds of content, that is, the instant replay and the television commerical. The boundaries of its content have not yet been reached.

Content for the New Medium begins with the attributes of television as we know it, for television already combines representational motion images of reality, representational still images, still and motion images that have been created, text as a part of images and text imposed upon images and all kinds of audio. An amplification of the *See It Now* title would be: *See and Hear It Now and Read and Hear All About It.*

What a palette to use to produce content—to provide information!

EYES AND EARS. Throughout our lives we experience multiple stimuli simultaneously. We enter a room, see the furnishings and relate its occupants to each other, hear their conversation and the street noise outside, smell the coffee and glance at the newspaper headlines. Our minds are accustomed to this. Television provides much the same experience artificially.

Narrow-band and *broadband* are terms used in communication technology jargon to describe how much data can be sent over a channel. In a mass media context, text is narrow band, radio is narrow band, text plus pictures is somewhat broader, but television is vastly broader, encompassing text and audio along with all the rest. We are exposed to a lot of information and a lot of different kinds of information all at one moment by television.

Because of this bountiful informational palette, the techniques developed by scholars and professionals in the use of television is at the center of creating content for the New Medium. A sampling of techniques is illuminating.

CINEMATOGRAPHY. A stagecoach rattles into a dusty western town, passing a general store, the marshal's office, and a saloon. One of the drivers grips his shoulder, which has an arrow protruding from it. When the stage comes to a stop, a beautiful woman steps to the ground, where she is confronted and mauled by a drunken man. A tall cavalry officer steps forward and cuffs the drunk into submission. By now we know that a romance is possible and that our hero will likely have to lead a brave band out to confront some angry renegades.

An *establishing shot* has given us historical context and a map of where the action will occur. *Intermediate shots* have allowed us to size up the characters and begin to establish relationships. *Closeups* have given us further insights into the individual characters. To these basics, the genius of the motion picture and television writers, producers, directors, cameramen, editors, and others, have added great sophistication. Dialogue, background sound, and music are blended with the visual stimuli. The goal is to move the story along compellingly, coherently, and efficiently.

TALKING HEAD. A fundamental method for getting into and out of a message, of explaining what cannot be shown or heard directly, and of giving information quickly is to put a person with a microphone in front of the camera. This provides an on-screen experience that we confront in our daily lives when we talk to a grocery clerk, a boss or a best friend. Indeed we probably became best friends because of repeated face-to-face conversations in which we established credibility and rapport. This tendency for persons who communicate with an audience with direct eye contact to become familiar and often trusted is a valuable communication tool in television. The talking head is more than a conveyer of words. He or she may be a source of credibility and of nonverbal information as well.

UP CLOSE AND PERSONAL. On television we have seen the planet Jupiter, up close; human cells, up close; the hulk of the sunken *Titanic* at the bottom of the ocean and just about everything else, up close. In a few scores of seconds, television can show us the birthplace, schools, training facilities, and family of a figure-skating star with comments from family, friends, and associates about almost any aspect of the star's life. TV stimuli in a few hours' viewing take us where our ancestors never dreamed of going in their entire lifetimes.

SEE IT ALL. From a communications point of view, television (and radio) allow us to be in three or more places at once: (1) where our bodies are, (2) where the anchorperson is, (3) with the "on-scene" reporters to whom the anchorperson is talking. We can see the empty popcorn bowl on our coffee table, the multiple television monitors behind the anchor, and, in a window on the screen, smoke rising from a disaster site behind a reporter.

Some television sets allow us to view more than one channel at once. Some stations (and perhaps by the time this book is published, networks) will put four pictures on the screen at once and allow viewers to select one to fill the entire screen. This is an introduction to hypermedia.

Through this ability to put the User of the media at more than one place at a time, mass media professionals can instantly begin to provide perspective and context to far-reaching events.

ELASTIC TIME. By recording videotape or exposing film at a speed different from that at which it is played back, the illusions of slow motion or time lapse are created. The bud opens to full flower in a matter of seconds, or the diver floats languidly above the board then drifts toward the water below. New ways of dissecting actions are created.

THE GLOBAL VILLAGE. Throughout the discussion on television have been interspersed terms that come directly from television: *hear it now, see it now, the thrill of victory, the agony of defeat, up close and personal.* The terms are used because many readers will immediately recognize them and have a grasp of what they mean. Thirty years ago Marshall McLuhan expounded the concept of the Global Village. In this metaphor, the village well of the late twentieth century where everyone gathers to swap information is the television set. As a result, television has created a new rhetoric. Since so much identical information is shared with so many people, this shared field of television experience enhances our ability to communicate.

Saturday Night Live, the satirical television program, depends upon its viewers' familiarity with what has been in the mass media in developing its skits. In the 1960s a Doris Day movie included a segment that took place during a television commercial's filming: a man in a harness was being wafted through the air into a convertible so Hertz could "put him in the driver's seat"—a visual satirical joke about television. The clichés of television and the movies have become the driving force behind a battery commercial. In the first versions, a bunny beating a drum interrupted the various clichés (a diet formula commercial, a furniture commercial, a cold remedy commercial) to announce that Energizers keep going, and going, and going . . . The interruption was refreshing to viewers tired of the clichés. Then the bunny sandwiched a real commercial between two segments of the "going, and going" bit. More recently the bunny has escaped the wrath of King Kong, Goldfinger, and bad guys in a Western. No doubt many viewers are beginning to hope he has drummed his way into the sunset of television commercial clichés.

When three television networks dominated the media landscape, a consensus of what was important could be established. The assassination of President John F. Kennedy is the classic example of an entire nation remaining focused on unfolding events. The widespread availability of CNN through cable television created a different environment during the Persian Gulf War: viewers deserted other channels to watch the conflict.

This shared field of television experience is a powerful communication tool. Moving to dozens of television channels has changed the way it manifests itself. Are we losing what used to be a strength of the mass media: the ability to articulate and explain the broad values and goals of society? That is an issue to be dealt with later in the chapter.

WEAKNESSES OF THE EXISTING MEDIA

When horses were the only way to speed up transportation and haul heavier loads, no one considered their inherent disadvantages: it took a long time to grow one; they had to be fed every day; they had to be trained; they deposited residue that had to be cleaned up. When a substitute came along, the horseless carriage (a.k.a. the automobile), the inherent weaknesses of animal-powered transportation became apparent. In earlier chapters the weaknesses of the mass media have been described in the context of why new forms of the media are likely to emerge. We can summarize them briefly:

Mike Gordon sees the *Atlanta Constitution*'s online project he is developing as a way the newspaper can offer more information than it can squeeze into the current news hole. "When you cover the latest survey, you can also give the Users the raw material and let them make decisions."

VARIED CHANNELS. Print, audio, and video each has its own production machinery and distribution system. Using traditional methods, they cannot be created, stored, distributed, and consumed together. As a result, they cannot easily be mixed.

MANUFACTURED PRODUCTS. Newspapers, magazines, books, audio disks and tapes, videocassettes, and even reels of motion-picture film are manufactured products used to provide a service: information including entertainment and cultural enlightenment. Manufactured products add an expense to providing the service; they are of finite capacity and in most cases they cannot be modified, only replaced. When Users are through with them they must be returned to a library or rental agency, or disposed of.

SCHEDULED SERVICES. Movies, television, and radio provide content on a schedule determined by the producer, requiring the User to conform. If the User misses the beginning of a message or any part of the message, it is irrevocably gone.

The results of these limitations are the limiting of content, duplicating successful content, appealing only to the universal desires, ignoring individuals, and slavery of producers and consumers to time and space constraints.

STRENGTHS OF THE NEW MEDIUM

The nature of the New Medium has been discussed at length. Here are some of the perceived opportunities it offers:

- All kinds of subject matter with less restriction on amount of content.
- More sources of content.
- Release from manufacturing and tight scheduling.
- Ability to pay attention to the individual,

- New ways of combining information and of moving about in the content.
- A chance for a new beginning.

Other technical qualities that strengthen the New Medium in relation to content: many entry points, use of a thesaurus (individually created) and keywords, prompting, purging, archiving, querying, contributing, revising/updating, and processing/analyzing.

Indeed User participation and control are enhanced.

WEAKNESSES OF THE NEW MEDIUM

One advantage of the oral tradition was that people carried the encoding and decoding devices around in their heads. Now we carry newspapers and Walkman radios around with us, and sometimes even a portable television. The New Medium requires a computer, screen, and some way to hook it to the information superhighway. Although computers aren't much bigger than some daily newspapers, we haven't yet figured out how to fold them up and stick them in our coat pockets. In short, the New Medium still has to be invented in the context of existing media and society.

DECODING. A key shortcoming of the potential New Medium is an effective decoding device including display and speakers. Just as important is the software to make it ultra user-friendly. Then there is the problem of educating the public on how to operate it. Once that is done, the content itself must be considered.

CREDIBILITY. There is a credibility problem because the device is used for everything from preparing the grocery shopping list and gossiping with Aunt Ida to preparing one's income taxes. All data look the same, meaning that the traditional mass communication cues for establishing credibility are not present. We now depend on high production values in movies and television programs to cue us as to their potential. We know what to expect when we pick up the familiar hometown newspaper or when we read the headlines at a supermarket checkout line. We know that a book jacket displaying a man and woman in flamboyant embrace is fiction, and that David Brinkley's face on the television screen means serious discussion of important issues. New credibility cues must be developed.

SERENDIPITY. Channel surfing with a TV remote device, leafing through the Sunday papers, and wandering about a bookstore are pleasant activities that lead us to information we would not otherwise encounter. How can the structured environment of the New Medium provide us with this kind of serendipity? Some new kinds of slothful habits will have to be developed.

PRIVACY. Barry Hollander's comment (see margin) regarding serendipity in the New Medium appeared on my computer screen one day while I was going through messages from persons who subscribe to the Computer Assisted Reporting and Research list on the Internet. Hollander, a University of Georgia faculty member, was commenting on an earlier message from another list member. His comment was in the form of a memo or note; it certainly was not part of a book or research report he had written.

Regarding electronic newspapers, Barry Hollander of the University of Georgia worries "that readers will lose that serendipity that comes from the version of the newspaper we now enjoy. Not only are readers exposed to important stories they might normally ignore, they also can come across an offbeat story that wouldn't appear in a customized version."

Memos, even those circulated in an office, are considered private messages or at least semiprivate. What if they are put on an electronic highway where dozens or hundreds of near-strangers will see them? Am I justified in referring to that memo in this book without asking Hollander's permission? (I did ask, and he gave it.)

Two kinds of privacy issues emerge in the digital information environment: (1) that previously private messages unwittingly will become public; (2) that previously public information (such as driver's license records) will be withheld from public view because computers make it so easy to get access to the information. We face the need for new ways of dealing with public/private information conflicts.

Joe Shoemaker, press aide to U. S. Representative Rich Boucher (who is sponsoring legislation on development of the information superhighway) believes that "It's going to be a lot harder to be an investigative journalist. Privacy on the network is going to be important."

THE WIDE WORLD OF CONTENT

One of the computer world's earliest adages was GIGO—"Garbage In, Garbage Out." Its meaning was that if the information fed into the computer was useless, then the information coming out of the computer would be useless. An example: In an early attempt to computerize the translation of languages, the idiom "out of sight, out of mind" was fed into a computer that was programmed to translate it into Russian and then retranslate it into English. The giant computer, housed in an air-conditioned bunker far underground on a giant university campus, applied the existing software to the task at hand and after some time came up with "blind idiot."

The computer could not comprehend the nuances of English and Russian grammar or the intuitive knowledge that we have regarding the difference between "out of sight" and "out of your mind." Garbage in, garbage out.

No matter how technically advanced and easy to use the New Medium is, it is the content that will determine its value to society and to individuals. This is a criticism of information technology that goes beyond mass media functions. One social scientist, Lester Thurow, has noted that "computerization has not increased productivity." And another social scientist, Wilson Dizard, has said, "There is growing

SCARLETT O'HARA ❧ MINNIE MOUSE ❧ MARY MARY QUITE CONTRARY ❧ HESTER PRYNNE ❧ MARY WORTH ❧ ELIZA DOOLITTLE ❧

TELLING STORIES: THE TRADITIONAL WAY. . .

The border of this page is composed of the names of some of the most famous women who have *never* lived. We know their names because they are the central characters of the familiar stories that have enriched our lives. On the other hand, few of us know anything about Eliza Johnson, Lucy Hayes, or Florence Harding, although those women knew the excitement of living in the White House. The stories are the difference.

Mass communications professionals are all engaged in one way or another in the enterprise of creating and disseminating stories. Whether it be the video montages set to the music of MTV or the almost intolerably gray stock tables of the *Wall Street Journal,* there's a story there that satisfies the needs of an audience. Today's sophisticated professionals are not far removed from the balladeers who spun out tales for the locals around the campfires during the Dark Ages.

One tells good stories by taking advantage of whatever medium is a hand. The Greek dramatists used the chorus: a group whose voices could bring forth the emotions as well as the meanings of the words. The Psalmists recognized the strength of thoughts told in rhythm and repeated with different words. Writers fearing the wrath of despots have hidden social commentary in children's stories. Great novelists like Charles Dickens in *A Tale of Two Cities* can weave an absorbing story of romance, danger, and treachery, and at the same time develop characters of strength, debauchery, and cunning evil, so that at the end we shed tears over the courage and selflessness of the reprobate Sidney Carton and hate to bid farewell to the happy members of the family of Charles Darnell. The story moves on several planes: the adventure, the recounting of historical events and their impact on the people of those times, the nobility and crassness of the human condition.

Masters of the cinema such as George Lucas can take us to galaxies far, far away for the otherworldly adventures of three gallant young people (and one old one) and some charming androids and a big alien against a very evil empire in *Star Wars.*

The writer places one word, then another. The stage offers a broader medium of action, sound, scenery, costumes, props, and dialogue. The motion picture and television are as big as outdoors. Yet the mass media creator still works by and large in a linear, beginning-to-end environment. But the New Medium is different.

The New Medium offers mass communications professionals a vastly expanded palette for telling tomorrow's stories. Ideally stories will be told without interruption and without space or time constraints.

As a case study for creating a New Medium story we will take the fiftieth anniversary, in 1995, of the detonation of two nuclear weapons over Hiroshima and Nagasaki in Japan. The two bombs killed more than 150,000 persons, resulted in the end of World War II within a month, changed the nature of international relations, and introduced a new form of usable energy as well as a new threat of environmental poisoning.

As the words forming the border of the following page indicate, a new nuclear vocabulary entered the language, attesting to the vast store of information available as documents, film, and living sources.

In all previous media, the creator of the story would proceed linearly. Embellishments in the form of sidebars or subplots would be possible, but the creator would determine when and where all the information was presented.

In our case study, using the multimedia and hypertext capabilities of the New Medium, the creator must take into account the ability of the User to enter the story at many points, to move in any

Box 9.1

cont'd...

JULIET ❧ OLIVE OYLE ❧ SLEEPING BEAUTY ❧ BRENDA STARR ❧ JO MARCH ❧ PRINCESS LEIA ❧ TINKERBELL ❧ NELLY FORBUSH ❧ TESS ❧ JILL ❧

MISS MARPLE ❧ LITTLE MISS MUFFET ❧ ANNE OF GREEN GABLES ❧ GOLDILOCKS ❧ BLONDIE ❧ HELEN OF TROY ❧ CINDERELLA

❧ MARY POPPINS ❧ BETTY BOOP ❧ LITTLE RED RIDING HOOD ❧ JANE EYRE ❧ SNOW WHITE ❧ MADAM BUTTERFLY ❧ DOLLY LEVY ❧ WENDY ❧

* MANHATTAN PROJECT * $E=MC^2$ * OAK RIDGE * URANIUM 235 * HALF LIFE * ALAMOGORDO * TRINITY * WHITE SANDS *

THE ROSENBERGS * FAT MAN * LITTLE BOY * MUTUALLY ASSURED DESTRUCTION * ENOLA GAY * SUPERFORT * PLUTONIUM * CRITICAL MASS

BIKINI * NEVADA DESERT RANGE * FALLOUT SHELTER * BAN THE BOMB * NUCLEAR CLUB * NUCLEAR SUB * DR. STRANGELOVE * THE BRINK

AND THE NEW MEDIUM WAY

direction, and go to related data at any point.

The New Medium storyteller bases the presentation on a chronological "main story." Almost any interested User will peruse this narrative. It begins before World War II and continues to the present.

For ease in organizing, and to offer the User appropriate options, some categories are established: the biographies of some people important to the story (Premier Tojo, President Harry Truman, scientist J. Robert Oppenheimer, and pilot Paul Tibbets). Each biography may be absorbed from beginning to end, or examined in turn, revealing the early lives of each of the four persons, then their wartime experiences. then their postwar lives. In a sense (looking at the accompanying chart), the User can move horizontally through each biography, or vertically.

Biography	Science	Politics	Culture
Robert Oppenheimer, built the bomb	How nuclear fission and fusion work	Wartime allies; Cold War foes	One world dream ends and Third World awakens
Paul Tibbets, dropped the bomb	Planes, missiles, subs, and defense	Axis powers win, lose, and thrive after defeat	Hiroshima and Nagasaki, before and after
THE BASIC NARRATIVE			
Hideki Tojo, ordered attack on Pearl Harbor	Health and survival in the nuclear age	Conquering and losing an empire; democracy	Japan: The story of an ancient island race
Harry Truman, ordered attack on Hiroshima	Building weapons and power plants	From isolation to superpower	USA: New World land of diverse ethnicity

BEFORE WORLD WAR II → DURING WW II → SINCE WW II

Other categories are science/medicine, politics/history, and culture. Each subcategory of each category could be either examined chronologically (horizontally), or compared (vertically) with one another.

Another way of using this story would be to move from right to left across a set of subcategories. One could read about the culture of prewar Japan, then the political and diplomatic climate in Japan, then the early life of Premier Tojo. This is a more fluid method of storytelling, with the User allowed to follow the trail that curiosity creates. The storyteller will use ingenuity and creativity to organize the material in multidimensional ways.

Not indicated are the many cross-indexing cue buttons in the information. They are to provide as many options for the User as are appropriate. Some cues will be for a different medium (audio, video, photo, text); other cues will be to related information in another part of the story. The storyteller will keep in mind that no two Users will absorb the story in exactly the same way.

This is indeed a New Medium for storytellers. Their diligence will determine the New Medium's success.

Box 9.2

* THREE MILE ISLAND * SZILARD * SALT TALKS * STAR WARS * WEAPONS * CUBAN MISSILE CRISIS * CHERNOBYL * AEC *

evidence to suggest that communications and information resources will have to be reassessed if they are to realize their full potential in the current re-industrial effort."

Noted editor Gene Roberts has pointed out that the dominant newspapers in New York, Philadelphia, Boston, Washington, Chicago, Dallas, and Miami achieved that position by out-reporting the competition. He says there is no substitute for substantive reporting.

Starting with Day 1 and continuing every day thereafter until Day Infinity, professional mass communicators will have to achieve high standards of performance or the New Medium will wind up performing like a blind idiot.

Mass communicators will be called upon to feed into the New Medium a greatly expanded range of information and also greater detail on each item of information. The goals will be

- To meet all the information needs of individual Users, rather than the common needs of most information Users.
- To present this information efficiently, compellingly, and in context.

A national information service is "not a matter of designing twenty screens of information that will be utilized a billion times. It's a matter of designing information so that four or five people in Los Angeles County get an answer to a very specific question."
—William H. Dutton, Annenberg School for Communication, Southern California

This greatly expands the kinds of content. For example:

- New modes of dramatic art and entertainment may emerge using multimedia, virtual reality and other computer techniques that more intimately involve the User than do theater, motion pictures, music videos, and so forth.
- As indicated earlier, new techniques of advertising may well combine functions of classified advertising, direct mail, catalogs, television commercials, coupons, and door-to-door selling.
- The big-city journalist may find himself involved with the kind of journalism practiced on rural weeklies, and the rural journalist may have the resources to better interpret the broader world to his community.

Content may well range from what we are now exposed to when we visit a great museum or read a great book to what we expect to find taped to the refrigerator door. (The refrigerator door is where really important communications are placed because that is the place those most important to us routinely visit.)

Gilberte Houbart of the MIT Media Lab notes that serendipity depends on individuals' wants, needs, attitudes and energy-level at any given time. The medium of the future, he says, should permit "assisted browsing."

Here is a random list of topics tomorrow's communicators may be sending along to the public: where to get help, sports schedules, school calendars, transportation schedules, movies and plays, novels, magazines, game shows, computer games, market quotations, catalogs, coupons, subscription contests, political columns, satirical cartoons, comics, jokes, crosswords, the State of the Union address, tax forms and deadlines, county budgets, births, marriages, divorces, obituaries, bar mitzvah announcements, economic indicators, weather reports and forecasts, reproductions of paintings, reruns of everything, poetry readings, music, recipes, charts of the stars, maps, gardening tips, birdwatching news, golf help, muscle building, crime reports, reviews of new cars, computer software updates, real estate transfers, new water-meter hookups.

In addition Users may be taking advantage of the New Medium for greeting cards, phone conversations, letters, and wake-up calls. The kinds of information that artists of all kinds, county clerks, librarians, reporters, telephone operators, beauticians, and taxi cab drivers now impart could all be content thousands of Users of the New Medium will turn to.

SUMMARY

Providing the kind of content that will make the leap from the decoding device to the User's mind is the key to a successful New Medium. The strengths of existing media—such as credibility and high production standards—should be carried into New Medium content. Weaknesses of the New Medium—lack of familiarity, difficulty of serendipitous access to information, and problems of privacy and secrecy, for example—must be overcome. Vastly expanded content will characterize the New Medium.

PROJECTS, DISCUSSION TOPICS, AND EXERCISES

1. If possible, secure a copy of the *San Jose Mercury News* for a given day and put a copy of *Mercury Center* for the same day on floppy disks. Read different sections of each and compare the experience. Did your familiarity with newspapers make them easier to read? Did you notice things in one version you did not notice in the other? (Any of the online editions of metropolitan papers could be compared to the print version.)
2. With a group of students, play Trivial Pursuit with the two versions of the San Jose paper. Create some questions about the content that are insignificant but interesting to some people. In which is it easier to find specific information?
3. Bring to class an example of what you regard as compelling media content and report on why it is compelling: a clipping, a description of a television drama, or news story or a musical selection.
4. Discuss the implications of being freed from "space" constraints in the print media and "time constraints" in the electronic media. Also, discuss the implications of top management realizing that what the firm is selling is information, not paper on ink or air time.

SELECTED READINGS

Bliss, Edward, Jr. *Now the News*. New York: Columbia Press, 1991. In 575 pages Bliss tells the story of broadcast news.

Dennis, Everette E., and Edward C. Pease, eds. *Media Studies Journal*, 8:1 (Winter 1994). Titled "The Race for Content," the issue contains a wide variety of information and comment on the development of content for digital media.

Ernst, Martin L., et al. *Mastering the Changing Information World*. Norwood, N.J.: Ablex, 1993. An insightful comparison of advantages and disadvantages of the print and digital platforms.

Parker, Edwin B., et al. *Rural America in the Information Age*. Lanham, Md.: The Aspin Institute, 1989. Content needs of rural areas are included; these micro-information topics will be universal in a digital environment.

Tomorrow's Media Professionals

Facilitating and Maintaining the New Medium and Its Content

> *Twenty years from now, people will look at the 1990s with some bemusement. They will wonder how we put up with daily two-hour commutes. They will find our dependence on inadequate educational resources archaic. . . . They will wonder why the ingenious application of knowledge technologies in the commercial sector lagged so noticeably in the personal sector.*
>
> **—Alfred C. Sikes**

The commercial sector, referred to above, is one of great energy, competitiveness, and ingenuity. Business people very quickly realized the potential of what Alfred Sikes calls knowledge technologies and bent them to their commercial needs. During the next few years mass communicators must acknowledge what is going on in knowledge technologies and bend them to the needs of the public. The alternative is that others not oriented toward the wants and needs of individuals may create a less than desirable New Medium.

Information Technology brings up questions of "Determinism or Choice?","Actors in the Drama," "Control and Power," "Access and Participation," and "Future of the Human Spirit: Depersonalization or New Development?"

—Ruth Finnegan

Business professionals have an important role in our society and they take it seriously. They view the economic sector of society as being its most important function. Maintaining its health is of paramount importance. Expanding the economy means more jobs and more products and services. That improves the lot of all individuals in the society. Marxist proponents view planned economies as the best way to serve society. Private-enterprise proponents view the initiative and competition of business as the best way to serve society.

There are other professions. Our clergy, for example, view the spiritual life of women and men as being more important than the material life. Obviously they view society from a decidedly different point of view.

Here we have two professions with seemingly opposite goals, yet many a business professional turns to his or her priest, pastor, rabbi, or other spiritual guide for counsel. The clergy do not hesitate to approach the business community for support of the temporal needs of organized religion. In fact these professions, along with law, medicine, and others, share certain attributes. Here are some of those attributes:

- Most important, professionals view their callings as essential to society.
- They have a commitment to their callings beyond the profit motive.
- They have a holistic approach to their callings.
- They have standards of performance they strive to attain and maintain.
- They enforce through codes and other means the standards of their profession.
- They have a body of knowledge and a regimen of training that members of the profession are expected to master.

PROFESSIONAL RESPONSIBILITY

Mass communications professionals recognize the importance of providing information of all kinds to every person. They recognize the benefits to society of an informed populace, and they recognize the need people have to know what is going on, to be intellectually challenged, to be entertained.

Beyond recognition, mass communications professionals assume the responsibilities of facilitating the acquisition of information by Users. That is what we do.

What this generation of professionals must do goes far beyond adapting the media of the past to the technologies of the present. That would be an Old World view. Instead the New World view of exploration and development as described previously will send media professionals exploring new ways of communicating. We can be as excited about what lies in our immediate future as our sci-fi grandpa, Eric, was about the prospects on New World.

New Medium mass communications professionals have several responsibilities, and the first is to make sure that their ideals as expressed above are as much a part of the New Medium as are the ideals of the business professionals.

Tomorrow's mass communicators have two additional roles to fill: first, to be creators of the the New Medium (the explorers); second, to be facilitators of the New Medium (the settlers).

CREATING THE NEW MEDIUM

HARDWARE AND SOFTWARE. A decade and a half ago at a wonderful newspaper that no longer exists, I saw a couple of guys loaf around in a newsroom and help create a new kind of editing. This was at the *Arkansas Gazette* in 1978 in Little Rock. The two guys were David Rapley and John Sarma, computer hardware and software technicians. They had changed the *Gazette* newsroom from a typewriter, paper, pencil, and pastepot environment to a state-of-the-art Hendrix computerized writing and editing system and were the resident experts. One of the qualities that set them apart from most computer experts was that they were as sensitive to the Users of the computers as they were knowledgeable about computers. They visited all departments of the newspaper consistently, conversed informally with the people who used the computer, and honed the system to fit the needs of the Users.

One day a reporter pointed out that after making a revision in the story he was writing, he could strike two keys that would take him to the end of the story to resume composition, but the cursor always went to the right margin of the last line instead of to the end of the last word on the last line. He had to peck on the backspace key to get to where he wanted to work. The next day that changed, thanks to the sensitive computer technician who made a slight change in the software. The system was easier to use.

The next generation of mass communicators must reverse this process. They must hang around with the computer experts and be the advocates of the people who will use the New Medium. They must make the New Medium so user-friendly that Users will indeed consider it their friend.

> For 35 years information technology has permeated every business activity. End-user productivity is tied directly to functionality and ease of learning and use. An understanding of Human–Computer Interaction (HCI) is needed during systems design. Only when system functions fit actual work and the system is easy to learn and use will the system be adopted.
>
> —*MIS Quarterly,* December 1991

USERS. Why would a User of the New Medium want to pay attention to it? What happens when an item comes to the User's attention? What discourages the User from pursuing additional information? Those are the kinds of questions that moviemakers, advertising people, and journalists have been asking themselves for years and years.

Two portions of the Shannon–Weaver communication model shown in Figure 10.1 on the next page are pertinent to User friendliness: understanding the receiver (or User) and understanding noise. In our model of communications these questions center around the nature of the Users—the box on the far right—and the nature of noise—that box underneath that has all but been ignored till now.

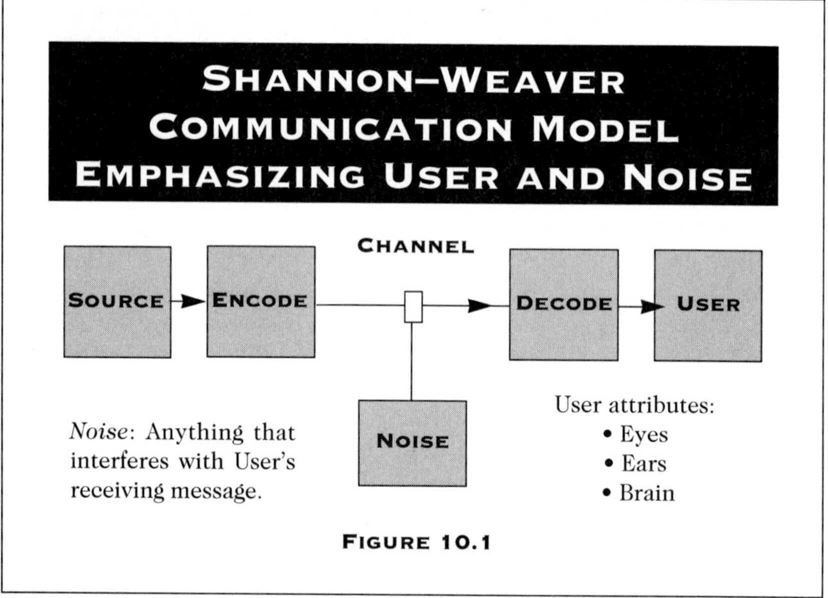

FIGURE 10.1

RECEIVER ATTRIBUTES

As indicated previously, all that the User learns depends upon the five senses. They provide the stimuli that we receive from our environment. The senses we are concerned with are sight and sound (audio and video). The New Medium can't provide stimuli of smell, taste, and touch. However, a good writer or speaker can provide descriptions that approach those sensations and allow the User to suspend disbelief and experience them in the mind.

So the first thing a mass communicator brings to the creation of the New Medium is an understanding of writing, charting, and speaking. Text, graphics, and talk can provide descriptions of the full range of sensory perceptions. Text, graphics, and talk can also link other kinds of communications (such as audio and video), can summarize, and can interpret. They are the most flexible tools the New Medium will have.

In addition, it is the mass communicator who must understand the communicative values of pictures and sounds. Pictures and sounds provide the User with sensory perceptions closely simulating what the User experiences in life outside the media. They require less re-creation of a scene by the User than do speech and writing. They seem more real or "vivid," as described previously.

These professionals also must be the authorities on how these stimuli are combined to provide the best possible message.

What can the various tools do?

- *Text.* Text describes things that were not video- or audio-recorded; compresses information into summaries; adds needed information that video or audio does not provide; interprets and analyzes in relation to theories and abstractions; provides chronology or narration; imparts the observer's reactions; offers the opportunity to read and reread with ease.
- *Speech.* Except for the last item, speech can do the things text does with the added information that inflection and tone provide—the non-verbal aspect of speech. Speech allows verbal information to accompany video with little distraction, since one stimulates the eyes and the other the ears, and people are used to that.
- *Map.* A map relates space and location (and often time) in a nonlinear fashion.
- *Drawing.* A drawing allows something that was not photographed to be depicted; can disassemble complicated items and maintain their relationships in three-dimensional form; allows imaginary images to be communicated.
- *Chart.* A chart allows for easy comparison of textual items; lessens the linear nature of writing.
- *Graph.* A graph shows quantitative relations in spatial rather than numerical form. Comparing blocks of space or lines is often easier for the mind to grasp than comparing numbers.
- *Photograph.* A photograph captures an instant with pictorial realism; permits lengthy examination of detail, allowing the User to draw independent conclusions.
- *Video.* Accompanied by audio, video most nearly re-creates a period of time. Video provides a virtual visual experience; allows the User to make an independent analysis of what was seen; can incorporate many of the other tools described above.
- *Audio.* Audio does for the ears what video does for the eyes, allowing the hearer to interpret what the sounds mean; reinforces what is being read or viewed; allows an original source to describe and analyze directly using abstractions or theoretical language.
- *Design.* In the New Medium, design (how the various elements are put together) must provide both order and serendipity. That is, the User proceeds at an individual pace and experiences elements somewhat as the User chooses. Yet there must be order to the design. The User must not be confused.

The encoding, channel, and decoding devices of the New Medium will have to provide quality text, graphics, still pictures, video, and sound, and effortlessly move from one to another. If it fails to do so, Users will reject it. It is the mass communications professional who plays a major role in determining when technical standards are adequate for all these necessities.

Thus far we have only gotten stimuli into the mind of the User. What happens then? No one can answer that question definitively. However, as has been noted, philosophers, biochemists, and social scientists have been delving into the mind for a long time. Mass communicators have been using their findings effectively in the traditional media. Now we are trying to combine communication tools into integrated messages, to offer vast amounts of information in an orderly way, and to allow the User to participate in the process. Some insight into how the human brain processes information is vital to this effort.

PERCEPTION, COGNITION, DISSONANCE

A few pages in one chapter cannot hope to even introduce this subject. However, a taste may whet the appetite and give an indication of what the subject offers. Consider three psychological terms—perception, cognition, and dissonance—in the following example.

You are driving across the plains. Off to your right is a low purple image that spreads for miles. You are aware of it. That is perception (and that is the point to which we took the stimuli we mentioned above).

You take a closer look. Is the purple image a range of mountains or is it a bank of clouds? This is cognition. You are comparing the image to past images and making assumptions.

You have driven this route before. You have never seen mountains on these plains. For mountains to suddenly appear would be a strange phenomenon indeed. This is dissonance. The image you are seeing does not match your preconceived notions of these plains. You conclude the image must be clouds. Dissonance resolved.

As you continue, your route takes you closer to the low purple image. Rocks, crags, and green foliage take shape. The image is a mountain range. Dissonance returns with a vengeance. You have taken a wrong turn and are miles and miles off your route. You idiot!

Memory, logical reasoning, and emotion were involved in the mental process as well as the original and subsequent stimuli. What role did each play? This is the kind of question that intrigues and baffles the communication researcher.

COMMUNICATION RESEARCH

Here are some other baffling and intriguing questions: What is the relationship between interpersonal communication and mass communication? That question leads to how is information diffused through a social system? How does information in the mass media change attitudes and behavior? How does the interaction between the receiver of a message and the sender change ongoing communication? Is all language learned by stimulus and response? Or is there within our minds a language module that allows us to make a quantum leap from a few words to an entire language, and does this module disappear as we emerge from infancy?

For the ongoing answers to these and other questions, stay abreast of the many academic journals in communication, the books on the subject, the conferences held, and the constant dialogue between researchers. This is an environment of theory and abstraction, of examining theory by establishing hypotheses and testing them through clinical or field research, of creating models (like the ones used in this book) that have general applications across a range of communications situations, of moving from the specific to the general and back to the specific. It is a world where the mind is used to study the mind and communication is used to explain communication.

Not all studies of communication are as arcane as those described above. Here is one from *Newspaper Research Journal* (spring 1986) that is very straightforward.

Two researchers, Marlyss Schwengels and James B. Lemert, established a hypothesis: News reports of rapes in town X are not representative of the range of rapes occurring in town X. They did a content analysis of news stories involving rape. Then they did a content analysis of all police reports of rapes. Then they compared the two analyses and found that the news reports gave the definite impression that rapes usually involved strangers in unfamiliar places, as opposed to the police reports, which indicated that more often the accuser and accused knew each other and the incidents happened in the domicile of one or the other. Their hypothesis was supported. Their conclusion was that potential victims of rape were not being adequately informed concerning the nature of this crime.

An interesting aspect of this study is that it dealt with a subject few mass media researchers attempt: examining information that the mass media ignore. That sort of analysis is hard to do because so often we cannot know what the media have not revealed.

Study of communication theory and research is essential to the mass communicator, particularly in the area of User perception, cognition, and dissonance. Such study offers insight, new ways of thinking, and new skills for dealing with the complicated world we live in and the sophisticated New Medium that may help people understand that world.

Let us now turn to that great enemy of communication: noise.

NOISE ATTRIBUTES

It's raining. The bus has turned the corner and is coming closer. You need an umbrella. You shout: "Mom, where's the umbrella?"

But suppose:

- There is always a 30-second delay between the time you ask a question and when your mother answers.
- You always have to say, "Please, Mother, would you take a moment from your busy day and . . . " before you ask for help.
- You have to be more descriptive and very specific in what you ask for: "Mom, I need foul-weather gear, water repellent, overhead, collapsible."
- Your mother ignores your question and asks if you've brushed your teeth with Crest and if you are wearing your Sportos.
- A tornado is bearing down on the back of the house and your mother can't warn you to run for the basement because you keep blabbering about an umbrella.

If any of the above situations take place, your options are:

1. Miss the bus.
2. Get wet.
3. Get blown away to the Land of Oz.

What you need is a fast answer: "Behind the couch" or "Run for your life!"

All of the above are examples of noise that could take place in a domestic interpersonal communication setting. Noise is much more than unpleasant, interruptive sounds. In a communication context it is anything that keeps a person from receiving an accurate version of a message another has sent.

Mass communications professionals are sensitive to the kinds of things that cause noise in the media. They more than any other group will determine whether the New Media will be able to minimize noise.

Each of the situations described above is a problem in a computerized mass media context.

The first is *delay, poor response time.* The User needs to be able to get information on demand without waiting. Both computer power and capacity at the User's end of the model are required. A shortcoming of the 1980s' attempts at interactive computerized communication was to provide a minimum of power and capacity at the User's end and to depend on the User to go to the sender's computer for everything.

Janette Dates, associate professor at Howard University, sees the need to market information services to the information-poor so they can perceive the value of the information.

The second example is *having to remember alphanumeric codes* to get a response in a computer setting. In a business setting, codes work well. The employer can require employees to use and learn the codes. The employee who has learned them and can use them is more valuable to the employer than an untrained person. It's a win–win situation. But in a universal and voluntary system like the New Medium, intuitive guides to operating the system are necessary.

In learning to read, twenty-six letters, ten numbers, and a dozen or so punctuation marks are all one has to memorize. Everything else is combinations of those. If the New Medium is equally simple and as useful as reading, Users will flock to it.

The third example is *having to go through a series of categories* to get to a specific message. In writing this book I constantly use my word processor's "Find" utility to leap about in the manuscript or bibliography. At the library using key-words and Boolean characters is a great improvement over card catalogs and classification systems preconceived by someone else. However, the classification system has the advantage of being something a person can become familiar with. If the User is assisted in creating an individual classification system based on needs and desires, the receiving device's software can be adapted to bring those categories of things to the User's attention automatically.

The fourth example is *having the message one is intent upon interrupted* by other messages. There is a great difference between offering a tantalizing hint and blatantly intruding upon a person's concentration. In promoting products and services, the New Medium needs to use the former and abolish the latter.

The fifth example is the necessity for providing access to important available *information of which the User is unaware.* Headlines and invitations to view snippets of entertainment programming or of advertising messages are items that Users will eagerly choose. In Kansas, when a little sketch of a tornado appears in the corner of the television screen, people pay attention, especially those who have had their homes demolished above their heads as they cowered in a basement.

Mass communicators can be the catalysts for creating a user-friendly New Medium. Computers already are being used to reduce "noise" in the production (encoding) of contemporary mass media.

Four of the five categories of noise described above exist because the existing computer and media systems have been designed to match the short-range, expedient needs of the senders. The fifth category is a new kind of noise created because the User plays a large role in the selection of information. Reduction of these kinds of noise is essential if the New Medium is to be successful. To achieve this reduction the creators of the New Medium need to understand the potential Users and how their minds operate as well as they understand computers, networks, audio, video, writing, and graphics.

TOMORROW'S MASS COMMUNICATORS

"Most young journalists learn how to be obsequious flacks for the establishment" when they work for school newspapers supervised by journalism professors.
—James Benniger

Effective reduction of noise calls for mass communicators with all types of interests and abilities and of many specialties who are also able to understand the broad scope of what is being done. (See Figure 10.2.) Most of all it calls for mass communicators who take the trouble to find out all the information that is available, who find out all the

PROFESSIONALS' NEW RELATIONSHIPS WITH USERS

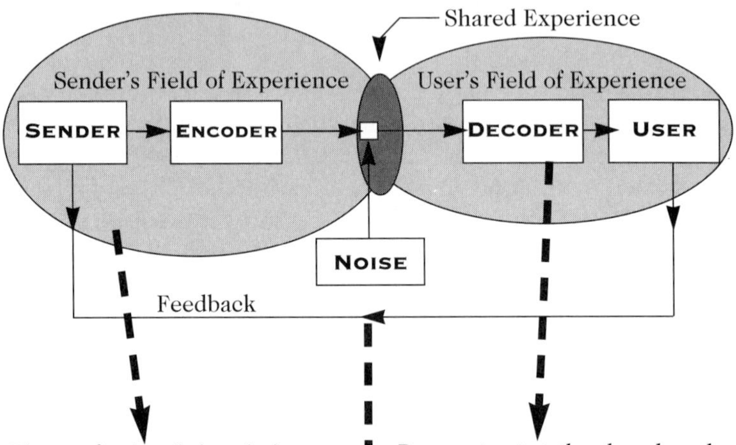

The professional (sender) stays abreast of what information (field of experience) is available to provide for specific User (receiver) needs.

By monitoring the decoder, the professional can create a profile of information interests and use, providing a basis for suggesting enhancements.

Feedback is now two-way interpersonal communication as professional assists User in setting up decoder and discovers what information the User needs.

The professional–User relationship outlined above creates a new responsibility for the mass communications professional, one more closely identified with doctor–patient, priest–parishioner, lawyer–client privilege. By counseling in person and by monitoring the decoding device, the professional establishes the User as the primary client. To take advantage of that relationship on behalf of an outside commercial interest or for selfish reasons would be an ethical breach similar to a doctor's prescribing unnecessary drugs or surgery, or a lawyer's incriminating a client.

FIGURE 10.2

things Users want, and who are astute enough to recognize the information that Users need. These mass communicators will be relieved of many constraints on the amount and subject matter of content that the contemporary media impose and that was previously described as noise.

Ratings, prime-time limitations, the cost of manufacturing, and distributing products all currently restrict what the mass communicator can do so that shrillness and the easily-recognized source, subject, or stereotype receive undue attention. This has led to criticisms like W. Lance Bennett's:

> As long as the distribution of power is narrow and decision processes are closed, journalists will never be free of their dependence on the small group of public relations experts, official spokespersons and powerful leaders whose self-serving pronouncements have become firmly established as the bulk of the daily news. [As long as] the public has little political access and even less power, there will be little substance behind the familiar democratic rhetoric that somehow equates all decisions of state with the public interest. [The news] provides little stimulus for enlightenment and few opportunities for expression should people attain their enlightenment elsewhere. In fact, the routine nature of news would seem to work against the elevation of civic consciousness by providing people with easy psychological escapes from the unpleasant reality of powerlessness. . . . Politicians, journalists, and the public are locked into a set of power relations that reinforces political deception, promotes journalistic narrowness and deference to authority and encourages public ignorance and retreat into a political fantasy world.

Frank Blethen, publisher of the *Seattle Times,* has expressed a similar view. He has noted that the breadth and diversity of the news media strengthens democracy. He sees three disconcerting trends working against this diversity: corporate ownership, concentration of ownership, and the attempt to control content, transmission, and access of information:

> Corporate ownership fosters short-term thinking, profit maximization. Concentrated ownership means too few are making too many decisions based on short-term profits, not based on local needs. The threat of controlling access, transmission and content can be remedied by creating a quality electronic conduit neutral to content and access. Failure to do so means further public alienation, less public participation and higher risk of government interference.

Perhaps the media professional of the future will be an independent operator, expert in what is going on in a geographical area or in specific issues and areas of interest. This expertise along with the professional's reputation for candor, lucidity, and completeness will gain the credibility necessary to attract Users to what he or she produces, gaining it access to the New Medium.

Paul Sagan of Time-Warner believes "people would even be able to create small businesses [reporting the news]; you could have hyperlocal news organizations that are essentially one- or two-person shops." Vincent T. Gross of AT&T points out that "people want to see little Johnny when he slid into home base."

USER AND VILLAGE PROVIDERS

The concept of some New Medium professionals being micro-operators meshes with the emerging realization that Users themselves will be providers of information for the New Medium. Users already use their home and office computers for mail, bulletin-board, and bulk-information communication. Many are adding mass communication reception to the menu of things their computers do. They are also taking advantage of the ancillary computer and audiotex services the traditional media are offering. The next step is to offer information for use in the mass media.

This step is of great concern to contemporary mass media professionals who are familiar with a unilateral kind of communication. The professional gathers, processes, and transmits information to the User. Feedback is very limited. How to handle large numbers of disparate messages from all kinds of Users is a seemingly overwhelming challenge.

A couple of models from today's world are enlightening. They combine User participation with independent communication specialists.

The first is a small weekly newspaper (or electronic bulletin board). The editor is a facilitator who encourages country correspondents to submit regular columns, welcomes all sorts of announcements and handwritten press releases, and publishes the minutes of public bodies and the week's additions to public records pretty much verbatim, just the way they arrive at the office. The editor is a conduit, a facilitator. In a New Medium context such a professional would be dealing with a small group, perhaps a village or neighborhood or, in the case of an interest group, members could be widely dispersed. The members know one another and this familiarity allows for easy User judgment of credibility from any individual source. (See Figure 10.3.)

The second example is the refereed academic journal. (See Figure 10.4.) Often the journal is published by the professional organization of an academic discipline, with the editor elected by the membership. The editor selects an editorial board from among the most respected members of the discipline. Submissions that look promising to the editor are sent to several appropriate members of the board; each member meticulously examines the report and suggests modifications for greater clarity and completeness, or recommends rejection. A report passing muster and suitably revised is published. The scrutiny by the editorial board gives the report credibility within the discipline and in the larger academic world.

This second example is not too different from what could happen in a community of geographical or subject-matter interest that is somewhat larger than a village. A mass communications professional establishes a list of known experts in various fields and confers with them about submissions by Users, publishing those that are approved.

In both these examples, the editors would be aware of the larger mass media world, and would pass to the next level information of interest to broader audiences than their own. The credibility of the editors themselves would be valuable in this instance. They also would scrutinize the larger information world and would pass to the Users of their service all pertinent items.

AN UNMEDIATED MASS MEDIUM

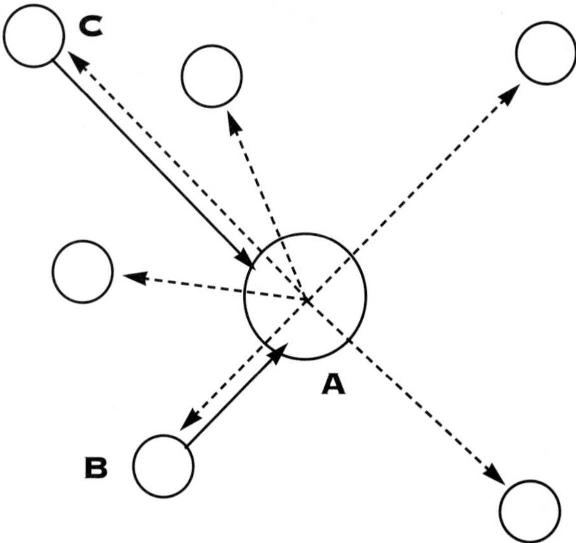

A is the editor of a very small weekly newspaper. He encourages readers, such as B and C, to submit items (solid arrows) for the paper and in most cases prints the stories word for word as they are submitted and distributes them (broken lines) to all readers. Unmediated mass media are credible in small groups, such as a village or a group of scientists, where everyone pretty much knows one another. Many electronic bulletin boards are unmediated. A, as a newspaper editor, is on the lookout for interesting items that larger papers would be interested in and submits them for wider distribution.

FIGURE 10.3

Although the examples above are taken from the print environment, the concepts could be applied to entertainment, music, drama, and the other areas of mass communications. Establishing grass-roots User-participation traditions in these areas would give great vitality to them.

The gamut of small-business arrangements would be appropriate for these grass-roots information enterprises. They could be mom-and-pop independents, franchisees, independent contractors, members of co-operatives or employees of large mass communications organizations. Motivating factors ensuring efficient, effective operation

A MEDIATED MASS MEDIUM

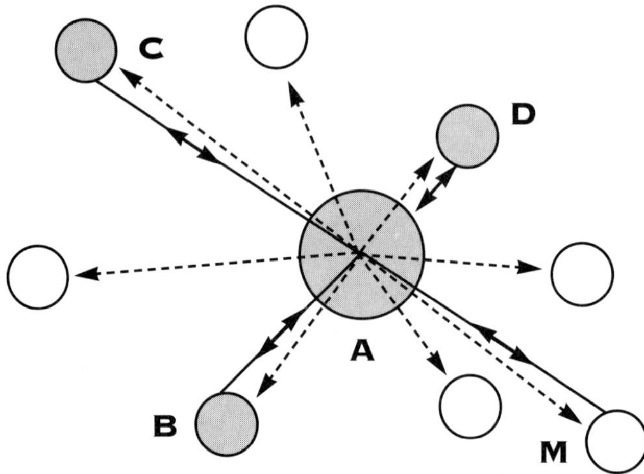

A is the editor of an academic journal. M offers a research report (solid arrow) for publication in the journal. B, C, and D are on the editorial board of A's journal. If A thinks the report has possibilities, A submits it to B, C, and D for review. If they approve it with reservations, A sends it back to M for revision, and, if the revisions are satisfactory, the report is published in the journal, which goes (dotted lines) to all subscribers. Mediated electronic bulletin boards also operate in this fashion. It is an appropriate way for a mass communication organization to operate in a modest-sized community (geographical or common-interest). The mediation process gives credibility to the operation. If A were an editor in a mass communication setting, he or she would be on the lookout for information that should receive wider distribution than the local medium provides.

FIGURE 10.4

would be the desire to be recognized as leading professionals, the opportunity to build careers, and the security of financially rewarding occupations.

These kinds of enterprises would be economically feasible because they would have relatively low overhead and capital investment in plant, requiring no large transmitters and expensive licenses and no presses or delivery trucks. They would use the generic computers used in all other business and personal enterprises. Their primary assets would be the effort they put into understanding the Users they serve, the information services they would depend on for outside information, their ability to provide information to those services, their credibility, and their effectiveness.

The larger information services, evolving from today's mass media, would assiduously cultivate these micro-enterprises as the basic source for Users of their services and for the information they would provide. The print media; motion-picture companies; and videocassette, audiocassette, and CD producers court the people who circulate their products in that way today, for example.

The relationship would be similar to what the AP bureau chief described in Chapter Seven does. Management would communicate constantly with the micro-professionals, keeping them abreast of new services, meeting their needs, encouraging them to participate in the development of useful information, and providing the nucleus of a support system. The professionals at the larger information services would also act as reference librarians, responding to the perceived information needs of Users.

ADVOCATE FOR THE PUBLIC

The professional mass communicator of the future may be an executive (like Frank Blethen), creating and implementing policy; a manager, ensuring the smooth operation of an information enterprise; or a practitioner, securing and creating information and preparing it for consumption or paying attention to the needs of Users. Wherever the communicator's name appears on the organization chart or whatever the skills he or she has, his or her first concern must be the easy availability of information. The mass media professional is the public's advocate for openness in society.

It is the professional obligation of these communicators to serve and protect freedom of expression and freedom of information and to expose and resist censorship and the tendency to think of information as exclusive property. Professional mass communicators must attend to these matters first of all—as a top priority.

Fortunately, the nature of the New Medium tends to narrow the focus of mass communications professionals. Instead of worrying about prime time or the high cost of publication, the professional can make information the Number 1 concern. It should be.

Mass communications professionals should make sure the law protects the rights of the public to public information. Where information is generated at the expense of all taxpayers, all taxpayers should have equal right to access. If the information is generated at taxpayer expense it should be easily and inexpensively available to all.

An ethic of openness should prevail in our society. Mass communications professionals should promote it. We all are born, live, and die on one planet. We all need the opportunities that learning offers. We all have the responsibility to make society as good as it can be; freely disseminated information is the key to responsible individual decision making. All of us and all our institutions are bound by the social contract described in the Declaration of Independence; being open about ourselves is the only way we can judge each other's fulfillment of the social contract.

The economy of plenty should supplant the economy of scarcity that has begun to erode the free flow of information. Squeezing news holes, abolishing news departments, predatory publishing, and paying a premium for early release of information are examples of short-term profit rather than long-term prosperity. The rampant success of the Internet is a positive sign. All benefit when all have access because all who are interested can then contribute, because competition of ideas promotes the emergence of truth and because the common welfare is served.

Broad-based support for openness already exists. Publishers and poets, actors and artists, librarians and journalists, philosophers and photographers, existentialists and even exotic dancers individually and in their organizations are the proponents of openness. Some organizations of mass media professionals supporting openness include the Reporter's Committee on Freedom of the Press, the Society of Professional Journalists, the American Library Association, and the Student Press Law Center.

Lance Bennett describes the constrictive nature of contemporary mass media. Frank Blethen warns that the public is alienated from the media and that government intervention is a threat. Perhaps the greatest hope the New Medium offers is an opportunity to regain a mutual admiration between mass communication professionals and mass media Users based on the expanded opportunities the New Medium presents.

FACILITATOR OF IMPROVED CONTENT

Mass communicators may have the opportunity to break out of the restrictions of contemporary media content if the content of the New Media is broadened, deepened, and made more convenient.

Tomorrow's mass media professional will need to be curious, reflective and energetic, as nearly a Renaissance Man or Renaissance Woman as it is possible to be. In addition these professionals must be highly proficient at the skills required by the New Medium. Here are some skills that come to mind.

Writing: This includes description, dialogue, narrative, excerpting, abstracting, transition, captioning, headlining, editorializing, persuasion, selling, paraphrasing, memos, instructions, logs, journals, critiques, satire, humor, pathos.

Language editing: This includes grammar, punctuation, spelling, word usage, style, and pronunciation.

Hypercommunication: The combining of all elements of communication into one message, requiring an understanding of the relationships between different kinds of communication; of when to use each; of how to blend them together; of how to allow the User to move freely within a message. Here are a dozen more skills just as important as those above:

Speaking	Interviewing	Photography
Design	Reading	Videography
Graphics	Drawing	Audio recording/editing
Listening	Observing	Negotiating

Understanding organizations: This pertains to formal structure, informal working relations, internal communication, and relating to outsiders. Tomorrow's mass communicators will work in isolation and as members of teams providing very complex services.

Understanding individuals: Motivation, reward, punishment, rejection, alienation, reinforcement, affection, self-delusion, self-realization, bonding, courage, fear, weakness, guilt, anxiety, contentment, solitude, companionship, gregariousness, infancy, childhood, puberty, adolescence, mating, maturity, middle age, menopause, retirement, senility, birth, death: these are the motivating and driving forces of life, the determinants of what information individuals want and need.

Micro–mass communication: The ability to provide the information that just a few persons want.

Areas of contemporary knowledge directly related to the skills above would include (subject to ongoing additions and changes):

Computers	Digital audio	Database	New technology
Software	Digital video	Relational database	Management
Word Processing	Multimedia	Online searching	Networks
Desktop Publishing	Spreadsheet	Digital archiving	Hypertext

Knowledge related to subjects communicated: This spans the whole realm of human experience. The communicator will seek out subjects of interest to him or her and of value to others and concentrate on them.

A new role for management: Management's role begins at the User's front door or when the set is turned on, rather than ending there. Management makes sure maximum information is transmitted; that all appropriate Users are connected; that Users have tools to get to information they want; that information is presented as clearly as possible. The concern with manufacturing and distribution of products and of scheduling for maximum audience is reduced. The manager's attention is focused on information, its producers, and its Users.

During the years immediately ahead, future mass communicators will be scrambling for educational opportunities appropriate to the New Medium. Formal curricula in traditional educational settings will come later. However, many opportunities to study multimedia, hypertext, computer networking, database operations, and related subjects already exist. Some enterprise on the part of the forward-looking student is required to find them.

The traditional areas of mass media "skills" and mass communications "research" are merging. The skills are changing and becoming more sophisticated and intellectual, and research itself is becoming an intellectual tool that the mass communicator must have.

Enterprises of all types are entering periods of transitional communications. Future mass communicators can seek internships and jobs with people like Rick Smolen, who produced the three versions of *From Alice to Ocean,* or like Clement Mok, a California pioneer in multimedia. In the 1980s he was designing packaging, brochures, videos, interactive computer-based presentations, events, business theaters, corporate seminars, rollouts of products, and conferences. An advocate of the printed page, he related concepts of print design to other media.

Awesome Responsibilities; Awesome Rewards

A reading of the awesome lists above might lead to the question why would anyone want to be a mass communicator? That is, what are the motivations and rewards of a mass communications career? Consider the following:

- Information is power. The mass communicator is close to the power.
- Providing information is democracy at work. It is important to the public and it protects freedoms.
- Meeting the challenge is fun.
- A mass communications career provides one with a life-long tour of the interesting people, issues, places, and things of our world; it results in an increasingly heightened understanding and fascination with life.
- It is a dynamic way to explore one's own capacity for expression and empathy.

And now for a personal note from the author to all of you who have waded through this book: Good luck as you create the New Medium. I hope to live to be a hundred years old so I can have the thrill of watching you do it.

A REVIEW FOR THE NEW MEDIUM PROFESSIONAL

The Communication Model

Chapter One describes the Shannon–Weaver Communication Model, categorizing steps in the process. Chapter Two demonstrates how all kinds of information can now flow in the same channel. Chapter Seven describes the vast field of experience that allows the professional to understand the User. In Chapter Ten, noise and decoding are discussed.

The User

Chapter Two discusses "logical man" and "experiential man" and how these concepts relate to communication. Chapter Seven is devoted to the nature of audiences, viewers, and readers. Chapter Ten discusses perception, cognition, and dissonance.

The New Medium Decoder

Chapter Three gives a cartoon example of the New Medium decoder device, describes what it needs to do, and presents the Viewpoint Computer in the Seattle Museum of Art as an early prototype. Chapter Six details what digital decoding involves.

The Professional and the User

Chapter Three gives an example of a User inventory of information, and discusses how the New Medium personalizes information.

Presenting New Medium Content

Chapter Three discusses multimedia as a way to integrate text, graphics, pictures, and sound, and gives an example of a multimedia project. Chapter Six presents a further discussion of the nature of multimedia and also discusses the nature of messages and the nature of advertising in the New Medium. Chapter Nine is devoted entirely to content.

Freedom of Information

Chapter Five is devoted to the concepts of freeing information, keeping it affordable, returning to an omnibus information environment, and meeting the media's social contract as outlined by the Hutchins Commission. This calls for universal access to the channel, the decoder, and information. Chapters Eight, Nine, and Ten also discuss this topic.

The New Medium Enterprise

Chapter Four describes how the New Medium enterprise would *not* be concerned with manufacturing and transporting products, would *not* be concerned with scheduling information into prime time or morning drive time, would *not* be concerned with interrupting the User with advertising messages. Chapter Seven discusses models for the New Medium enterprise and gives an organizational outline for a local information enterprise. Chapter Ten discusses micro–information enterprises.

Professional Skills

Chapter Ten is devoted to the New Medium Professional. Chapter Seven tells why the professional will be concerned with databases, indexes, keywords, records, multimedia, and Users as providers of information.

The Professional and Technology

Chapter Three says the New Medium Professional will standardize, organize, and schedule. Chapter Nine notes how creativity in content is related to technology.

BOX 10.1

SUMMARY

Persons trained and experienced in the mass communications field are best qualified to judge the standards of performance of the New Medium. They have an understanding of what Users will expect and require. They are sensitive to the various kinds of media and technology noise that interferes with User friendliness. It is mass communications professionals who will create the broader and more detailed base of information that Users of the New Medium will expect. Without an adequate base of information, well chosen and well presented, the New Medium will fall far short of its potential. A rigorous and challenging period of education and training faces potential mass communicators as they prepare for the changes ahead. Ingenuity and enterprise will be required to secure the knowledge and experience needed. But the rewards of carrying out interesting and important responsibilities are there.

PROJECTS, DISCUSSION TOPICS, AND EXERCISES

1. Examine the General Catalog of your school to see what courses would help prepare you and your fellow students for emerging mass media careers. Create a database or scrapbook of your findings.
2. Search appropriate CD-ROM indexes for research articles on the following topics: (1) audience use of the media, (2) uses of personal computers in the home, (3) comparison of the ease of using various computer operating systems.
3. Invite a communications researcher or a panel to discuss research in relation to technological change. Prepare questions ahead of time and be prepared to participate.
4. See what enterprises, including advertising and public relations agencies, in your city are involved with desktop publishing, videotoaster production of videotapes, and multimedia. Plan one or more field trips to promising sites.

SELECTED READINGS

Bennett, W. Lance. *News: The Politics of Illusion.* New York: Longman, 1980. Discusses shortcomings of contemporary media in providing a thorough picture of society and the issues affecting it.

Lynn, Kenneth S., ed. *The Professions in America.* Boston: Houghton Mifflin, 1965. An examination of how various professions view professionalism.

Pool, Ithiel de Sola. *Technologies of Freedom.* Cambridge, Mass.: Harvard University Press, 1983. What Pool wrote more than a decade ago is what contemporary professionals need to heed.

Rosen, Jay. *Community Connectedness Passwords for Public Journalism.* St. Petersburg, Fla.: Poynter Institute for Media Studies, 1993. A discussion of public discourse as the source and strength of democracy.

Thurow, Lester. "Is Telecommunications Truly Revolutionary?" *The Telecommunications Revolution.* New York: Routledge, 1992. Discusses the shortcomings of computers in increasing productivity.

Conclusion

"I think, therefore I am."

—René Descartes

Self-realization is a sign of humanity, of intelligence. Pediatric psychologists examining a baby for signs of normal development wait for the child to touch its own face rather than the face in the mirror. When the baby is old enough to spend an hour combing in front of the mirror, then indeed realization of self and of an ability to change has taken place.

A corollary to our thesis would be: "I am what I think (perceive, believe, act upon)." The environment in which our brains operate shapes us as people. A 1992 movie, *White Men Can't Jump,* involved inner-city playground basketball. The number of whites relative to the number of blacks playing basketball in the movie was quite low, and was an accurate representation of life. If one watches sports on television in June, one notes that the National Basketball Association is full of black basketball players and the Professional Golf Association is full of white golfers. Whether genetic differences help blacks put a big ball through a hoop and whites put a little ball in a hole is debatable, but there is no doubt that for many black youths, a basketball goal is about all the recreational equipment they are exposed to. More white youths come from the suburbs where golf courses abound.

Are we to think that our brains are different from our other organs and tissues? A child exposed to 10,000 hours of Nintendo is going to be a Nintendo adult. There is reality—the truth—out there in the universe. Then there is my reality, your reality—our individual truth—up there in our memories. This internal reality is the one we live our lives by. It is built incrementally by the information we are exposed to, just as basketball and golfing abilities develop.

We have discussed the dramatic changes printing and reading brought to society. Obliquely we have referred to the high expectations for broadcasting to be a great educator and enlightener. But by the 1960s Newton Minow, chairman of the FCC, was calling television "a vast wasteland." He found those words to be still true just a few years ago.

Now is another time of high expectation. Because computerized databases can remember such infinite detail and provide it so conveniently, some have described mental activity in conjunction with computer memory as a third kind of reasoning—inductive, deductive, and data-ductive, or something along those lines.

For the ordinary person will the computer be a mystery, a toy, or a tool?

To a large extent the answer depends upon what the ordinary person finds in the computer. If the truth in the computer is arcane, computers will remain a mystery. If the truth in the computer is inane, computers will be a toy. If the information in the computer is enlightening and compelling, computers will be the most fantastic tool ever devised for relating the reality out there in the universe to the reality inside our heads.

Freedom is knowing what the options are and being able to take advantage of them. For us to be free the world in our heads must be closely related to the world out in the universe.

A half-millenium ago the hallowed monks in their monasteries, carefully preserving as scribes the wisdom of the ages, were largely unaware that a new age was dawning, Indeed, the printers of the sixteenth century, up to their elbows in ink, were barely conscious of the revolution in information and knowledge they were fomenting. Surely the changes now under way are just as radical. Will the historians of five hundred years from now look at our dawning century as the New Enlightenment? That is a dream worth pursuing, and that is why the next generation of mass media communicators will be the most important ever to enter society.

INDEX

A

academic journal, 164, 166
Advanced Network and Services Inc., 100
advertising, 91
Albuquerque Tribune, 8
Allsport, 84
AM/FM radio, 25
America Online (online sevice), 100
American Telephone & Telegraph. *See* AT&T
Amos 'n Andy, 28, 57
AP. *See* Associated Press
Apple Computer, 21. *See also* Macintosh
Apple, R. W., 44
archiving, 82
Arkansas Gazette, x, 155
Armstrong, Edwin, 27
Arsenio Hall Show, 120
Aspen Movie Map, 12
Associated Press (AP), 72, 80, 84, 105–108
AT&T, 28, 67, 68, 82, 85–86
Atlantic Bell, 87
audio, 10

B

Baltimore Sun, 22
bandwidth, 139, 142
Baran, Paul, 100
Barnum, P. T., 10, 100
Bellows, James, x
Bennett, W. Lance, 163
Benniger, James, 161
binary mathematics, 9
Blanchard, Robert, 93
Blethen, Frank, 55, 163
Bogar, Tony, 135
Bogart, Leo, 72, 102
Bonisteel, Steve, 126
Brazeal, Donald,136
Brinkley, "Dr." John Romulus, 26
British Telecommunications, 87
broadcasting, 24–25
Buchanan, Edna, 71
Bulkley, Christy, 57
bulletin board, 8, 124–125

C

Cable News Network. See CNN
Cable Satellite Public Affairs Network. *See* C–SPAN
cable television, 30, 55
Capital Cities Communication, 29
carrier wave, 25
Carter, Hodding, Jr., x
Cater, Douglass, 30
CB (Citizens' Band) radio, 25
CBS, 28, 80, 134
CD–ROM (Compact Disk–Read Only Memory), 11, 13, 33, 34, 42, 81, 92–93
channel, 6, 21, 37, 66–67, 85–89
channel surfing, 53, 122
"Chicago" (Microsoft Windows version 4.0), 64
Churchill, Winston, 44
CNN (Cable News Network), 29, 54, 72, 111, 144
coaxial cable, 27
cognition, 158
Cole, David M., 138
Colliers, 56
Columbia College, 93
comfort factor, 118
Commission on Freedom of the Press (Hutchins Report), 73
communication, 5
communication research, 158–159
Communications Act of 1934, 28
compression (digital), 89
Compact Disk. *See* CD–ROM
CompuServe (online service), 45, 100
Computer Assisted Reporting and Research List (CARR–L), x
Conner, Joan, 93
content, ix, 25, 40, 168–169
Continental Cablevision, 86
copyright, 65
The Corpse Had a Familiar Face (Buchanan), 71
Council Grove [Kansas] *Republican,* 71–72
credibility, 135, 136–137
critical mass, 116

Cronkite, Walter, 28
C–SPAN (Cable Satellite Public Affairs Network), 55, 72
The Cuckoo's Egg (Stoll), 99

D

Daniels, Frank, III, 137
"Dark Ages," 17, 30, 31
database, 34, 37, 71, 84, 109, 110–111, 124–124
A Day in the Life of Japan (Smolen), 42
"The Day the Universe Changed," 19
Declaration of Independence, 67
decode, 5, 6, 22, 38–40, 89–92
DeFleur, Melvin, 103–104
Denson, John, x
Descartes, Rene, 175
desktop publishing, 35, 81
The Diary of Anne Frank, 43
Digital Electronics Corp., 65, 84
digitization, 3, 82
digitized photography, 7, 35
direct broadcast service, 30
"Disabilities Act of 1990," 63
dissonance, 158
Dizard, Wilson, 147
Don, Abbe, 20
Donne, John, 71
Dow Jones News Retrieval Service, 42, 96
Dutton, William, 74, 150

E

Edison, Thomas, 63
electronic (as term), 22, 23
electronic journals, 94
e-mail, 4, 41, 72, 100, 124–125
encode, 5, 6, 8, 21, 35, 81–84
entry points, 138
environment, 53
Esrey, William, 86
"experiential man," 23–24, 30, 35
EXPRES, 84

F

fax, 4, 66, 72
FCC (Federal Communications Commission), 25, 28, 55, 59, 68, 85, 87–88
feedback, 103, 104
fiber optics, 25, 81, 85, 87, 88
Fidler, Roger, 99, 105
field of experience, 103
Fincham, Robin, 79
Finnegan, Ruth, 153
First Amendment, 55, 62
Fleming, Ambrose, 27
Foote, Shelby, 129–130
For Whom the Bell Tolls, 71
Ford, Henry, 63, 65
de Forest, Lee, 27
Freedom Forum, x, 72
Franklin, Benjamin, 22
Franklin, Jon, 104, 128
Friendly, Fred, 28, 140, 141
From Alice to Ocean, 42, 170

G

Gannett, 50
Gates, Bill, 63–65
gateway, 80, 82, 84
General Electric, 28
Georgia Tech, 93
global village, 144
Gordon, Mike, 145
Gore, Al (Albert, Jr.), 70
Graphical User Interface (GUI), 64
Grolier's Encyclopedia, 50
Gross, Vincent T., 163
Grossman, Lawrence K., 74
GUI (Graphical User Interface), 64
Gutenberg, Johannes, 4, 19, 22, 49
Gutenberg Bible, 19
"Gutenberg Man," 19, 21–22, 30

H

Haber, Alan, 90
Hale, Jim, 96
hardware, ix
Hartford Courant, 65
Hear It Now, 140
Hemingway, Ernest, 71
Hertz, Heinrich, 27
"High Performance Computing Act of 1991," 69, 101
Hiroshima, 100, 148–149
Hollander, Barry, 147
Holocaust, 43
homogenization, 119
Hoover, Herbert, 26
Houbart, Gilberte, 150
Houston Chronicle, 6
Howard University, 88
Hudson, Heather, 75
Hutchins Report, 73
Hypercard, 83
hypertext (hypermedia), 82, 83, 91, 93, 109, 148–149

I

IBM, 65, 90, 100
indexing, 20, 109

information, 40
information overload, 120–121
"information superhighway," 69–71, 126
interactive, 37, 59, 66, 87, 121, 122
Internet, 37, 84, 86, 99–102
Interstate Highway System, 69, 88, 101
Intuitive communication. See "Smileys"

J, K

James, Matt, 121
Johansen, Johannes, 105
Kahan, Robert, 42
Kansas City Star, x, 95–97
Kansas State University, 1, 40
Keats, John, 31
Kennedy, John F., 25–26, 29, 144
keywords, 34, 83, 109
Kilmer, Joyce, 31
Kodak, 42
Knight–Ridder News Syndicate, 50, 80

L

Lansing State Journal, 95
Laventhal, David, 56
Lavine, John, 47
left brain–right brain, 30
Levy, Steven, 74, 120
Library of Congress, 70
Life, 56
Lincoln, Abraham, 3
linear logic, 19, 30, 35
literacy, 4, 20, 21, 32
Locke, John, 68
Los Angeles Times, 56
low salience, 118
Lyon, David, 79

M

Macintosh (computer), 9, 42, 64, 83, 90
Marconi, Guglielmo, 27
Marsh, Ellie, x, 94
mass media, 2, 4
MCI, 87, 100
McLendon, Gordon, 30
McLuhan, Marshall, 21
media gap, 123–125
Medialink, 94
media strengths, 137–139
  print, 139–141
  audio, 141–144
  television, 145–146
  New Medium, 145–146
media user target, 126–127
media weaknesses, 145–147
Miami Herald, 71
Microsoft Corporation, 34, 82, 86. *See also* Gates, Bill; MS–DOS
microwave, 27
Middlesex News, 8
Minow, Newton, 29, 176
MIT (Massachusetts Institute of Technology), 82
MIT Media Lab, 10, 12, 93
Model T, 64
Mok, Clement, 170
Morse, Samuel F. B., 22
Morse code, 22, 23
Mosaic, 84
MS–DOS (Microsoft Disk Operating System), 64–65
multimedia, 20, 40, 81, 82, 83, 91, 93–94,112, 148–149
multimedia magazines, 51
Murrow, Edward R., 28, 140, 141

N

National Geographic, 42
National Information Infrastructure Advisory Council, 67
The National Information Infrastructure: Agenda for Action, 75
National Research and Education Network, 69–70
National Science Foundation, 84, 100
NBC, 27, 28, 82, 136
Neuman, W. Russell, 115, 123, 129
network, 20, 35, 37, 53, 54, 55, 62, 63, 69, 70, 71, 74, 75
New England Courant, 4
New Medium, ix, 35–36
newsletters, 21
newspaper, 7, 52, 55
  weekly, 164, 165
New York Daily News, x
The New Yorker, 30
New York Herald Tribune, x, 112
New York Sun, 26
NEXIS, 84
Noam, Eli, 88
noise, 5, 6, 156, 158–161
North American Presentation Level Protocol Syntax (NAPLPS), 80
NorthWestNet NodeNews, 94
NSNFT, 100
NYU (New York University), 93

O

Okerson, Ann, 94
online, 8, 33, 84
online services. See America Online, CompuServe, Prodigy
Online Videotex Service, 80
oral tradition, 18, 25
Oukrop, Carol, x

P, Q

paper, 50
Parker, Everett, 68
PBS, 29, 55
PC (personal computer), 9, 49, 90
Pearce, Charles, x
perception, 158
Pinkerton, Tad, 121
Podium, 40
point-to-point communication, 24
Power Macintosh, 64
Poynter Institute, x
"The Press" (as institution), 1
Prestel, 79–80
Price, Raymond K., Jr, x
printing, 19–20
privacy, 147
Prodigy (online service), 45, 73, 100, 120
Publish, 83
Pulitzer, Joseph, 102
Pythagoras, 65
QuickTime, 59, 83

R

Radin, Charles, 101
radio, 1, 26, 27–30
"Radio Act of 1912," 28
Radio Luxembourg, 30
Rather, Dan, 44
RCA, 27, 28
Renaissance Man, 20
Roberts, Gene, 150
Roberts, Eric, 74
Roosevelt, Franklin D., 26, 140
Rosen, Don, 121
Rosen, Jay, 54
Rousseau, Jean-Jacques, 68
Royse, Molly, 94

S

Sagan, Paul, 163
Sanders, T. C., x
San Francisco State Univeresity, 93
San Jose State University, 93
Sargent, Dwight, x
Sarnoff, David, 27, 100
satellite, 30, 33, 37, 71, 85, 88
Saturday Evening Post, 26, 56
Schecker, Fred, 96
Schramm, Wilbur, 103
Schwartz, Tony, 21
Seattle Museum of Art, Viewpoint, 34
Seattle Times, 55, 82
See It Now, 28, 141
Seiler, Lauren, 49
serendipity, 147, 150
Severin, Werner, x
Shannon, Claude, 5
Shannon Model of Communication, x, 5, 7, 8, 11, 14, 36, 82, 102, 134, 156, 162
Shapley, Barbara, 75
Shaw, Donald L., 33
Shoemaker, Joe, 147
Sikes, Alfred C., 33, 49, 79, 153
"smileys," 21
Smolen, Rick, 42, 170
social contract, 67
social responsibility, 73, 135–136, 167–168
software, ix
sound, 18
Southwestern Bell Telephone, 87
speech, 17
Sprint, 86
Stanley, Jack, 6
StarTouch (Kansas City Star), 95–97
Star Trek, 43–44
Stoll, Clifford, 99
storytelling, 148–149
St. Petersburg Times, 84
Stricklin, Michael, ix
Sullivan, Michael, 139

T

TCI (TeleCommunications International), 53, 86, 87, 88
telegraph, 22
Tele-Metropole, 12
television, 1, 26, 27–30
"Television Consumer Protection and Competition Act," 88
Telidon, 80
Templeton, Brad, 112
Texas Education Network, 37
The New York Times, 31, 44, 80, 134
Thurow, Lester, 147
Time, 56, 100
Times-Mirror Co., 80
Time-Warner Inc., 14, 29, 82, 86
Tomita, Tetsuro, 123, 125
Tracewell, Nancy, 96
transistor, 27
Turner, Ted, 29
    See also Cable News Network

U, V

USA Today, 97
User, ix, 123–130, 156
Venture One, 80
video, 10
videocassette, 53, 74, 82
video disk, 12
video toaster, 12
Viewtron, 80
virtual reality, 83

W

Waco Tribune–Herald, x
Wall Street Journal, 42
Walton, Sam, 63, 128
Washington, University of, 50
Washington Post, 40, 50
WEAF, 26, 28
Weather Channel, 54, 117
Weaver, Warren, 5
  See also Shannon, Claude; Shannon Model of Communication
Weiss, Dimitri, 104
Welles, Orson, 28
Westinghouse, 28
White, E. B., 30
White Men Can't Jump, 175
Whiteside, Scott, 96
Williams, Frederick, x, 68, 74
"Windows" (for DOS), 64
wood (as paper source), 50–51
World War II, 43
Wriston, Walter, 62
writing, 17, 21
WTBS, 29

X, Y, Z

Zeeck, David, 95
Zenith, 82